THE FULNESS OF SACRIFICE

By the same author:

CATHOLIC SOCIAL ACTION
PROPERTY AND POVERTY

THE FULNESS OF SACRIFICE

DOCTRINAL AND DEVOTIONAL SYNTHESIS
ON THE MASS
—ITS FORETELLING, FORESHADOWING
AND FULFILLING

A. M. CROFTS, O.P., S.T.Lt., M.A.

Os Justi
Press

Nihil Obstat: Fr. A. Moynihan, O.P., S.T.L.
Fr. J. F. Smith, O.P., S.T.L.

Imprimatur: Fr. T. E. Garde, O.P., S.T.M.
Provincialis

May 13th, 1953

Nihil Obstat: Georgius D. Smith, S.T.D., Ph.D.
Censor Deputatus

Imprimatur: E. Morrogh Bernard
Vic. Gen.

Westmonasterii, die 26a Maii, 1953

Republished by Os Justi Press
ISBN 978-1-965303-32-0

First published 1953

MADE AND PRINTED IN GREAT BRITAIN
BY NORTHUMBERLAND PRESS LIMITED
GATESHEAD ON TYNE

FOREWORD

MOST REVEREND JAMES M. LISTON, D.D.
Bishop of Auckland

A S one who listened with profit to the Conferences on the Holy Mass preached in St. Patrick's Cathedral, Auckland, by the Rev. A. M. Crofts, O.P., I welcome the publication of them in book form and heartily commend the reading of them to priests and layfolk. The discourses of the Dominican preacher were attractive in their profundity of doctrine, clarity of expression and fervour of heart, and when printed at the time helped many to take their part with understanding in the offering of the Sacrifice of the Altar. The Conferences in book form, unchanged in fundamental thought but largely rewritten, will give light and warmth to very large numbers.

We are witnesses in our time of a well-informed and devoutly fashioned approach of the faithful to the sacred liturgy of worship, and therefore to a love of the Mass which, though different from, is no less strong than that of Ireland through the centuries. Deeper search into the treasures of the Church's heritage along with enlightened preaching such as that of Father Crofts has brought out things old and new in doctrine and history, and has given intensity to devotional life. The beauty of Scriptural readings and the venerable prayers in the Missal, the dignity of the ceremonies of a High Mass, the drama of presentation in cathedrals and monastic churches of Benedictines and enclosed Orders, the concerted movement of priests and worshippers in supplication and love have stirred the heart of the Catholic world and brought it closer in the endless renewal of the Altar offering, as Our Lord Himself wished and ordered, to His sacrifice of redemption on the Cross: "Yes, if only I am lifted up from the earth, I will attract all men to myself" (John 12.32).

Whilst each one of us prays in his own heart before the Altar he forms as it were a separate thread in the woven garment of the Redeemer, but that is not the monumental greatness of the Mass. For it is not a private prayer, nor even an assembly of worshippers for prayer, nor a human service designed for instruction and exhortation: it is a sacrificial prayer, the central theme being the pierced heart of our Redeemer and His eternal Kingship; it is an offering of Sacrifice for the honouring of God Supreme and the sanctification of men, through and with and in Christ Jesus.

Many aspects of our Act of worship—its setting, foreseen in prophecy and fashioned reverently in the course of time; the heart of it, the Eternal Priest offering a Victim, which is His Sacred Humanity; the memorial in His daily return, as real as when He walked to death; the sharing by worshippers in that ceaseless Eucharistic action where the Church offers herself in Christ to God; the inexhaustible riches of the Redeemer's sacramental presence and sacrificial offering; the food of the soul on earth with a pledge of eternal life—these are lucidly explained by the author, their character and sanction derived from the Cross, and analysed to show how man's deepest religious longings carry him in adoration and thanksgiving to the Lord of all. In Liturgies of sixteen centuries ago we hear Catholic voices "with lips that keep not silence and hearts that cannot be still," giving thanks both for the magnificence of God and His Son's death for all men. This of course is the deep thought of the Church at all times, and therefore it is the spiritual temper brought by Father Crofts to these studies.

Under his guidance, as he unfolds Catholic doctrine, we see that our Altar memorial is made above all to the glory of God, and next as a due part and occasion of the Church's praise and thanksgiving. She knows that His Sacrifice of the Cross is the cause and cost of her existence, and therefore "calling to mind the Blessed Passion of the same Christ, thy Son, our Lord, likewise his resurrection from the grave and glorious ascension into heaven," she offers to "thy sovereign majesty, out of the gifts thou hast bestowed upon us, a sacrifice that is pure, holy, and unblemished, the Sacred Bread of everlasting life, and the Cup of eternal salvation."

It is Christ's Sacrifice, and the Church's, the Council of Trent defines, for He left it to her: and the Church, we know, is the whole Christian people under the leadership of proper authority. Our eyes travel from the altar table to the Cross above, to see in the Action of the Mass the great events of "the dense and driven Passion", and our worship is thus given more reverently, our love awakened and spoken more fully, and our heart opened wider to the Redeemer's sanctifying graces. We see Him, too, as His own memorial transfiguring every day temples that are not made with hands, for they are the souls of men. He comes, and we, creatures, can give the Lord acknowledgment of adoration, and find our souls pardoned, strengthened, comforted. He goes, but not before blessing us for His work in our life. And next day like the rising sun He returns to us.

The preacher dwelt, it seemed to me, with insight and joy on two essential features of the inexhaustible mystery of our visible Sacrifice. First, it is a fulfilment of Christ's: "Do this in commemoration of Me." He wished that the supreme event in His redeeming of us should be witnessed consciously by all men to the end of ages, so that its power of atonement and petition might be theirs.

Secondly, the Eucharist is a sacramental and sacrificial meal. The baptized, His own, receive at the Lord's table for spiritual strength, comfort and delight, His Body and His Blood, handed to them under the species of bread and wine. The author explains with clearness that this meal is not something complete in itself, but a part that fits into a larger entity, the climax of the Sacrifice. The offering of worship to God in the sacrifice is the proper preparation for the intimate, personal coming of the Lord to our soul in Holy Communion. "I am the living Bread", and in the receiving of It, especially at this time, we are given by divinely generous hands the very sources of spiritual life.

I count it a privilege to recommend this book of learning and piety to priests and the faithful.

CONTENTS

First Chapter

SHADOW OF GOOD THINGS TO COME
(Heb. x. 1)

Second Chapter

THE HIGH PRIEST OF OUR CONFESSION, JESUS
(Heb. iii. 1)

Third Chapter
THE OBLATION OF THE BODY OF JESUS
(Heb. x. 10)

Fourth Chapter
THE WAY INTO THE HOLIES
(Heb. ix. 8)

Fifth Chapter
THE LORD'S SUPPER
(1 Cor. xi. 20)

Sixth Chapter

PARTAKING OF THE BODY OF THE LORD
(1 Cor. x. 16)

Seventh Chapter

COMMUNICATION OF THE BREAKING OF BREAD
(Acts ii. 52)

PREFACE

THE Mass is the centre and heart of Catholic worship. Its unceasing celebration, its universal liturgy, its bond of sacrificial union, present unimpeachable testimony to the divine origin of Christian faith. Its sacred action, as it moves on with calm certainty, bears along with it the strong conviction that what is thereby accomplished on the altar transcends any merely human institution, rises above its own outward appearances, and in its essential effects is independent of the dispositions of minister or assembled congregation. The Holy Sacrifice came forth from the omnipotent hand of God through Jesus Christ, His Word Incarnate and eternal High Priest—at the Institution of the Last Supper. It relies unfailingly on that same omnipotent will of God as its unending offering is continued down the centuries of time through the empowered word of " Other Christs " —the ordained priests of the Catholic Church.

This phenomenon of Catholic faith and life emphasizes the wide gulf which separates the Catholic religion from all other substituted forms, which are designated, be it ever so sincerely, under the heading of Christian worship. The Mass is something more than a mere Sunday service of prayer, of readings, of the singing of hymns: for, over and above the presence of God's minister, there comes through the power of Consecration the real, bodily, though veiled presence of yet Another—the Incarnate Son of God. Over and above the voice of the people and priest, there is another voice—the voice of the precious blood of the ever-living Victim on the Altar which, in its unceasing mystic pouring and sprinkling: "Speaks better than that of Abel" (Heb. xii. 24).

Without the Mass Catholic churches would be reduced to what so many of them became, and still remain, under the Reformation—an empty tomb, a stable without the Divine Child, an altar-site without altar, victim, or sacrifice. Because of its strong conviction Catholic faith continues its calm way unshaken, though saddened, by the tragedy of inherited error, which still deprives vast numbers of human beings of the comfort and strength of so essential an act of religion. The efforts of some sections of Protestantism to bridge by mere external similation the chasm created by Reformist hatred of the Mass, reveals how powerful is man's natural instinct to express his religion by some external act of sacrifice. The Catholic Church to-day accepts, as did the Apostles in the Upper Room, and the people of God down the centuries, in their literal sense the words of Christ, Who declared: "Take ye and eat ye all of this; This my body—Take ye and drink ye all of this. This is the chalice of my blood." Down the ages of Christian history since the night of that Last Supper men have been consoled, encouraged and renewed by the undying pledge of God's infinite love. For wellnigh two thousand years Catholic life has been centred and built up on the strong truth of Him Who commanded: "Do this for a commemoration of me." Down the ages yet to come the same hope will ever brighten the darksome depths of human misery. "The world shall pass away, but my words shall not pass away." Our strength in the present is found in humble and loving acceptance of this mystery of God's goodness. "I believe all the Son of God has spoken; than Truth's own word there is no truer spoken" ("*Adoro Te*").

The Holy Sacrifice of the Mass can be understood only by those who believe. Faith is absolutely necessary, and with faith humility and prayerfulness, to approach so great a mystery. From God alone can we receive the grace of greater understanding. Jesus said of His Spirit: "He will teach you all things, whatsoever I have commanded." We need the light of the Holy Ghost to appreciate the most sublime and most holy of all Christ's commands, which is contained in the divine ordinance of the Holy Thursday night: "Do this for a commemoration of me." Yet, in this process of enlightenment, God deigns to use human instruments, be they ever so unworthy. "Faith cometh by hearing" (Rom. x. 17). It is hoped, in the grace of God, that these considerations on the Most Blessed Eucharist may provide some food for that thoughtfulness which is the normal prelude to the work of the quickening Spirit, Who stirs both mind and heart, and makes truth a living thing in the soul.

Of the Mass, someone declared, there is never enough. The abundant literature on the Most Holy Sacrifice is a sign in our times of a strong religious revival. It shows that men's thoughts are turning more resolutely in these days of world crisis to that centre of most perfect worship of God and of man's salvation, which must endure until the "end of ages" (Heb. ix. 25). The chief aim of this book is to present a synthesis of logical and compelling thought, which, it is hoped, will help the reader to appreciate the Sacrament and Sacrifice of the Eucharist, not merely as a truth isolated within itself, but as the culmination of God's vast and eternal design of Redemption, gradually unfolded down the ages of preparation, and, once fulfilled, for ever perpetuating the fulness of sacrifice in the redeeming mystery of the Messiah.

Written primarily for the Catholic laity, certain subtleties of discussion are intentionally avoided, which, however useful for theologians, might tend to obscure for the lay mind the great essential truth that the Mass is in the truest sense a real sacrifice—the daily sacrifice of the faithful in Christ in which they individually enjoy a perfect participation. The apologetic value of continual appeal to both the Old and New Testaments, whilst strengthening the faith of those who believe, should also prove of assistance in the instruction of non-Catholics by widening the horizon of their religious beliefs beyond the man-made barriers set up by the Reformers of the sixteenth century to God's established way of perfect worship.

First Chapter

SHADOW OF GOOD THINGS TO COME

(Heb. x. 1)

1

FIRST STIRRINGS OF THE CHURCH

THE early history of a believing and teaching Church, founded by Jesus Christ and sanctified in the power of His Spirit, provides a rich source of enlightenment in what concerns our Christian faith. It is apparent from that history that, dating from the first Pentecost Sunday, those who embraced the new religion, though for a while they continued to pray with their Jewish brethren in the Temple, became at once quite distinct from them through what was most characteristic in the new form of worship, namely the "Breaking of Bread". This Christian rite, together with the complete sacramental and prayerful life which was centred in it, quickly accentuated the cleavage between the old and the new, and emphasized the essential difference in worship between Jew and Christian. In his epistle to the Hebrews St. Paul stresses the contrast between the outmoded Jewish sacrifices and the new Christian altar. The latter, though, like the former, it included a consuming of the victim, yet debarred the unconverted Jew from participation in its ritual. "We have an altar whereof they have no power to eat who serve the tabernacle" (Heb. xiii. 10).

Of the first converts to Christianity we read: "They were persevering in the doctrine of the Apostles and in the communication of the breaking of bread and in prayers" (Acts ii. 42). Of the nature of this "breaking of bread" no doubt existed in the minds of the Apostles or in that of their first converts to Christ. The name by which they knew this new ritual brought them back in spirit to the Upper Room where the Saviour had first broken bread for them, and had given them to eat. St. Paul set his face against early abuses at the Christian meetings by reminding the faithful of what brought them together. "The chalice of benediction, which we bless, is it not the communion of the blood of Christ? And the bread, which we break, is it not the partaking of the body of the Lord?" (1 Cor. x. 16). What they witnessed at the altar was nothing less than a renewal of the Passion and death of Jesus. "For as often as you shall eat this bread and drink this chalice, you shall show forth the death of the Lord until he come" (ibid. xi. 26). In the power of this living, pulsating, life-giving centre of the abiding Christ, the primitive Church launched its campaign for the salvation of souls. Every stratum of Jewish life felt the inexorable shock of its spiritual impact and the compelling force of divine grace. Even the jealously guarded priestly caste was not immune from its influence. St. Luke furnishes us with a brief but impressive summary of this early stage of development. "The word of the Lord increased; and the number of disciples was multiplied in Jerusalem exceedingly. A great multitude also of the priests obeyed the faith" (Acts vi. 7).

It was not surprising that the Sanhedrin, represented by the Scribes and Pharisees, who had encom-
passed the death of the Founder, should vent their
wrath against the new menace to their status which
had risen up in His Name. Once again they foolishly
thought that physical punishment, imprisonment, or
even death as a last extremity, would eradicate this new
religious society; Gamaliel, one of themselves, had
warned them, though in vain, of the foolhardiness of
such an undertaking. "Refrain from these men and
let them alone. For if this council or this work be of
men, it will come to nought; But if it be of God, you
cannot overthrow it, lest perhaps you be found even to
fight against God" (ibid. v. 38, 39). The Apostles were
first warned, and then they were scourged. But the
results did not fulfil the expectations of their perse-
cutors. "They indeed went from the presence of the
Council, rejoicing that they were accounted worthy to
suffer reproach for the name of Jesus; and every day
they ceased not, in the temple and from house to
house, to preach Christ Jesus" (ibid. xli. 42). Each
new trial of the young Church tended to widen the
gulf between Jew and Christian. Jesus had more
than once warned His Apostles of what would happen
to them for His sake, and of the inevitable complete
break between themselves and ancient Jewish priesthood. "The servant is not greater than the Master.
If they have persecuted me, they will also persecute
you. They will put you out of the synagogues: yea
the hour cometh, that whosoever killeth you, will think
that he doth a service to God" (John xv. 20; xvi. 2).

Persecution, when it came, served but to enlarge
and strengthen the vine of Christ's Church. Once
expelled from the Synagogue, the Christians were

forced to lead a more independent life in their own meeting places, with an ever increasing distinction of worship between the new and the old. As the Church grew she became more and more an object of fear and hate. The first shedding of blood in the martyrdom of St. Stephen appeared as a signal to the powers of evil to mass their might against the work of God. " At that time there was raised a great persecution against the Church which was at Jerusalem. And they were all dispersed through the countries of Judea and Samaria, except the Apostles" (Acts viii. 1). The Twelve with their first ordained co-operators in the Priesthood, who had continually "broken bread from house to house", realized how firmly established was the new faith. Violence defeated itself. Priests went forth with their dispersed brethren, and prepared the new altars of Christian Sacrifice in the settlements of these fervent members of the Church. To this growing independence and early dispersal was due the first development of a distinctly Christian Liturgy.

To appreciate these primitive liturgical developments we must bear in mind that, whilst there was bitter hatred of the new faith, and violent persecution of the faithful by the Jews, the Christians, on the other hand, hated neither Jews nor what was Jewish. Though essentially different, their worship had come forth from the Jewish Temple. They did not reject the Jewish holy books which contained the prophecies of the Messiah, and preserved for them in divers ways " most great and precious promises " (2 Pet. i. 4). All that had been written beforehand and entrusted by God to His Chosen People, became theirs by right of inheritance and was absorbed into the new religion as the imperfect is absorbed into the perfect. They took the ancient Testament of God out of the ruined Temple, and joined it to the new which had fulfilled it, that they might possess in the fullest measure the loving and vast design of God. When the veil of the Temple was rent asunder at the moment of Christ's death on the Cross, the new—"the greater and more perfect tabernacle" (Heb. ix. 11)—superseded the old. "In saying the new, he hath made the former old" (ibid. viii. 13).

2

CHRISTIAN LITURGY

Even a superficial examination of Catholic liturgical books, such as the Missal, Breviary or Ritual, reveals a predominance of Psalms, canticles, prophecies and histories from the Old Testament. This marked characteristic of Catholic Liturgy is in evidence from the earliest times. The retaining of so much that was originally Jewish by the early Christians was not by mere chance, nor just a matter of convenience. Still less was it attributable to any inability on their part to provide something better of their own. To the early Church the shaping of a new worship presented no difficulty. The Divine Founder furnished them with the essentials of that worship, and promised, moreover, to remain for ever with them as its living source and centre. The fulness of that bequeathed worship is contained in Christ Himself. For that reason St. Paul bestows upon Him the beautiful title of "Liturge of the holy things" (Heb. viii. 2). His life on earth was all worshipful of His Father.

But in establishing this new religion He declared that He had "come to fulfil, not to destroy" (Matt. v. 17). During His life on earth He accomplished all that had had been written of Him, and brought to perfection all that had foreshadowed Him. By giving Himself for ever to the Church, He perpetuated this excellence of worship amongst men. This was the business on which His Father had sent Him.

By the gift of Himself the Church inherited and became the divinely appointed guardian of Divine worship, whether in its prophetic design of the past, or in the splendour of its fulfilment in the present. The old belonged to the new as the shadow to its substance; and the substance was Christ Himself, "of whose fulness we all have received" (John. i. 16). The arrangement of Christian Liturgy in detail was left to the Apostles and their successors. Just as it was natural to them to defend the truth of the Christian religion by appeal to the evidence of the Old Testament and the perfect fulfilment of God's promises in Christ, so from the same source they also built up a great body of praise to adorn and explain the mysterious living centre which they held in the abiding Christ. Worship naturally springs from faith. "*Lex orandi; lex credendi.*" Prayer is Christian Dogma received and cherished on bended knees.

The people of Israel were the original custodians of the first and preparatory revelation. "The words of God were committed to them" (Rom. iii. 2). What was revealed to them, however, being prophetic and Messianic in character, belonged to the future rather than to the present. For them God's word constituted a saving hope in the Redeemer Who was to come. The moment of perfect communication of God's Word arrived with the descent of the Person of the Word in human form. "The Word was made flesh and dwelt amongst us" (John i. 14). "In him dwelt all the fulness of God corporeally" (Col. ii. 9). Jesus was the embodiment of all that had been promised. Sent by the Father, He became the guarantor of the Father's promises. "My meat is to do the will of him that sent me, that I may perfect his work" (John iii. 34). He confronted the Jews, who sought to kill Him, with the testimony of the past in which they professed to believe: "Search the Scriptures; the same are they that give testimony of me" (John v. 39). The motive of all His actions is repeatedly stressed in the Gospels; "That the Scriptures might be fulfilled." He took upon Himself as His rule of life, "Obedience unto death, even unto the death of the cross" (Phil. ii. 8). He fulfilled all that had been written, and in the perfect form of its accomplishment He passed it on to His Brethren as the living completed Word unto the end of time. "All things must needs be fulfilled, which are written of me in the law of Moses, and in the prophets, and in the Psalms concerning me" (Luke xxiv. 44). By accomplishing His appointed task so perfectly He lifted the inspired prayer and praises of God in the Old Testament back to its source to the everlasting glory of His Father, from Whom it emerged again in the new brilliance of the Spirit in Whom with Christ we cry: Abba—Father. He Who was the perfecter of praise in Himself, bestowed that same Spirit of praise on His Church that the glory of His Father might be continued in like perfection until the end of time, and throughout eternity. "The words which thou gavest me, I have given to them, and they have received them. . . . And the glory which thou hast given me,

I have given them that they may be one, as we also are one" '(John xvii. 8, 22). What belongs to Christ belongs also to Christians as part of their glorious inheritance to the praise and glory of our common Father.

The Canticles of the Patriarchs, the Psalms of David, the words of the Prophets found their place in Christian prayer precisely because its purpose was to continue the prayer of Christ. What had been written was the work of the Holy Ghost, and held concealed the wonders of God's design, yet to be revealed. Jesus, God and man, alone fully comprehended the mysteries contained in this first revelation. He alone in the fulness of that comprehension could perfectly direct His life, Passion and death into the depths of these mysteries. His life on earth from the beginning to the end was epitomized in His symbolic action in the synagogue, when "He unfolded the Book" (Luke iv. 17). The Old Testament possesses in Him an entirely new light, since He has opened it to all men, that they may see "the mystery which had been hidden from ages and generations, but now is manifested to his saints" (Col. i. 26). "God, who at sundry times and in divers manners spoke in times past to the Fathers and the prophets, last of all in these days, hath spoken to us by His Son, whom he hath appointed heir to all things" (Heb. i. 1). In the Psalms and canticles of the Old Testament the Jews sang the glory of God in the hope of the Messiah. Christians resumed the divine harmony of that ancient praise in the perfect phase of its completion in Christ. The angels on Christmas night were the first to voice the silent worship of the Babe of Bethlehem—"Glory to God in the highest." That canticle of the angels absorbed into itself all that went before, and summarized the unending praise of Christ and His mystic Body the Church, which echoes still around the altars of our Christian Churches.

3

THE IMPREGNABLE ROCK

'The light cast from out the Old Testament on the worship of the New is something more than a general illumination. Its rays bring into relief even the details of our Christian Liturgy. The most Holy Sacrifice of the Mass, in particular, is revealed in greater splendour, when viewed against the background of the promise, which called it forth out of the past. The religion of the Old Testament not merely sang hopefully in praise of the Messiah, but prepared the way for His coming by a divinely appointed external ritual. The ancient sacrifices, with their accompanying psalmody, possessed a certain excellence of worship in so far as they foreshadowed the mystery of Redemption, and to attain to perfection they needed only to be enacted and fulfilled by the Incarnate Word. In the religion of the Old Testament we find the first flowering of the Christian cult—the germ of its Liturgy. The religion of the New Testament in the blood of Jesus Christ came forth from it as a perfect fruit from the flower which had announced and prognosticated it. Just as the fruit appears when the flower fades and its germ has been absorbed, so the worship established by Christ superseded the old ritual, and brought to full growth the germ which it contained.

Our Christian religion is impregnably founded on two great volumes—the Old and the New—of God's testimony. Of all the apologetic arguments in favour of the truth of our faith, there is none, perhaps, more cogent than that which emerges from the relation of these volumes to one another. We can best understand the Old in the light of the New, and, conversely, the grandeur of our Christian institutions becomes still more striking when viewed in the light of God's preparation down the ages which preceded them. This twofold testimony of God's truth is an open book, which may be examined by all men. There is nothing secret about it. It contains, indeed, many things which surpass the power of human understanding, but the exact fulfilment of its prophetic content, which stamps it with the inescapable evidence of truth, is a fact which can be grasped by the feeblest intelligence. In the first volume of this testimony of God inspired writers told of events hundreds and even thousands of years before they came to pass. During these long ages of waiting God commanded also a detailed ritual which foreshadowed the perfect religion which was to follow. All that was written spoke in one way or another of what the New Testament was to contain. To God alone could such things be known. He alone could speak through the mouths of His prophets of what He intended to do in the far-off future. There is nothing vague about the preparatory revelation. It foretells on behalf of the Messiah an immensity of labour, a detailed exactness of work to be done; it pictures a holiness of life, a perfection of accomplishment which only God could predetermine and so perfectly fulfil. In the full light of the New Testament in comparison with the Old, it is evident that the mysteries of the Incarnation, of the birth, life, Passion, death and Resurrection of Jesus Christ, together with the fulness of grace and worship inherited by His Church, correspond most perfectly to the grandeur of God's promise of salvation and sanctification down the ages of preparation.

This testimony to the truth of our Christian faith is indestructible. God's Word stands. The Bible represents the unassailable evidence of His omnipotence. No science, no power, no pseudo-philosophy can prevail against it. It is simple but inexorable. Those who receive it find life, and safe anchorage, since it bears to them the message of God's undying love. Those who in their pride would seek to destroy this rock of Divine truth, discover to their undoing how impregnable is its strength. Every evil force that has set itself against it has ultimately perished beneath the weight of its truth and power. "To you therefore, that believe, he is honour; but to them that believe not, the stone which the builders rejected, the same is become the head of the corner: and a stone of stumbling, and a rock of scandal, to them who stumble at the word, neither do believe, whereunto they are sent" (1 Pet. ii. 7, 8). "Whosoever shall fall upon this stone, shall be broken: but upon whomsoever it shall fall, it shall grind him to powder" (Matt. xxi. 44).

4

FORESHADOWING OF SACRIFICE

As one would naturally expect, the prophecies, whilst foretelling the entire life and work of the

Messiah, paid particular attention to the supreme and most tragic hour—" the hour so long desired "—of His Passion and death.   In graphic and detailed language they describe His sorrows and sufferings from the moment of His betrayal until His last breath upon the cross.   The prophecies emphasize Calvary because it is the culminating point of man's redemption, the unique source of all good, and the most perfect act of worship offered by the Saviour to the glory of His Father.   But whilst it was a culminating point in the work of Christ, for mankind it marked the beginning of a new and perfect religion.   Neither His priesthood nor His worship were extinguished in His death (cf. Heb. vii. 23).   What the Cross contained was to take root in the hearts of men through the merits of the Crucified.   The Church born of His open side is essentially a religious society, which, by the appointment and bestowal of power by her Founder, is enabled to continue on earth the worship of the Father, which reached its apogee in the Passion and death of the Incarnate Word.

Religion, or the relation between man and God, was the great theme of the Old Testament.   Its main concern was to lead men to the saving hope in the Messiah. As it took more and more definite shape down the thousands of years after the Fall, it desired to prepare men's minds for the perfect religion of the Son of God made man.   The universal character of the Kingdom of Christ, the conversion of the gentiles, the abundance of grace, the appointment of new teachers, of a glorious priesthood, were repeatedly emphasized in the prophecies.   The decrees of the Levitical Law of Moses, the detailed prescriptions of ritual observance, which determined the externals of the people's religious life, the striking events of God's merciful dealings and protection, all these things were replete with profound Messianic significance. The Jewish religion was essentially a religion of the future, since it depended for its efficacy on the fulfilment of God's promise. We can look back to it in the clear light of the Gospel in order to confirm our faith, not only in Christ, but in all that He established in His Church as the Founder of life and worship. The study of this reflection of the New in the Old is particularly profitable for our spiritual progress and a powerful aid to our appreciation of the Mass. The perpetual sacrifice which was to characterize the Christian religion holds a very particular place in the prophetic pronouncements of the Old Testament. Then, as now, sacrifice was an essential of worship, and its predominating place in ancient worship, as well as its splendid ritual, is eloquent in its message to ourselves of the still greater splendour which it foretold.

Acceptance of the Dogma of the Most Holy Eucharist rests principally on the words of the Saviour in the Upper Room. Yet faith in this mystery is strengthened and increased by viewing the act of sacrificial worship, which He there instituted, against the background of its divinely appointed prophetic preparation. God clearly foretold, not only the Passion and death of His Beloved Son, but the everlasting renewal of His sacrifice of the Cross, in which, through union with the self-same Victim, men would possess a most perfect form of worship, a most sure source of grace, and a pledge of everlasting glory. In this juxtaposition of the old and new is found also the answer to the Protestant argument against the Mass, that Calvary alone is sufficient. What is human judgment that it

C

dares to determine against the weight of such evidence what is sufficient in God's sight?   It is God's will alone which must decide.   That will, so manifest in the words of the Institution, was proclaimed also in the preceding revelation.   We admit that Calvary alone is sufficient, and the source of every grace.   But it must be remembered that Christ founded a religion for all men, and for all time, and that no religion is complete without sacrifice.   St. Augustine declared: "Whether religion be true or false, we always find sacrifice as one of its essential elements."   The Divine intention of the Saviour to provide at His Last Supper a perpetual renewal of Calvary in the Holy Mass is supported under three distinct headings of appeal to the Old Testament, firstly by Prophecy, secondly by Messianic types, and thirdly by ritual observances.

5

PROPHECIES OF THE MASS

The best known and clearest prophecy of the Mass is found in the Book of Malachy, who is reputed to have lived about 400 B.C.   Bearing the Word of God to the Chosen People, the Prophet spoke of God's displeasure with the sacrifices of half-hearted worshippers, who reserved the diseased and weaklings of their flocks and herds for the sacrifices of the Temple.   God rejected all such sacrifices: "I have no pleasure in you, saith the Lord of Hosts, and I will not receive a gift at your hand."   God, having turned away from the irreverent offerings of a stiff-necked people, spoke in the inspired word of the Prophet, and in loving expectancy of the future—of an era of continuous, universal, and most pleasing sacrifice. "From the rising of the sun even to the going down, my name is great among the gentiles: and in every place there is sacrifice, and there is offered to my name a clean oblation. For my name is great among the gentiles, saith the Lord of Hosts" (Mal. i. 10, 11). Only in the light of the New Testament can we perceive the full meaning of these words. Something great and holy is portended, which is fully satisfied in the daily ubiquitous sacrifice of the body and blood of Jesus Christ on our Christian altars under the appearances of bread and wine.

The requirements of the prophecy demanded a *clean oblation*. There can be no purer oblation in the sight of God than the death of His Beloved Son on the Cross; "Who in the days of his flesh with a strong cry and tears, offering up prayers and supplications to him that was able to save him from death, was heard for his reverence. And whereas indeed he was the Son of God, he learned obedience by the things which he suffered; and being consummated, he became, to all that obey him, the cause of eternal salvation" (Heb. v. 8, 9). But the actual sacrifice of Calvary is not of itself sufficient to fulfil this prophecy, since this most pleasing act of worship must be *from the rising of the sun even to the going down*. Christ died only once on the Cross. He cannot die again. "By one oblation he hath perfected for ever them that are sanctified" (Heb. x. 4). The prophecy demands that His immolation be in some mysterious way capable of renewal. The Most Blessed Eucharist provides fulfilment in a mysterious and sacred ritual which makes Him present on our Christian altars in the guise of death.

The new and most clean oblation spoken of by the Prophet was clearly unbloody in the form of its celebration.   It is apparently akin to the bloodless food offerings familiar to the Jews, and characteristic of the offering of Melchisedech.   The exact nature of this future act of worship is made clear from the Hebrew word used by Malachy, namely *Mincha*, which was used only for oblations of unleavened bread, as distinguished from the *Sebach*, which was reserved for sacrifices in the shedding of blood of animal offerings. In Christ both kinds of sacrifices are represented and united.   The substances of bread and wine, changed by Consecration into the all-holy substance of the once immolated body and poured out blood, makes possible the mystical renewal of the sacrifice in the actual shedding of blood on the Cross.   Consecration corresponds to the *Mincha*—Calvary to the *Sebach*.   Though the merits and power of Christ on the Cross passed beyond the limits of time and space, yet, the actual immolation of Calvary was measured by both, and could be witnessed by those only who stood by the Cross.   Jesus realized our need of visual renewal, and so arranged in the Mass that our association with His Passion and death might be made evident in a sacred sacrificial sign which would fill the measure of time foretold by the Prophet.   Likewise, the new form of worship necessitates a bridging of space—it must be "*in every place*".   It must pass beyond the confines of Golgotha for that very reason.   This prophetic rite could not refer to any sacrifice possessed by the Jews.   No worship within the walls of the Temple could satisfy the conditions of its fulfilment.   All Jewish sacrifices were exclusive.   This new oblation sends up praise to God, even from among the Gentiles.

This aspect of the prophecy of Malachy regarding Gentile participation in the worship to be established by the Messiah is a familiar theme in other prophecies also. Isaias emphasizes the universal nature of the Kingdom of Christ which would draw all peoples into its worship as in a great temple covering the earth, "And in the last days the mountain of the house of the Lord shall be prepared on the tops of the mountains, and it shall be exalted above the hills, and all the nations shall flow into it" (Isa. ii. 1). What the prophets saw from afar, Jesus Himself foretold from near at hand to the Samaritan woman at the well of Jacob. "Woman believe me, that the hour cometh, when you shall, neither on this mountain, nor in Jerusalem, adore the Father. But the hour cometh and now is, when true adorers shall adore the Father in spirit and in truth. For the Father also seeketh for such to adore him" (John. iv. 21, 22).

The rejection of the ancient sacrificial ritual in favour of the perfect Christian Liturgy is also a familiar thesis in the Epistles of St. Paul. We are, very appropriately, indebted to the Apostle of the Gentiles for an inspired interpretation of a prophecy of King David, somewhat akin to the Prophecy of Malachy. "Sacrifices and oblation thou wouldst not; but a body thou hast fitted for me: holocausts for sin did not please thee. Then said I: behold I come: in the head of the book it is written of me: that I should do thy will" (Psalm xxxix. 7, 8; Heb. x. 5-7). The rejected sacrifices here referred to were, St. Paul declares, those which were "offered according to the law" (ibid.). The prophet's announcement in the person of the Messiah implied the substitution of a new ritual for the old. "He taketh away the first, that he may establish that which followeth " (ibid. ix). The centre of the new worship is found in the " Oblation of the body of Jesus ". The purpose of His assuming of our flesh was that He might offer it in perfect obedience to the Father from Whom he received it. The sacrifice of Calvary is the one supreme act of worship of the new dispensation. "In the which will we are sanctified by the oblation of Jesus Christ once " (ibid. x). St. Paul would seem to have in mind the renewal of Calvary as well as Calvary itself. He is comparing ritual with ritual. He contrasts the old legal sacrifices with that "which followeth ". The immolation of the Cross is made an everlasting covenant of God with man through the Lord's Supper. The old sacrifices were but " a shadow of the good things to come, not the very image of these things " (ibid. i). The Mass, on the other hand, is the very image of Calvary. Again He declares that in Christ man has found "a new and living way which he hath dedicated for us through the veil, that is to say, his flesh " (ibid. xx). This new way leads "into the sanctuary through the blood of Christ " (ibid. xix). There is a new sanctuary established on earth, which is the prelude to the sanctuary of heaven. The old Temple has gone—its veil rent asunder. The new temple demands a new and everlasting ritual which will continue to apply to men the merits of Christ. That St. Paul has this new Christian ritual in mind is obvious from the whole text. The oblation of the body of Jesus Christ is continued in the sign which renews it. Moreover, he takes occasion from his exposition of such sublime doctrine to remind the faithful of the conditions necessary for approach to so holy a participation with Christ in this new sanctuary. "Let us draw near with a true heart in the fulness of faith, having our hearts sprinkled from evil conscience, and our bodies washed in clean water" (ibid. xxii). At the same time he reminds them of the necessity of being present at the offering of the Holy Sacrifice—"not forsaking our assembly" (ibid. xxv). The Christians knew well what these assemblies meant. St. Paul refers otherwise to these same Christian assemblies as their "coming together in the Church . . . to eat the Lord's Supper" (1 Cor. ii. 18. 20).

6

PROTOTYPES OF CHRIST

The promise of a Redeemer, first given to Adam, was renewed at various stages of man's subsequent history. God appointed the Patriarchs of the Old Testament to be His messengers of hope in the future Messiah. Many of them not only spoke of the coming, but in various appointed ways became themselves figures or types of Christ. Their Messianic character was appreciated by the Jews, as is apparent from the New Testament, where Our Lord and, later, the Apostles, frequently appealed to the mysterious likeness of their vocation, or status, or achievements, to certain phases of the Messianic fulfilment. The varied parts to which they were divinely assigned during the preparatory period of revealed religion emphasize the power and headship of Christ, and the splendour of His redemption on behalf of mankind. In the light of the divinely inspired word of the New Testament we are enabled to draw instruction for ourselves from the history of the past, particularly in relation to the sacraments and the Mass.

St. Peter brings our minds back to the days of Noe, who, in building the Ark, foreshadowed the founding of the Church and the sacrament of Baptism. "Whereunto baptism being of a like form, now saveth you also" (1 Pet. iii. 20). Abraham, with whom begins the history of the Chosen People, received from God a renewal of the primitive promise. He was appointed the head of a new race. "I will bless thee, and I will multiply thy seed as the stars of heaven, and as the sand that is by the sea shore" (Gen. xxii. 17). From him according to the flesh was to descend the Messiah. "And in thy seed shall all the nations of the earth be blessed" (ibid. xviii). We are again indebted to St. Paul for an inspired interpretation of this promise. "To Abraham were the promises made and to his seed. He saith not, *And to his seeds*, as of many: but as of one, *And to thy seed*, which is Christ" (Gal. iii. 16). Of the same Patriarch Jesus declared: "Abraham your father rejoiced to see my day: he saw it and was glad" (John viii. 56). In him was typified the mysterious relationship between the Father and His Incarnate Son, Who was sent to be obedient unto death. Abraham was commanded to sacrifice his only son Isaac, on whom depended the fulfilment of God's promise. God's acceptance of his willingness to obey was couched in terms which proclaim the love of the Father in sending His Son for a redemption. "Now I know that thou fearest God, and hast not spared thy only begotten son for my sake" (Gen. xxii. 12). Like Moses, who was not permitted to enter the Promised Land, but received the privilege of at least viewing it from afar on Mount Nebo before he died, so the Patriarchs, and Abraham in particular, beheld from the heights of their privileged association in the design of redemption, something of the mystery to come. "All these died according to the faith, not having received the promises, but beholding them from afar off and saluting them" (Heb. xii. 13). To Abraham was granted the special honour of saluting the Christian Sacrifice in an oblation of bread and wine, offered on his behalf, and of reverencing Christ's most excellent priesthood in the person of Melchisedech, the mysterious "priest of the most high God". King David was later to sing prophetically of the glory of that priesthood, and of the solemn oath sworn by God to fulfil it in His Son. (cf. Chapter 2.)

When confronted with the incredulity and even bitter hatred of His own people, Our Divine Saviour charged them with betrayal of all that Moses had done on their behalf. "Think not that I will accuse you to the Father. There is one that accuseth you, Moses, in whom you trust. But if you did believe Moses, you would perhaps believe me also. For he wrote of me. But if you do not believe his writings, how will you believe my words?" (John v. 46, 47). On yet another occasion he showed how Moses had been privileged to salute His death on the Cross: "As Moses lifted up the serpent in the desert, so must the Son of man be lifted up" (John iii. 14). By his appointment as leader over the people of Israel, Moses bore likeness to Christ. "The Lord thy God will raise up to thee a Prophet of thy nation and of thy brethren like unto thee. Him thou shalt hear" (Deut. xix. 15). This prophecy of Moses was well known to the Jews, and should have been for them a guiding light in their accepting of Jesus. But for the most part their hearts were hardened, and their eyes were blinded by their own self-love. It was otherwise with those whose hearts were open to believe, such, for instance, as with Philip, who declared to Nathanael: "We have found him of whom Moses in the law, and the Prophets did write, Jesus the son of Joseph of Nazareth" (John i. 45). In his first defence of the Christian religion St. Peter appealed to the fulfilment of the same prophecy in Jesus Christ: "Whom heaven indeed must receive until the times of restitution of all things, which God hath spoken by the mouth of his holy prophets from the beginning of the world. For Moses said: *A prophet shall the Lord your God raise up unto you of your brethren like unto me*" (Acts iii. 21, 22). This likeness of Moses to Christ appeared in many different ways—as leader, as teacher, as deliverer, as liturgist, as law-giver. But most striking of all was his privilege to foreshadow in two distinct ways the Most Holy Eucharist and the Mass. The Manna which he obtained by his prayer from God to feed the people in the desert was compared by the Divine Saviour to the heavenly bread of eternal life which He received from His Father and gave to mankind; "My Father giveth you the true bread from heaven" (John vi. 32). In prescribing the ritual of the Passover Moses approached nearest of all the Prophets to the ritual repast and sacrifice of the Upper Room.

The Manna was a sign of the Eucharistic Communion rather than of its essential act of Sacrifice. Even as Moses provided his people with a copious supply of water from the rock—"And the rock was Christ" (1 Cor. x. 4), so also of the food, which he received from heaven for their sustenance, we may say: "The Manna was Christ." For the Jews the Manna betokened the greatest sign of God's favour. It also represented for them the genuineness of Moses' claim to be their divinely appointed leader. In their minds it possessed a symbolic Messianic meaning which would be eventually fulfilled. They challenged Christ's claim to be the Messiah by appeal to what Moses had done for their people. "They said therefore to him: What sign therefore does thou show that we may see and believe thee? What dost thou work? Our fathers did eat manna in the desert as it is written, *he gave them bread from heaven*" (John vi. 30, 31). Jesus accepted the challenge, and in reply showed how He was indeed the Messiah, Who would provide a still more abundant and more excellent bread than that which they had received from Moses. "Moses gave you not bread from heaven, but my Father giveth you the true bread from heaven. For the bread of God is that which cometh down from heaven and giveth life to the world" (ibid. 32, 33). "Your fathers did eat manna in the desert, and are dead. This is the bread which cometh down from heaven and giveth life to the world" (ibid. 32, 33). "Your fathers did eat manna in the desert, and are dead. This is the bread which cometh from heaven; that if any man eat of it, he may not die. I am the living bread, which cometh down from heaven. If any man eat of this bread, he shall live for ever: and the bread that I shall give, is my flesh for the life of the world" (ibid. 49-52).

Christ's way of fulfilling the prophetic portent of the long expected Messianic food was not favourably received by the materially minded Jews, who sought only for free bread to support the body. "You seek me because you did eat and were filled. Labour not for the meat that perisheth, but for that which endureth unto life everlasting, which the Son of man will give you" (ibid. 26, 27). Their refusal to believe, their murmuring, and final desertion have at least for us the advantage of showing how well they grasped the meaning of the Saviour's words. They were under no misapprehension regarding the nature of His promised gift, as a fulfilment of their prophetic Manna. Having up to then refused to consent to His Divinity in spite of all His miracles, they were not prepared to accept the supreme miracle of His love for men. In one breath they expressed their disbelief in the mystery of the Incarnation and of the Blessed Eucharist. "How then, saith he, I am come down from heaven?" (ibid. 42). "How can this man give us his flesh to eat?" (ibid. 53). Our Christian faith in the mystery of the God-man, and in the Real Presence, rallies us to the side of Peter and the Apostles; "Lord to whom shall we go? Thou hast the words of eternal life. And we have believed and have known that thou art the Christ the Son of God" (ibid. 69, 70).

7

THE SACRIFICE OF THE PASCH

God appointed Moses to liberate His people from their long-sustained Egyptian bondage. By means of ten plagues of increasing severity Pharao was finally constrained to set them free. The final plague marked the day of deliverance. God told Moses that He would send a destroying angel to slay the first-born of every Egyptian family. At the same time He prescribed a sacrificial ritual which would distinguish between Jew and Egyptian, and so prevent harm from falling on His people. This ritual was known as the sacrifice of Pasch or Passover, so called because the angel passed by the houses of the Israelites. Amidst the splendour of ancient sacrificial types this Pashcal rite stands supreme in the perfection of its foreshadowing power. According to St. Thomas, all the ancient sacrifices predicted one or other characteristic of the sacrifice of Christ and the Blessed Eucharist. Melchisedech, in offering bread and wine, foreshadowed the matter of the sacrament. The ancient Levitical sacrifices, especially those of expiation, prefigured the ends for which Mass is offered. The Manna which constituted the food of the Chosen People in the desert signified the Communion of the faithful. But all these separate symbols are found grouped together in the one sacrifice and ceremony of the Passover, which, he declares, " is the principal figure of the Mass and the Blessed Eucharist " (iii; Q. 73, 6).

A year-old lamb without blemish was the chosen sacrificial victim of the rite of the Passover, which was separately offered in each household. In other Jewish sacrifices the sacrificial act was the sole privilege of the priestly tribe of Levi. In the paschal sacrifice the father or head of the household officiated. There was thereby a widening out of priestly power. Once the lamb was slain, its blood was poured out on the doorposts of the home as a sign to the destroying angel. The Israelites were commanded to stand by with loins girth, staff in hand, as if ready for the journey. The flesh of the lamb provided their sustenance for the way. It was to be eaten with unleavened bread and wild lettuce; so that the celebration became subsequently known as the Feast of Unleavened Bread. In commanding the first celebration of this rite, God laid down strict laws for its future commemorations, as "a feast to the Lord in your generations with an everlasting observance" (Exod. xi. 14). The annual celebration was to last for seven days, and marked the beginning of the Jewish year. Special care was to be taken that no leavened bread be found in the houses, once these days of festivity had commenced, under threat of dire penalties for those who dared to transgress. "Seven days there shall not be found any leaven in your houses, he that shall eat leavened bread, his soul shall perish out of the assembly of Israel" (ibid. 19). So severe a penalty for a breach of what would otherwise seem a trivial observance can only be explained by the importance of the Messianic symbolism attached to it, pertaining to the Passion and the Institution of the Blessed Eucharist. St. Paul emphasizes this relation of the Old to the New: "Christ our Pasch is sacrificed. Therefore let us keep festival, not with the old leaven, nor with the leaven of malice and wickedness, but with the unleavened bread of sincerity and truth" (1 Cor. v. 8).

Other details connected with the ritual gave further strength to its Messianic character. The partaking of this food of the paschal sacrifice was strictly reserved to the people of Israel. "No foreigner shall eat of it" (ibid. 43). Circumcision, which foreshadowed the sacrament of Baptism in the new dispensation, was enjoined as a necessary condition of being admitted to the repast. A further significant command accompanied the preparation: "Neither shall you break a bone thereof" (ibid. 46). This prophetic prohibition regarding the paschal lamb was later to stay the sacrilegious fury of the Roman soldiery to whom Pilate gave orders to break the bones of the crucified. "But after they were come to Jesus, when they saw that he was already dead, they did not break his legs" (John xix. 23). The desire of the Jews to dissociate the Victim of Calvary from the paschal celebration by hastening His deposition from the Cross served only to perfect its accurate fulfilment. "For these things were done that the Scriptures might be fulfilled: You shall not break a bone of him: and again another Scripture saith; They shall look upon him whom they pierced" (ibid. 36, 37).

The Jews were well aware of the Messianic significance of the "Lamb without blemish". The prophet Isaias spoke of the Messiah in the silent endurance of His Passion as the "Lamb before his shearer" (53.7). St. John the Baptist expressed both the expectation of his people and the certainty of its fulfilment in Christ. "John saw Jesus coming to him, and he saith: Behold the Lamb of God, behold him who taketh away the sins of the world" (John i. 29). Jesus is the Paschal Lamb of the new and more perfect testament, Who fulfilled minutely the paschal portent of God's mercy and love. He is the "Lamb that was slain" (Apoc. v. 12). Who delivered Himself for the liberation of His people from the servitude of sin and Satan, Who shed His blood "unto the remission of sins" (Matt. xxvi. 28).

In the Gospel we witness a kind of crescendo of fulfilment of the ancient Passover, mounting towards an inevitable climax. Significant events occurred during the three paschal celebrations, which coincided with the public life of the Savour. At the first Pasch he drove the buyers and sellers out of the Temple, and purified it in His Father's Name. "My house shall be called the house of prayer, but you have made it a den of thieves" (Matt. xxi. 13). The old Temple was a figure of the more perfect sanctuary which He was to establish on earth to His Father's glory. He purified what was figurative before establishing the reality. During the following year's feast of the Passover He made a still more immediate preparation for its fulfilment by the multiplication of the loaves and fishes, and by announcing in plain words how the ritual of unleavened bread and the flesh of the Lamb would be combined in one consuming. He spoke in terms of flesh and blood, which brought to mind the ancient ordinances of the Paschal sacrifice, which even at that moment they were preparing to offer to God. "Amen, amen, I say unto you: Except you eat the flesh of the Son of man, and drink his blood, you shall not have life in you. . . . For my flesh is meat indeed; and my blood is drink indeed" (John. vi. 54, 56).

The final feast of the Passover coincided with His last days on earth. He chose the actual feast of the Pasch on which to become the Pasch. With clear vision He saw what He must do, and as the great Liturge, or supreme Master of Ceremonies, He set Himself resolutely to the task. "The day of the unleavened bread came, on which it was necessary that the Pasch should be killed. And he sent Peter and John, saying, go and prepare for us the Pasch, that we may eat" (Luke xxii. 7, 8). Jesus longed with all His heart for the time of this accomplishment, which was to mark the final phase of His work on behalf of man's redemption. The new Pasch, once established, was to constitute a perfect act of worship until the end of time, and was to find eternally in the kingdom of His Father a still higher perfection "as an everlasting observance".

"He said to them: With desire have I desired to eat this Pasch with you before I suffer. For I say to you, that from this time I will not eat it till it be fulfilled in the Kingdom of God" (ibid. 7, 8).

God ordained the yearly celebration of the feast of unleavened bread to be an unceasing ritual which would renew the memory of the first sacrifice of actual deliverance. The institution of the Blessed Eucharist had a like commemorative purpose— "that the Scriptures might be fulfilled". Jesus established a perpetual sacrifice in the midst of His Church, which would renew for all time the actual redeeming sacrifice of the Cross. "Do this for a commemoration of me." By bestowing power of Consecration, and thereby of offering the self-same sacrifice of His body and blood under the appearances of bread and wine, Jesus shared His priesthood with men. He thus provided for a vast number of bishops and priests of every tongue and tribe, who would be the fathers and heads of His family of brethren until the end of time. Simultaneously, he furnished both priests and people with a strong nourishment to sustain them in their journey towards the Promised Land of His eternal Kingdom. This food, which is the flesh of the Lamb that was sacrificed, is the exclusive possession of the faithful of His Church. Entrance into this Divine ritual and repast of the new Pasch is possible only through the regenerating waters of Baptism, whereby men are born again in the Holy Ghost as the chosen children of His Father. The Holy Mass, being the perfect renewal of the redeeming sacrifice of the Cross, delivers us by its inherent power of satisfaction from the bondage of sin and of the Devil. By its atoning power it makes reparation for us in the sight of God

D

for our manifold transgressions. When present at the Holy Sacrifice, we become associated in the privilege of St. John the Baptist, who "saw Jesus coming to him", and with him we fervently cry out: "Behold the Lamb of God; Behold him who taketh away the sins of the world."

8

ANCIENT SPLENDOUR

With the freedom of the Chosen People from the bondage of Egypt, the worship of the Jews grew by Divine ordinance into an ever more splendid ritual. The books of Leviticus, of Deuteronomy, and others of the early Old Testament, which contain detailed directions from God to Moses for the various sacrifices, reveal an amazing wealth of ceremonial. The intercessory power of this ancient ritual consisted in its expression of Messianic hope. Through a magnificent diversity of Levitical sacrifices, through solemn rites and significant ceremonial, through various types and figures, the mind of the people was joined to the Saviour to come. Almighty God deigned to accept these ancient sacrifices, not merely because He had prescribed their ritual, but because they foretold the most pleasing offering of His Eternal Son upon the Cross. St. Thomas Aquinas declared: "It is true to say that Christ was sacrificed even in the figures of the Old Testament: Hence it is stated in the Apocalypse (xv. 8): *Whose names are not written in the book of the life of the Lamb, which was slain from the begin-*

ning of the world" (iii, Q. 83. 1). St. Paul calls these sacrifices "the patterns of heavenly things, not the heavenly things themselves . . . having a shadow of the good things to come, not the very image of these things" (Heb. ix. 23, 10, 1).

It would seem to have been God's intention in prescribing such a wide diversity of sacrifice, such a multiplying of victims, so abundant a shedding of blood, to show forth the infinite efficacy contained in the one supreme sacrifice of the God-man, "of whose blood one drop can cleanse the whole world of all stain" ("*Adoro Te*"). In the ancient ritual there was a diversity of victims to suit all occasions according to the manifold needs of the people. All manner of beasts were offered. There were holocausts, and partial sacrifices, rites of thanksgiving, of expiation, of sin, of peace. Jesus Christ is the unique victim who by offering Himself once, raised adoration of God to new and immeasurable heights, and expressed therein the entirety of human needs. "This man offering one sacrifice for sins, for ever sitteth on the right hand of God" (Heb. x. 12).

Recalling the grandeur of the foreshadowing which foretold what was to come, the splendour of ritual, the multitude of victims which spoke so eloquently in blood of the future, we may well ask, Whither all this has led? What is to be expected from such magnificence of types and figures? It is evident that what followed should be more splendid than what went before. "If that which is done away is glorious: much more that which remaineth is in glory" (2 Cor. iii. 11). Even as the promised Messiah should be more perfect and more holy than the prophets who foretold Him, so also the sacrifice, which He established in His new and perfect religion, should excel the multitude of sacrifices, which were but shadows of the reality. "For if the blood of goats and oxen, and the ashes of an heifer being sprinkled, sanctify such as are defiled to the cleansing of the flesh: how much more shall the blood of Christ, who, by the Holy Ghost, offered himself unspotted unto God, cleanse our conscience from dead works to serve the living God. And therefore he is the mediator of the new testament" (Heb. ix. 13-15). In the light of the fulness of the new dispensation it would be absurd to place the religion of Christ in a position of inferiority to that of the Jews of old. Christians also require some visible act of sacrifice, such as comforted the Chosen People. Without it the Christian religion would not be complete. In our approach to God through Christ, considering the love of God which His coming on earth revealed, we must likewise expect the assurance of a visible and divinely appointed sign of His continued love and favour. For we are a "chosen generation" in a far higher sense than were the Jews.

In rejecting the Holy Sacrifice of the Mass, under the plea of a purer religion, the Protestant Reformers not only robbed the Christian religion of its most essential act, but, in so doing, declared meaningless and useless all the preparatory splendour that had gone before. God's work of preparation over thousands of years was made by them the foreshadowing of a lesser shadow—and Christ did not attain to the greatness which was promised. The so-called Communion Table of their Sunday Service, which they substituted for the Christian Altar of sacrifice, and on which lie unchanged the mere common substances of bread and wine, presents a sorry spectacle when compared with the magnificence of the ancient Jewish ritual. Such a result, viewed in the immensity of the foreshadowing which called it forth, would be a deterioration of worship instead of an increase and a perfecting. It would have been far better to have retained the old splendour, rather than to end in so cold and comfortless a ceremonial. Jesus Christ established a perfect religion, a perfect worship of His Father, in a perfect and most acceptable sacrifice. Nothing less than the real and true sacrifice of the Mass, which places on our altars the all-holy Victim of the Cross, which renews for us through the transmitted power of Consecration all the merits of His death in the actual shedding of His blood, can satisfy the claims of the Old Testament.

Such was the foreshadowing, such now is its bountiful fulfilment in the reality of Christian sacrifice. The immensity which was foretold during the long period of expectation and preparation is all ours to offer and consume to God's glory and our own salvation. One Mass is the gathering together of all the ancient sacrifices. The daily sacrifice of our Christian altars contains the fulfilment of myriads of religious acts which preceded and promised it. The Mass is the perfect sacrifice of the Lamb without blemish, Who, "being made a curse for us" (Gal. iii. 13), offered Himself, "that we might be made the justice of God in him" (2 Cor. v. 21). It is the duty of Catholics to appreciate the glory of their inheritance in Christ. "If thou didst but know the gift of God" (John iv. 10). The Saviour said to His Apostles: "Many prophets and just men desired to see the things that you see, and have not seen" (Matt. xiii. 17). We have not only seen—"we have tasted also of the heavenly gift" (Heb. vi. 4).

Our Christian faith, which opens the door to this sanctuary of God on earth through Jesus Christ, is strengthened by the thought of the new glory, so wonderfully reflected in the old, "of which we are heirs according to the promise" (Gal. iii. 29). "You are come to Mount Sion, and the city of the living God, the heavenly Jerusalem, and the company of the many thousands of angels, and the church of the first-born, who are written in the heavens, and to God the judge of all, and to the spirits of the just made perfect, and to Jesus the mediator of the new testament, and to the sprinkling of blood which speaketh better than that of Abel" (Heb. xii. 22-4). In the Mass is fulfilment. In the Mass, too, is what yet remains to be fulfilled. What it accomplishes in time is the guarantee of what it will infallibly complete in eternity. In the Mass is the pledge of God, in part fulfilled, and in part still promised. "He that eateth my flesh and drinketh my blood, hath everlasting life: and I will raise him up in the last day" (John vi. 55).

Second Chapter

THE HIGH PRIEST OF OUR CONFESSION, JESUS

(Heb. iii; 11)

1

ORDAINED FOR MEN

FROM the cradle to the grave Catholic life comes under the benign influence of Christ's priesthood. The exercise of priestly power marks the stages of our growth from childhood to maturity; from maturity to death. It accompanies us along the entire road of life. Brought to the Baptismal font of living water, the priest sets us on our journey of Christian living. When, as yet barely able to lisp the name of God, we assisted with our parents at Holy Mass, the priest was associated with a certain solemnity, which impressed our youthful and immature minds. Through that solemnity we grew to know, even though vaguely, that we were in the house of God, and that the priest at the altar was in some mysterious way concerned with Him and us. As we reached the use of reason, and began to know good from evil, we were taught to kneel at this representative of God's mercy, and tell him our sins with the assurance of Divine pardon. Later still we knelt at the Communion rail, that we might receive from his anointed, consecrating hands the living body

of Jesus Christ. As the years rolled on, we were grateful beneficiaries of his constant and watchful care.
Looking forward down the years yet to come, we are
not ashamed of our sense of dependence on the
ordained of Christ, who is what his sacerdotal name
implies, "the giver of good things". Finally, when
death threatens, this "Other Christ" will, we hope,
be at our bedside to give us the final comfort of the
Last Anointing. The Catholic attitude to the priesthood presents a problem to those outside the Church,
and many, failing to understand its true meaning,
reject it as unwarrantable interference with personal
liberty.

A Catholic does not need to be reminded of the
words of St. Paul: "A priest is one taken from amongst
men." Like all men he is subject to infirmity and the
frailties of human nature. Like all other Christians
he must live by the grace of God. Yet, we know by
our faith that the sacred oil of Ordination and the
imposition of hands have consecrated him to God
and bestowed on him supernatural powers. "He is
ordained for men in the things which appertain to
God" (Heb. v. 1). He is enabled thereby to confer
what no earthly agency can bestow, namely, a spiritual
richness of sanctifying grace, which is not lost in death,
but is "laid up as a treasure in heaven" (Matt. vi. 20).
From birth to death, from Baptism to the Last Anointing, he is devoted to our care. When we wander away,
he seeks us as did the Good Shepherd his lost sheep,
and brings us back to the loving fold of Jesus Christ.
His labour on our behalf does not cease until he com-
mits our bodies to the blessed grave to await our
resurrection from the dead. The Catholic priest is,
like the Church herself, set for the whole world unto

a universal salvation. Like Christ from Whom he springs, he is ordained to "give life, and give it more abundantly". By reason of this Christ-like appointment we find in him something that is independent of likes or dislikes, which rises above class distinction or social standing, and is untrammelled by exigencies of racial boundaries. The priest must be "all things to all men". He has freely received; he must freely give, as commanded him by Christ.

This phenomenon of the Catholic priesthood is one well worthy of our study and meditation. It is the centre of a great mystery, which can only be understood as part of the vast design of God's eternal plan of redemption. Jesus Christ is the unique source of this divine agency—of this "Admirable commerce" between God and man. In Him through the mystery of the Incarnation the priesthood is found in its perfect fulness. Through His omnipotent power He willed to share that fulness with His chosen of earth, that what He began, and established, might be continued until the end of time. He willed that all human life should be charged with this priestliness, at once active, or ministerial in His Ordained, and passive or receptive in all His faithful. He planned by this means that the world might once again be gloriously raised to God, from Whom it came in the beginning. Our immediate concern in this chapter is the ministerial participation in the priesthood of Christ. In a later conference we shall examine the lay participation in that same priesthood (cf. Fourth Chapter). The sublime gift of active sacerdotal power, like the Most Holy Sacrifice, which is its essential act, depends for its truth on the words of Christ—"Do this for a commemoration of me"—pronounced at the

Last Supper, but it also, like all other "good things to come" was ushered in prophetically down the ages of preparation.

2

THE FALL AND ITS CONSEQUENCES

"The first man Adam was made into a living soul" (1 Cor. xv. 45; Gen. ii. 7). The "breath of life", breathed into the first man by God, made him to the image and likeness of his Maker, and bestowed upon him a power to know and love God, and serve Him by religion. Adam was superior to all the other creatures of the earth through God's gift of intelligence and will. By reason of his rational nature, he, in a manner, contained within himself all earthly things, which were ordained to his use and benefit. In him all matter was made to serve an intellectual soul. He was made the Lord of Creation, and was given "dominion over the whole earth" (Gen. i. 26). Creation was immediately followed by a wonderful token of his Maker's love. God raised him from the merely natural state to a supernatural life of union with Himself by granting him an intimacy of revelation, and a corresponding closeness of union in love. The Book of Genesis gives us some glimpses of the familiar conversational communication which existed between man and God. "They heard the voice of the Lord walking in paradise in the afternoon air" (ibid. iii. 8).

Man's original happiness was closely linked with the maintenance of this order of subjection and love to His Creator, from Whom came all the good that he possessed. It was his duty by nature and by grace to express that indebtedness and love in adoration, thanksgiving, and petition through prayer and sacrifice, as God directed him. Adam was the first priest of creation, whose privilege it was to voice intelligently the entire earth and its fulness to God's glory and his own everlasting good.

The Fall disrupted this initial priestly order between man and God. He, who by nature and appointment was the natural mediator between earth and heaven, lost his familiarity of association with his Creator through pride and disobedience. His expulsion from the garden of Eden symbolized the abyss, created by his sin, between himself and God. By the severance of friendly relations, and the loss of sanctifying grace, man became dumb, and all matter, represented in him, was made mute in the sight of the Almighty. Earth's hymn was silenced. Adam had no means within himself of restoring that shattered order, since he was incapable of offering atonement for his sin, or of presenting satisfaction which would be worthy of Divine acceptance. St. Augustine describes Adam's efforts to express sentiments of religion immediately after the Fall, as "the barking of a dog". "Wherefore as by one man sin entered the world and by sin death: and so death passed upon all men in whom all have sinned" (Rom. v. 12). Adam's guilt was pride, which urged him to establish an independent lordship over the earth, and to reject his priestly obligation, as steward of His Creator, of offering himself and all created things back to God from Whom they had come. He foolishly endeavoured to wrest supreme dominion from God by seeking to be a god himself.

The temptation of the serpent, to which both he and Eve consented, entailed a complete usurping of the Divine prerogatives. "Your eyes shall be opened: and you shall be as Gods, knowing good and evil" (Gen. iii. 5). Thus, with the Fall, the primitive priestliness inherent in human life collapsed, and there was nothing left to man but to hide himself from the wrath of God. By his sin Adam lost for himself and for posterity all that had been granted him by grace. The havoc of his guilt penetrated even into the natural good of his created nature by disrupting the order of his lower appetites to the higher order of his reason. "The creature was made subject to vanity" (Rom. ii. 20), and all Adam's children "were by nature children of wrath" (Eph. ii. 3).

God, Who is wonderful in His works, became most wonderful of all in His design of redemption through His Beloved Son. "O happy fault," cries out the Liturgy, "that has merited so great a Redeemer." God restored priestly power to Adam and his children in the promise of a Messiah. The first priesthood having failed, it was necessary that another priesthood should be conferred, which would both atone for the first failure, and restore the good order that was lost. Adam was received back to grace in the merit of the great High-priest to come, Who would expiate sin, and constitute Himself the new Adam in a spiritual headship over the human race. By destroying the reign of the serpent, He would take away sin and death. "I will put enmities between thee and the woman, and thy seed and her seed" (Gen. iii. 15). Through His sacrifice this new priest would change "the children of wrath" into "the children of the promise" (Rom. ix. 8). "When we were enemies we were reconciled to

God by the death of his Son; much more being reconciled, shall we be saved by his life " (Rom. v. 10). "For if by the offence of one many died: much more the grace of God and the gift, by the grace of one man Jesus Christ, hath abounded unto many " (ibid. 15).

3

THE PRIESTHOOD IN PROPHECY

The promise made to the first man took shape down the centuries of expectation. Just as Almighty God foreshadowed the Sacrifice of the Cross, and of the Blessed Eucharist, which perpetuates it, so He willed also to prepare the world prophetically for the perfect priesthood of the New Testament. In general, the priests of the Old Testament present but dim shadows of the splendour which was to come. The appointment of Aaron and his companions, and their solemn consecration to God in the priesthood, marked the first setting apart of a priestly caste (cf. Exod. xxix. 1). Their priesthood, however, like the sacrifices which accompanied it, was but temporary and imperfect. It ceased to exist once death claimed them. "By reason of death they were not suffered to continue " (Heb. vii. 23). In the time of Isaias, and even more emphatically in the time of Ezechiel, God manifested His displeasure with the appointed priests, and under the figure of the Good Shepherd, so dear to Christ, spoke of what was to come. "Thus saith the Lord God: Behold I myself will seek my sheep, and I will visit them . . . and I will set one shepherd over them and he shall feed them " (Ezech. xxxiv. 11, 23). Though Jesus according to the flesh descended, as did the Levitical priests, from the stock of Abraham, His priesthood was not according to theirs—"not to be called according to the order of Aaron" (Heb. vii. 11). God gave Abraham the promise of a priesthood which would be infinitely superior to that of his own descendants of the tribe of Levi. The priesthood of the Incarnate Son would not be transmitted "according to the law of carnal life" through earthly generation, but as proper to the Son of God made man, "according to the law of indissoluble life" (ibid. 16). His priesthood would be such as was sung of by psalmist, "Thou art a priest for ever according to the order of Melchisedech."

There is a deep mystery surrounding the brief appearance of the "Priest of the Most High", who met Abraham at the vale of Mambre. The significant event was accepted by the Jews as a portent regarding a priesthood to come, surpassing all other priesthood, and of eternal duration. Its Messianic character was emphasized by King David. "The Lord hath sworn, and he will not repent: thou art a priest for ever according to the order of Melchisedech" (Psalm cix. 4). Other prophets also insisted on the everlasting character of Christ's priestly mediation. How much this prophecy meant to the Jews is clear from the Gospel of St. John. Shortly before His Passion, Jesus spoke of the restorative power of His death. "And I, if I be lifted up, will draw all things to myself." Such an admission of mortality—of death by crucifixion—seemed to the Jews to contradict His Messianic claim to be the promised "priest for ever". "The multitude answered him: We have heard out of the law, that Christ abideth for ever; how then sayest thou: The Son of man must be lifted up?" (John xii. 34). Jesus vouchsafed no further explanation, except to admonish them to walk in the light He had already given.

The excellence of Christ's priesthood compared with that of the sons of Levi was further emphasized by St. Paul: "If then perfection was by the Levitical priesthood (for under it the people received the law), what further need was there that another priest should arise according to the order of Melchisedech . . . the law brought nothing to perfection. . . . By so much is Jesus a surety of a better testament. And others indeed were made many priests, because by reason of death they were not suffered to continue: But this, for that he continueth for ever, hath an everlasting priesthood, whereby he is able to save for ever them that come to God by him: always living to make intercession for us" (Heb. vii. 11, 22-5). Far from being extinguished in His death, the priesthood of Christ reached the zenith of its dignity and power, and merited to be perpetuated on earth as in heaven, through the triumph of the Cross.

Melchisedech was King of Salem. His name and title, meaning King of Justice, and King of Peace, were prophetic of Christ, Who restored justice in the sight of the Father, and established peace between God and man. "He is our peace" (Eph. ii. 14). "Surely salvation is near to them that fear him; that glory may dwell in our land. Mercy and truth have met each other: justice and peace hath kissed" (Psalm lxxxiv. 11). The account of the meeting in the vale of Mambre, as related in Genesis, shows how clearly God intended the event to be "a pattern of heavenly things", and how closely it approached the foreshadowed reality in Christ. Abraham, who was the father of the Levitical priesthood, acknowledged the superiority of Melchisedech in a twofold way, namely, by accepting his blessing and paying him tithes. "Without all contradiction, that which is less is blessed by the better . . . and even Levi, who received tithes, paid tithes in Abraham: For he was yet in the loins of his father, when Melchisedech met him" (Heb. vii. 7, 9). "Now consider how great this man is, to whom also Abraham gave tithes out of the principal things" (ibid. 4). The Old Testament mentions nothing of the genealogy of this mysterious priest, who owed his appointment solely to God. The Scripture is purposely silent about his pedigree, because he was appointed by God to foreshadow the ineffable generation of the Eternal Son made man, of Whom the Prophet declared: "Who shall narrate his generation?" (Isa. liii. 8). For the same reason St. Paul writes of him: "Without father, without mother, without genealogy, having neither beginning of days nor end of life, but likened unto the Son of God, continueth a priest for ever" (Heb. vii. 3).

To this likeness of Mechisedech to Christ according to priestly power and dignity, there must be added also his likeness in the matter of sacrificial worship. In the sacrifice of bread and wine, which Melchisedech offered on behalf of Abraham and his posterity, there is a clear figure of the perpetual sacrifice which Christ instituted at His Last Supper, and which by His Sacred ordination of "other Christs", He commanded to be done until He should come again. By this institution, Christ, Who has entered into His glory, continues on earth through the abiding presence of His sacred Humanity His everlasting priesthood. By maintaining the power of His sacrifice on the altars of the world, and by abiding with us in our tabernacles, He pre-

serves for us by His real presence the pledge of the
New Testament between God and man.   We may
conclude with St. Paul: "Now of the things which
we have spoken, this is the sum: We have such a high-
priest, who is set on the right hand of the throne of
majesty in the heavens, a minister of the Holies, and
of the true tabernacle, which the Lord hath pitched,
and not man" (Heb. viii. 1, 2).

4

THE FAITHFUL HIGH PRIEST

"Wherefore, holy brethren, partakers of the
heavenly vocation, consider the apostle and high priest
of our confession, Jesus" (Heb. iii. 1).   Acceptance of
so holy an invitation brings us into the heart of the
mystery of the Incarnation. The Incarnate Word, conceived of the Holy Ghost, and born of the Virgin Mary,
became the High Priest, so long foretold and expected,
in the instant of His conception in His Mother's
womb.   At that moment the words of the angel were
fulfilled.   "The Holy Ghost shall come upon thee, and
the power of the Most High shall overshadow thee.
And therefore also the Holy which shall be born of
thee shall be called the Son of God" (Luke i. 35).   St.
Paul declares membership of the human race to be
necessary for the priesthood.   Jesus is one "chosen
from amongst men" (Heb. v. 1).   From the moment
of His assuming of our human nature, He assumed
also all the dignity and power of mediator between
God and man.   His priestly work began when God
fitted a body for Him—"A body thou hast fitted for

E

me." By the Incarnation He became "the engrafted Word which is able to save our souls" (James i. 21). He is the vine engrafted on the old stock of a fallen race, whereby all the branches become fruitful for the Father, Who is the "husbandman". The perfection of His priesthood is derived from His eternal Sonship with the Father. Though clothed in our flesh, and housed as it were within the narrow confines of our human nature, His relation with the Father lost nothing of its infinite power and dignity. He is the new temple of humanity—the new house of God on earth by reason of the body which He assumed, and we by His grace of mediation form part of that living temple of God. "Christ as the Son in His own house: which house are we" (Heb. iii. 6). The intimate connection between the Incarnation and His office of high priest is emphasized by St. Paul: "Therefore because the children are partakers of flesh and blood, he also in like manner hath been made partaker of the same. . . . Wherefore it behoved him in all things to be made like unto his brethren, that he might become a merciful high priest before God, that he might be a propitiation for the sins of the people" (Heb. ii. 14, 17).

This priest of the New Testament, "Who emptied Himself, taking the form of a servant, being made in the likeness of man, and in habit found as a man" (Phil. ii. 7), established for all men a newness of life most pleasing to His Eternal Father. Through the power of the Holy Ghost, in Whom He was conceived, all that was merely human in Him was sanctified, and linked in most holy hypostatic union with the Person of the Word, and in Him with the Father in the mutual unifying love of the Spirit. He was not less the Son of God, when He became the Son of Man. "I and my Father are one" (John x. 30). Through the Incarnation He assumed our intelligence, our will, our senses, our entire human body and soul, unto an everlasting and most perfect union with the Godhead. He lived a perfectly human life on earth, yet His human activity was always a divine activity, because His every action was that of the Second Person of the Most Holy Trinity. This is the highest point of perfection to which any created nature can be raised. From the point of view of religion, it is the culmination of glory and worship ascending from a human heart. Every act of love of the heart of Jesus Christ was of infinite merit, since it was the loving act of the Divine Son, though expressed through the created medium of His human will. The Father's acceptance and pleasure was made manifest at the very outset of Christ's public life; "Behold a voice from heaven, saying: This is my beloved Son, in whom I am well pleased" (Matt. iii. 17). All that the Incarnate Word said and did on earth had the glory of His Father for its highest and final purpose. "Father, I have glorified thee on earth" (John xvii. 4). Its secondary purpose, no less efficiently secured, was man's salvation and sanctification, which in turn redounds to the glory of His Father. The religion of Jesus Christ has ever the same twofold purpose, namely, to worship and to save.

St. John the Baptist declared: "The Father loveth the Son: and he hath given all things into his hand" (John iii. 35). The priestly lordship of man over the earth, which Adam lost by sin, was restored through Jesus Christ. In Him was re-established the harmony of the entire earthly creation in its order to the Creator. In Him, by reason of the perfection of His life as the

Man-God, there was complete exemption from the
original disorder which had been set up in man after
the Fall. "In him there was no sin" (1 John iii. 5).
In His humility was found the antidote to the pride
of the first man. "He emptied Himself, taking the
form of a servant" (Phil. ii. 7). He taught man this
great lesson of human living: "Learn of me, because
I am meek and humble of heart" (Matt. xi. 29). Man's
pride was expressed in his disobedience. By way of
contrast, Christ's life consisted in the perfect observance of His Father's commandments. "I have run
the way of thy commandments" (Psalm cxviii. 32). In
His Father's will He found the work of His life. From
the beginning He set Himself on that road; "He hath
rejoiced as a giant to run the way" (Psalm xviii. 6).
When but twelve years old, His answer to His Blessed
Mother in the Temple revealed the essential purpose
of His coming: "Did you not know, that I must be
about my Father's business" (Luke ii. 49). The perfection of His life was found in this perfect conformity
of will with the will of His Father. "My meat is to do
the will of him who sent me, that I may perfect his
work" (John iv. 34). Through this perfect fulfilling
of God's will there was established a new familiarity
between man and the Father. "He that sent me is
with me, and he hath not left me alone, for I always
do the things that please him" (John viii. 29).

The intimacy which Christ enjoyed can be shared
in by all through attachment to Himself in charity.
"If any man love me, he will keep my word, and my
Father will love him; and we will come to him, and we
will make our abode in him" (John xiv. 25). The
certainty of all men's prayer being heard is founded on
the ever attentive ear of the Eternal Father to the voice

of His Beloved Son: "Father, I give thee thanks that thou hast heard me. I know that thou hearest me always" (John xi. 41). He assured His followers of a like hearing; "If you ask the Father anything in my name, he will give it you" (John xvi. 23). Passing in review the thirty years of His life, Christ could send up His fervent and assured prayer, which is an epitome of the religion which He established for mankind. "I have glorified thee on earth: I have finished the work which thou gavest me to do" (John xvii. 5). In the power of His conquest, He passed on that same task to His followers: "As thou hast sent me into the world, I have also sent them into the world" (John xvii. 18).

5

SACRIFICE IN OBEDIENCE

Before the gift of "partaking in Christ" could be shared in by men, there was need of reparation. In assuming our human nature Christ assumed also the responsibility of atonement, which was inherent in it by reason of the Fall. Of this heavy burden of human guilt the Prophet foretold: "The Lord hath laid upon him the iniquity of us all" (Isa. liii. 6). There was need to establish a new obedience and humility, which would leave no doubt concerning man's future attitude to God and his complete reparation for past injustice. The new High Priest presented to the Father the highest measure of this assurance and satisfaction. "He learned obedience by the things which he suffered" (Heb. v. 8). "He humbled himself, becoming obedient unto death: even unto the death of the

cross" (Phil. ii. 8). The priesthood of the Divine
Saviour reached its climax in His Passion and death.
He assumed our flesh and blood that He might offer
it back to God in a perfect sacrifice as a holocaust of
love and atonement on behalf of men. This was His
supreme act of worship, to which He set Himself from
the beginning. It was the sacrifice so long foretold.
" Wherefore when he cometh into this world, he saith:
Sacrifice and oblation thou wouldst not: but a body
thou hast fitted for me. . . . Then said I: Behold I
come: in the head of the book it is written of me; that
I should do thy will, O God" (Heb. x. 5, 7). The
physical sufferings of the Saviour and their purpose
were foretold by the Prophets. " He was wounded for
our iniquities, he was bruised for our sins: the chas-
tisement of our peace was upon him, and by his bruises
we were healed" (Isa. liii. 5). Through His Passion
and death the body of Jesus became the link joining
heaven and earth: " Who in his own self bore our sins
in his body upon the tree" (1 Pet. ii. 24). For this
reason St. Catherine of Siena call Him the "Bridge".
St. Paul establishes the perfection of His priesthood in
the sanctifying power of His sufferings, " How much
more shall the blood of Christ, who by the Holy Ghost
offered himself unspotted unto God, cleanse our conscience from dead works, to serve the living God? And
therefore he is the mediator of the New Testament:
that by means of his death, for the redemption of these
transgressions, which were under the former testament,
they that are called may receive the promise of eternal
inheritance" (Heb. ix. 14, 15). The priesthood of the
New Testament, in which we all share through our
Baptismal character, was sealed in the precious blood
of Jesus Christ, poured out in the various phases of

His bitter Passion. "Him hath God the Father sealed" (John vi. 27).

"The oblation of the Body of Jesus" was a most perfect sacrifice by reason of the conformity of His will with that of His Father, the immensity of His sufferings, and the completeness of the shedding of His precious blood (cf. Chapter 3). His sacrifice of the Cross was of infinite merit because it was the death of the Son of God made man. It contained the infinite and everlasting act of the Second Person of the Most Holy Trinity. "This man offering one sacrifice for sins, for ever sitteth on the right hand of God. . . . For by one oblation he has perfected for ever them that are sanctified" (Heb. x. 12, 14). Just as His priesthood is everlasting, so is the Divine act of sacrifice which it called forth. "Whereas indeed he was the Son of God, he learned obedience by the things which he suffered: and being consummated, he became, to all that obey him, the cause of eternal salvation; called by God a high priest according to the order of Melchisedech" (ibid. v. 8-10).

6

CHRIST'S PRIESTLY PERFECTION

"Every high priest is ordained for men in the things that appertain to God, that he may offer up gifts and sacrifices for sins: who can have compassion on them that are ignorant and that err: because he himself also is compassed with infirmity" (Heb. v. 1, 2). Priestly perfection is found in the call of God and in the fulfilment of the duties demanded by that vocation. First of all, there must be some kind of ordaining, or of divine deputing, whereby the priest is recognized as an acceptable mediator between God and man. Such appointments are found in the Old Testament, as, for example, when God commanded Moses to set aside Aaron and his sons unto the ministry. It is evident that, since God is concerned, no man can be self-appointed. "Neither doth any man take the honour to himself, but he that is called by God, as Aaron was" (ibid. 4). The eternal decree of redemption through the sending on earth of the Incarnate Word, contained also the priestly mandate given to Him by the Eternal Father Who sent Him. The Saviour of men repeatedly asserted His claim to be recognized as the supreme mediator with the Father. "The Father himself, who hath sent me, hath given testimony of me" (John v. 37). "This is the will of my Father that sent me: that every one who seeth the Son, and believeth in him, may have life everlasting, and I will raise him up on the last day" (ibid. vi. 40).

St. Paul appeals to the Old Testament to show how intimately the High priesthood of Christ was linked with His Sonship. "Christ also did not glorify himself that he might be made a high priest: but he that said unto him, *Thou art my Son, this day have I begotten thee;* As he saith also in another place: *Thou art a priest for ever according to the order of Melchisedech*" (Heb. v. 5, 6). The priestly pact between the Beloved Son and the Father in the love which is the Spirit, was first promulgated to Abraham. It was decreed in a far more solemn manner than was used for the Levitical priesthood, since it was promulgated under oath. "God making promise to Abraham, because he had no one greater by whom he might swear, swore by himself, saying; *Unless blessing I shall bless thee, and multiplying I shall multiply thee.* . . . For men swear by one greater than themselves: and an oath for confirmation is the end of all controversy. Wherein God, meaning more abundantly to show to the heirs of the promise the immutability of his counsel, interposed an oath" (ibid. vi. 15-17). By reason of this solemnity the priesthood of Christ is to be judged superior to all others. "Inasmuch as it is not without an oath (for others indeed were made priests without an oath; but this one with an oath, by him who said unto him: *The Lord hath sworn, and he will not repent, thou art a priest for ever*): By so much, is Jesus made a surety of a better testament" (ibid. vii. 20-2).

With divine appointment there must also be demanded holiness of life through personal union of the Priest with God.   In Jesus Christ, as the Son of God, there is the infinite sanctity of the Godhead in the all-holy mystery of the adorable Trinity.   As God He is holiness itself. "Holy, holy, holy, Lord God Almighty, who was, and who is, and who is to come" (Apoc. iv. 8). As man through the sanctifying power of the Holy Ghost, in Whom He was conceived and sanctified, His human body and soul became what St. Thomas calls "the conjoined instrument" of the Divine Person of the Word.   This sanctity of the Sacred Humanity of the "Mediator of the New Testament" was foretold by the Prophet: "The Spirit of the Lord shall rest upon him: the spirit of wisdom, and of understanding, the spirit of counsel, and of fortitude, the spirit of knowledge, and of godliness, and he shall be filled with the spirit of the fear of the Lord" (Isa. xi. 2, 3).

The Gospels bear ample witness to the workings of

the Holy Ghost in the manhood of Christ. This in-fluence of the Spirit was found particularly in His supreme priestly act of sacrifice on the Cross: "Who by the Holy Ghost offered Himself unspotted unto God" (Heb. ix. 14). The Eternal Father gave public testimony on three solemn occasions to the good pleasure which He found in the life and work of His Beloved Son. The last of these occasions coincided with His Passion, and emphasized the glory of His supreme sacrifice. Jesus, on Palm Sunday, gave expres-sion to His sorrow and desire. "Now is my soul troubled. And what shall I say? Father save me from this hour? But for this cause I came unto this hour." Then, with all the love of that troubled soul, He ex-pressed the true purpose of His death, so close at hand. "Father, glorify thy name." His desire was met with instant response. "A voice therefore came from heaven: I have glorified it, and will glorify it again" (John xii. 27, 28).

Jesus Himself claimed sinlessness and holiness which were a necessary condition in the mind of the people of His being accepted as the Messiah. "Which of you shall convince me of sin" (John viii. 46). "Be-lieve you not that I am in the Father, and the Father in me (ibid. xiv. 11). St. Paul stressed the spotless purity of Christ, Whom he calls the "throne of grace" (Heb. iv. 16). "It was fitting that we should have such a high priest, holy, innocent, undefiled, separated from sinners, and made higher than the heavens: who needeth not daily (as other priests) to offer sacrifice first for his own sins, and then for the people's, for this he did once in offering himself" (ibid. vii. 27, 28).

Priestly perfection also supposes an intimate union of priest with the people for whom he is appointed mediator in holiness. Not only must the priest be "taken from amongst men", but he must be in complete sympathy with their needs and circumstances, so that he may with sincerity and compassion represent them faithfully in the sight of God. He must be in some way, as St. Paul demands, identified with the infirmities of the human race. Jesus admirably fulfilled these obligations of the priestly office. The source of His perfect representation on behalf of mankind is again found in the mystery of the Incarnation. "Both he that sanctifieth, and they who are sanctified are all of one. For which cause he is not ashamed to call them brethren. . . . Therefore because the children are partakers of flesh and blood, he also himself in like manner hath been partaker of the same. Wherefore it behoved him in all things to be made like unto his brethren, that he might become a merciful and faithful high priest before God, that he might be a propitiation for the sins of the people. For in that, wherein he himself hath suffered and been tempted, he is able to succour them also that are tempted" (Heb. ii. 11-18). The life of the Saviour proclaims throughout the pages of the Gospel His marvellous compassion for His fellow men. He was never aloof from the crowd; rather did He draw them compassionately to Himself. "Come to me, all you that labour, and are burdened, and I will refresh you" (Matt. xi. 28). "He saw a great multitude, and had compassion on them, and healed their sick" (ibid. xiv. 14). So closely did He identify Himself with us, that He took even our sins upon Himself. "Surely he hath borne our infirmities, and carried our sorrows" (Isa. lv. 4).

It is the essential duty of the priest to offer up "gifts

and sacrifices to God ". This demands yet another perfection pertaining to the priestly office. Not only the priest himself, but the victim of his sacrifice must be acceptable to the Most High. In the ancient sacrifices the victim offered was by way of substitution. Its death and destruction was a ceremonial, yet true representation, of man's nothingness, and an acknowledgment of his debt to God. The more perfectly the victim represented this disposition, the more acceptable was the sacrifice. The holocaust, or whole burnt offering, was for that reason the most complete of ancient Jewish sacrifices. The representative character of the Levitical ritual by way of substitution fades before the glory of self-immolation in the sacrifice of the Incarnate Son of God. In Christ there was no substitution. Priest and victim are identical. "He hath appeared for the destruction of sin by the sacrifice of himself " (Heb. ix. 26). There can be no more perfect sacrifice than that of the all-pure living body and blood of the Incarnate Word. In the immensity of His suffering, and total shedding of His blood, there is found the most perfect holocaust of Himself in the consuming fire of His infinite love for God and man. The redeeming power of the sacrifice of the Cross is expressed by St. Paul: "In the days of his flesh with a strong cry and tears, offering up prayers and supplications to him that was able to save him from death, was heard for his reverence. . . . And being consummated, he became, to all that obey him, the cause of eternal salvation " (Heb. v. 7, 9).

The sacrifice of the Cross was the achievement of Christ—"the first-born of many brethren". It inaugurated by its merits the birth of a new race of the sons of God. Man, and in him the whole earthly creation, was voiced once again in the strong redeeming cry of the Crucified. "I, if I be lifted up from earth, will draw all things unto myself (John xii. 32). The immolation of Calvary was in the body and soul of the Saviour, representing both matter and spirit. Even as He assumed our human nature by taking flesh, so did He renew it by surrendering it to death on the Cross. He joined all human souls to His own soul. He sanctified all flesh in His own tortured body. "Know you not your bodies are the members of Christ" (1 Cor. vi. 15). In this way the immolation of Calvary is all-embracing. Christ restored man, and in man are all things restored, in so far, as St. Thomas says, that in man all things are in a manner contained. St. Paul speaks of this universal effect of redemption: "God indeed was in Christ, reconciling the world unto himself" (2 Cor. v. 19). The same Apostle speaks of the entire material world being unwillingly involved in man's fall, since it was for his benefit that God created it, and he alone could consciously voice its debt of glory to the Creator. For that reason all nature is figuratively described as groaning and in travail in expectation of redemption by Christ. (cf. Rom. viii. 19-23).

7

THE ORDAINED OF CHRIST

Jesus offered a real sacrifice in the Upper Room. Having celebrated His First Mass, He gave power to the Apostles to do what He had done. The divine command of the Last Supper entailed a conferring of

priestly power on the twelve, whom He had chosen as
the foundation of His Church.   Considering the universal and enduring character of God's redemptive
design, such an appointment is not surprising.   It
appears as the necessary adjunct to the mission of the
Saviour, Who came that men "might have life and
have it more abundantly", until the end of time.
Christ established a perfect and permanent religion in
the new and glorious worship of the Father.   Divinely
appointed and visible agents of that worship are an
essential part of that new ritual, which through Christ
binds men to God.   Overwhelming evidence in the
Gospel points to His actual establishment of such an
agency.   He left no doubt regarding the priestly
powers which He conferred on the Twelve, and which
He commanded them in turn to pass down to their
successors, the Bishops of the Church and their priestly
coadjutors in the ministry.

"Do this for a commemoration of me."   These
sacred words were a command which presupposed the
conferring of corresponding power.   They represent
the formula whereby Christ ordained His Apostles,
and bestowed on them an active sharing in His own
ministerial and mediatory power in its most sublime
sacrificial act.   Charged with this power, the Apostles
and their successors were to take in their hands the
living Crucified Christ, and bear Him with the good
tidings of the Gospel to the farthermost parts of the
earth.   The powers conferred by Christ on the priests
of the New Testament fulfil the promise of priestly
perfection foretold by the Prophet David (Psalm
cxxxi. 16).   "I will clothe her priests with salvation"
(Psalm cxxxi. 16).   Christ shared the priestly excellence which was divinely bestowed on Him by His

Father. " He hath obtained a better ministry, by how much also is he mediator of a better testament, which is established in better promises " (Heb. viii. 6) .

The need of proclaiming the truth of Christ's priesthood has been made more imperative to-day, by reason of the widespread ignorance which prevails in its regard. This ignorance is a sequel to the inherited darkness of the error of Protestantism. Realizing that the priesthood and the Mass were the rock on which was built the Catholic Church, the Reformers of the sixteenth and following centuries set out to eradicate both one and the other. Luther went so far as to say: " The sacrament of Orders is not known in the Church of Christ; it has been invented by the Pope's Church." The violence of the reformist persecution against the priests of the Catholic Church provides ample evidence of their hatred. The Penal Laws, which Bourke described as " the most inhuman ever invented by human ingenuity ", put the same price on the head of a priest as on that of a wolf. Some of England's ancient Cathedrals, even to this day, show how bitter also was their hatred of the Mass. Altar Tables on which the Most Holy Sacrifice had been celebrated were desecrated and broken, or in some cases placed as pavement stones in the porches of the Cathedrals, that they might be trampled on irreverently. Historical documents show how real was the intent which inspired such acts of vandalism and sacrilege. In 1571, for instance, Grindal, Protestant Archbishop of York gave orders that " the altar stones be broken, defaced and devoted to some common use ".

Toleration has in great measure softened the hatred of these past centuries. But the error which gave rise to it still remains, and still bears its melancholy fruit. The abyss, which in the beginning divided all the various sects of the Protestant Churches from the one true Church of Christ, still stands in the way of reconciliation. The issue still lies in the rejection of both sacrifice and hierarchical priesthood. For the old sacrificial rite the Reformers substituted a non-sacrificial Communion service, and for that reason purposely suppressed in their Book of Common Prayer all references to the Real Presence or sacrificial ritual. Instead of priests, with whom is intimately associated the idea of sacrifice, they appointed what they called ministers, whose ordaining was not in the conferring of power, but in a simple authorization to preach, and administer the few sacraments which they agreed to retain. Cardinal Newman in his time pointed out the weakness of their position, which has become more apparent down the years. "They conscientiously shudder at assuming the real episcopal or sacerdotal powers, who resolve, *Receive ye the Holy Ghost* into a prayer, *Whose sins you shall remit, they are remitted,* into a licence to preach, and, *This is my body* into an allegory."

The Council of Trent solemnly decreed against Luther and his followers: "If any man saith that by these words—*Do this in commemoration of me*—Christ did not institute the Apostles priests, or did not ordain that they and other priests should offer His own body and blood; Let him be anathema." The Fathers of the same Council also lucidly explained how God's design, foreshadowed in the Old, found its completion in the New Testament, and how vital it was for the Christian religion to possess a continuance of both the sacrifice and the priesthood of Christ. "There was need, the Father of mercies so ordaining, that another priest should arise, according to the order of Melchisedech, Our Lord Jesus Christ, Who might consummate and lead to what is perfect as many as are sanctified. . . . Because that His priesthood was not to be extinguished in death, at the Last Supper, that he might leave to His own beloved Spouse, the Church, a visible sacrifice, such as the nature of man required, whereby the bloody sacrifice, once accomplished on the Cross, might be represented. . . . He offered up to God the Father His own body and blood to be received by the Apostles, whom He constituted priests of the New Testament."

Distance from the Upper Room in time or space does not lessen our sense of security in the Divine institution of the priesthood. Our Catholic Hierarchy to-day—Pope, Bishops, and priests—through perfect continuity with the Apostolic college, possesses the fulness of the sacerdotal power which was bestowed on that night by Christ. Our Catholic priesthood is still the great spiritual and vivifying power in the world. St. Catherine of Siena summed up the essential office of all priests by saying that they possess "the keys of the blood of Jesus Christ". Like Christ Himself, they are appointed shepherds of the flock. Like Him, they are appointed to serve, not to be served. What they have to give is not their own. The inheritance of truth and life, of which they are the dispensers, belongs to the people of God, for whom Christ's blood was shed. Of all the powers which they possess on behalf of the faithful, there is none more sublime than that which engages both themselves and the people in the Holy Sacrifice of His body and blood. All other priestly powers radiate, as it were, from that sacrificial centre,

F

even as the source of all grace and power comes from Calvary itself. " When generations demand where are to be found the marvellous fruits of salvation given by the Redeemer, where is the blood that was shed for all men, where are granted the pardons which wash away the sins of the guilty, we must be able to reply that these benefits still remain. . . . Marked by a divine seal, men will go forth to their brothers, by them Christ will teach, will pardon, will offer for ever a victim of expiation, by them will redemption be continued, they shall be other Christs." (Gégout.)

Intelligent appreciation of God's gifts is an essential factor in the development of the Catholic mind. The heritage of the priesthood in the Church, and all that is included in it of eternal life, is God's gift to every Christian soul. We must receive it with admiration, with thanksgiving, with confidence, and with reverence. Those who are sealed with the divine sacerdotal character are set aside for the service of God and of His holy altar. Raised as they are to the highest dignity which it is possible to confer on any human being, and at the same time weighted down with tremendous responsibility, they need our prayers that they may be worthy of " His holy calling " (2 Tim. i. ix). Modern paganism knows nothing of this sublime vocation. Surrounded by so much indifference to religion, there is a danger that Catholics also may forget how sacred is the character which seals all priests, and establishes them as divinely appointed intermediaries between the people and God. " The sure foundation of God standeth firm, having his seal " (ibid. 19). Our Catholic priests are not mere ecclesiastical functionaries who have chosen a profession, like any other of a worldly kind, to earn a respectable livelihood. They are " men

who have given their lives for the name of our Lord
Jesus Christ" (Acts xv. 26).   They are "the ministers
of Christ and the dispensers of the mysteries of God"
(1 Cor. iv. 1).   "They watch as being to render an
account of your souls; that they may do this with joy
and not with grief" (Heb. xiii. 17).

Third Chapter

THE OBLATION OF THE BODY OF JESUS

(Heb. x. 10)

1

THINK DILIGENTLY UPON HIM

THE High-Priesthood of Jesus, which is so closely knitted to the mystery of the Incarnation and the Hypostatic Union of our human nature with the Incarnate Word, launched the Saviour of men on the road of His obedience. "In the head of the book it is written of me: that I should do thy will" (Psalm xxx. 8). His priestly life as intermediary between man and God was consummated in the perfect obedience of the sacrifice of Calvary. "Being consummated, he became to all that obey him, the cause of eternal salvation" (Heb. v. 9). Neither our Catholic priesthood, nor our sacrifice of the Mass, nor any source of grace in our Church can be separated from the Passion and death of the God-Man. "We are sanctified by the oblation of the body of Jesus Christ once. . . . By one oblation he hath perfected for ever them that are sanctified" (Heb. x. 10, 14). Our Catholic religion links us inseparably to the one infinitely meritorious sacrifice of the Cross. Without continual recurrence in thought and affection to the Passion, we would fail altogether to appreciate the Christian life and its sources without and within the soul.

"There is nothing more advantageous, nothing more adapted to ensure our eternal salvation," says St. Augustine, "than daily to contemplate the sufferings which Jesus Christ bore for our sakes." St. Paul exhorted the early Christians to "think diligently upon him that endured such opprobrium from sinners against himself: that you be not wearied, fainting in your minds. Looking on Jesus the author and finisher of faith, who, having joy set before him, endured the cross, despising the shame" (Heb. xii. 3, 2). The only knowledge in which St. Paul rejoiced was that of the Passion; "For I judged not myself to know anything among you, but Jesus Christ, and Him crucified" (1 Cor. ii. 2). Love of the Passion is the essential foundation of devotion to the Holy Mass which renews it on our altars. St. Thomas received Our Lord's own encomium for His treatise on the Eucharist. "Well hast thou written of me Thomas." It was appropriate that such words of praise should come from the Crucifix, since to write on the Mass was to write on the Passion. Though Jesus can no longer suffer, He renews in the sign of the Consecration what was once accomplished on Calvary. He thereby releases the efficacy of His sacrifice of the Cross, and opens the floodgates of His infinite merits. He is lifted up again in the Mass, though in an unbloody manner. With Him is lifted the world, where men continue to live and die on their way towards eternity, and need amidst the trials of life to be joined to the Eternal Priest and Victim, that, thereby, they may be able "to fill up those things that are wanting of the sufferings of Christ" (Col. i. 24).

2

PROPHECIES OF THE PASSION

Seeing, as St. Jerome reminds us, that "in the Passion all other mysteries are contained", it is not surprising that the prophecies which foretold these mysteries should emphasize in a particular way the sufferings of Him Who was to become the "Man of sorrows". The Divine Saviour knew well the meaning of these prophetic utterances, which, inspired by the Holy Ghost, expressed the Father's will in His regard. He frequently spoke of His desire to fulfil them in obedience to His Father's command. His Apostles also were acquainted with them, though they did not understand their full import until later. The chief priests and scribes, who were the custodians of the word of God, possessed in their own sacred writings a forewarning of their crime in condemning Him to suffering and death. They, who at His birth so readily directed the Magi to seek Him in Bethlehem, might just as easily have read of the opprobrium they would heap upon Him in His Passion in Jerusalem. Self-interest and hate blinded them to the truth revealed by God concerning the Messiah, for Whom they pretended to wait in expectation. Jesus quoted the words of Isaias against them: "The heart of this people is grown gross, and with their ears they have grown dull of hearing, and their eyes they have shut; lest at any time they should see with their eyes, and hear with their ears, and understand with their heart, and be converted, and I should heal them" (Matt. xiii. 15; Isa. vi. 9). In their blindness they foolishly thought that the crucifixion would end for ever Christ's threat to their perverted power. They rejected His kingship while He lived and refused to have part in it. They refused to see what was so clearly foretold of the establishment of that kingdom through suffering and death. Caiphas the High Priest, intent solely on His destruction, sought solace and assurance in words, prophetically revealed to him, which should have convinced him and others of the Divine purpose of Christ's Passion and death. "One of them named Caiphas, being the high priest that year said to them: You know nothing. Neither do you consider that it is expedient for you that one man should die for the people, and that the whole nation perish not. And this he spoke not of himself: but being the high priest of that year, he prophesied that Jesus should die for the nation, and not only for the nation, but to gather together in one the children of God, that were dispersed " (John xi. 49-52).

Throughout the various phases of His bitter Passion Christ was the omnipotent Master. Those who were guilty of His death were but blind, hate-ridden agents of Satan, who unwillingly became instruments of the Divine inexorable will for the fulfilment of the prophecies and the good of man's redemption. The secret of this embitterment of the leaders of His own people against Christ had been foretold long before: "Let us therefore lie in wait for the Just, because he is not of our turn, and he is contrary to our doings, and upbraideth us with transgressions of the law, and divulgeth against us the sins of our way of life. He boasteth that he hath the knowledge of God, and calleth himself the son of God " (Wis. ii. 13). The final clamour of the Jewish mob for his death literally fulfilled the prophecy: "He ought to die, because he made himself the Son of God" (John xix. 7).

So detailed is the account of the sufferings of Christ in the Prophecies that the manner of His death could be reconstructed from them, were no other account available. The plotting of His enemies is frequently referred to: "The rulers take counsel together against the Lord and against his anointed" (Psalm ii. 2). His betrayal by Judas after the Last Supper is the burden of the Psalmist's lament. "Even the man of my peace, in whom I trusted, who ate my bread, hath greatly supplanted me" (ibid. xl. 10). The price of that perfidy was announced by the Prophet Zacharias: "They weighed for my wages thirty pieces of silver" (xi. 13; Matt. xxvii. 9). The same prophet referred to the flight of the Apostles at the moment of Christ's arrest: "Strike the shepherd, and the sheep shall be scattered" (xiii. 7; Matt. xxvi. 31). The false accusations made against Him in the court of the High Priest were also the subject of prophecy: "Unjust witnesses have risen up against me, and iniquity hath lied to itself" (Psalm xxvi. 12). "My enemies have spoken against me: and they that watched my soul have consulted together" (ibid. lxx. 10). Isaias described His silence as well as the shame that was heaped upon Him: "He shall be dumb as a lamb before his shearer, and he shall not open his mouth" (liii. 7). "I have given my body to the strikers, and my cheeks to them that plucked them: I have not turned my face away from them that rebuked me and spit upon me" (l. 6). "He was wounded for our iniquities, he was bruised for our sins" (liii. 5; Matt. viii. 17). His death by crucifixion, the dividing of, and casting lots for his garments, and other details were also graphically foretold: "They

have dug my hands and my feet. They have numbered all my bones. They have looked and stared
upon me. They parted my garments among them:
and upon my vesture they cast lots" (Psalm xxi. 17
seq.). "In my thirst they gave me vinegar to drink"
(ibid. lxviii. 22). The voices of the jeering crowd
beneath the Cross were heard long before; "All they
that saw me laughed me to scorn, they have spoken
with lips and wagged the head. He hoped in the
Lord, let him deliver him: let him save him, seeing
he delighteth in him" (ibid. xxi. 8, 9). The prophet
Zacharias laid the blame of His death by crucifixion
on His own chosen people; "And they shall say to
him: what are these wounds in the midst of thy hands?
And he shall say: With these was I wounded in the
house of them that loved me" (xiii. 6). The prophecy
of Isaias referred to the thieves who were crucified
with Him; "He hath delivered his soul unto death,
and was reputed with the wicked" (liii. 12; Mark
xv. 28). The same prophecy spoke of His prayer on
the Cross for His enemies: "He hath borne the sins
of many, and hath prayed for the transgressors"
(liii. 12).

3

THE HOUR SO LONG DESIRED

The hour of the Passion was a divinely appointed
hour, which no human agency could either hasten or
delay. Jesus waited until His body had attained to the
perfect age of manhood and its full growth in His
thirty-third year before rendering to His Father the

supreme homage of its sacrifice. The body which the
Father had formed for Him, and which was "conceived of the Holy Ghost and born of the Virgin
Mary", was providentially adapted to its essential
purpose of sacrifice, and in sacrifice of acute suffering.
By Divine decree and by His own free and holy will
He was destined to be "made obedient unto death,
even unto the death of the cross" (Phil. ii. 8). "He
was offered because it was his own will" (Isa. lviii. 7).
When the fulness of time had come, He set Himself
to the divinely appointed task of offering as a holocaust
to His Father both His body and soul for the Redemption of mankind. He warned His Apostles beforehand
of what awaited Him in Jerusalem. "You know that
after two days will be the Pasch, and the Son of man
shall be delivered up to be crucified" (Matt. xxvi. 2).
More than once before His appointed time the chief
priests and scribes had attempted to kill Him. Once
they would have cast Him from the "brow of the hill
on which their city was built"; yet another time, they
tried to stone Him to death, but He passed out of their
midst, because His time had not yet come.

Referring to the wealth of detail concerning His
death, as it had been decreed eternally by God, and
announced by the Prophets, Jesus said to His Apostles:
"The things concerning me have an end" (Luke xxii.
37). Once the time of His sacred Passion had arrived,
He looked forward lovingly to the great accomplishment. "I have a baptism," He said to His Apostles,
"wherewith I am to be baptised, and how am I
straitened until it be accomplished" (Luke xii. 50).
He expressed the same longing for His consummation
in prayer to His Eternal Father at the Last Supper:
"Father, the hour is come. . . . I have glorified thee

on earth: I have finished the work which thou gavest
me to do" (John xvii. 1, 4). He accepted each separate
phase of His suffering as it had been prescribed. "I
am come not to do my own will, but the will of him
who sent me" (John v. 30). When Peter sought so
impetuously to defend His Master by a violent attack
on the servant of the High Priest, Jesus commanded
him to put back his sword into its scabbard.
"Thinkest thou that I cannot ask my Father, and he
will give me presently more than twelve legions of
angels. How then can the scriptures be fulfilled, that
so it must be done" (Matt. xxvi. 53). In the Upper
Room on Holy Thursday night He had already pre-
celebrated in the new and permanent sacrificial rite
of the Most Holy Eucharist the oblation of His body
and blood. The sacrifice which was unbloody, though
real, in the Last Supper through its sign of immolation
and perfect submission of His will, was made in actual
shedding of blood on Good Friday by His death on
the Cross. During His agony in the Garden of Olives
in solemn declaration of perfect obedience He clearly
identified the ritual chalice—"The new testament in
my blood"—with the chalice of actual suffering in His
Passion and death. "My Father, if this chalice may
not pass away, but I must drink it, thy will be done"
(Matt. xxvi. 42).

4

THE PASSION OF CHRIST

"When Jesus had said these things, *he went forth*
with his disciples over the brook Cedron, where there

was a garden, into which he entered with his disciples" (John xviii. 1).   The resoluteness of will with
which Jesus entered into the three distinct phases of
His Passion is apparent from the words used by the
Evangelist.   Three times is used the phrase: *"He
went forth."*   It emphasizes the determination of One
Who was set to the offering of Himself, because it was
His own will.   He went forth to the agony and sorrow
of the garden.   He went forth after that agony to meet
His enemies and the traitor's kiss.   He went forth finally
under the heavy weight of the Cross to the place that
is called Golgotha.   The Royal Psalmist had stressed
that triumphant firmness of purpose.   "Sacrifice and
oblation thou wouldest not: but a body thou hast
fitted for me: holocausts for sin did not please thee.
Then said I: behold I come: in the head of the book
it is written of me: that I should do thy will O God"
(Psalm xxxix. 7, 8; Heb. x. 5-7).

According to St. Thomas, Christ assumed the
greatest sorrow compatible with reason that He might
atone for the sins of all men.   That sorrow was in part
caused by the anguish of physical pain and death, but
had still deeper root in His soul which accepted responsibility in the sight of His Father for the guilt of
mankind.   "All ye that pass by the way, attend and
see if there be any sorrow like unto my sorrow"
(Lam. i. 12).   St. Thomas again gives two reasons why
this sorrow of the Saviour exceeded that of all contrite
human hearts.   First of all, by reason of His greater
wisdom and charity, He saw at once the enormity of
sin and how grievously it offended God, Who called
man into being, because He is love.   Secondly, because
His sorrow was not successive, nor confined to the sin
of any one person.   He sorrowed in the hour of His

sacred Passion simultaneously for all men from the beginning until the end of time (cf. III, Q. 46; A. 6). Such a sorrow could only find its complete and satisfying expression in the total sacrifice of Himself as a holocaust to God by way of reparation. He declared to His Apostles, who were quick to notice the external signs of that grief on His countenance, that it alone was sufficient to cause His death. " My soul," He said, " is sorrowful even unto death " (Matt. xxvi. 38).

Jesus opened wide His Divine Heart to the inrush of this sorrow in the Garden of Olives, where really began the actual oblation of His body and blood. " He began to be sorrowful and to be sad " (Matt. xxvi. 37). There He poured out His soul to the Father in the great pact between Them of human redemption. He and the Father willed the Passion. The Father commanded and the Incarnate Son obeyed. The pact identified Jesus with a sinful race. " Him that knew no sin, for us he hath made sin, that we might be made the justice of God in him " (2 Cor. v. 21). " The Lord hath laid upon him the iniquity of us all " (Isa. liii. 6). Pilate was indeed to sentence Him to death, but only as an evil agent of the powers of darkness which sought His destruction. The sentence of death had been eternally decreed in the courts of God. " He spared not even his own Son, but delivered him up for us " (Rom. viii. 32). The decree was primarily one of love, and in love of justice. Christ responded to its command in the same order with an exceeding thirst after justice born of His tremendous love.

The agony in the Garden was all His own. It was the prelude to the great eternal offering. He delivered Himself into the hands of the Father before delivering

Himself into the hands of His enemies, who were already gathering around Him in the darkness of that terrible night.   In that complete self-surrender the first stage of the oblation of His body and blood was reached.   " His sweat became as drops of blood trickling down upon the ground" (Luke xxii. 44). The heart of Jesus was crushed down with weight of sorrow such as no other man could have.   He knew all the horror and a savagery which lay before Him on that night and the next day.   But over the fear which He allowed to dominate His sense faculties, there triumphed in His soul the longing to obey and to fulfil.   The first shedding of His precious blood in that agony of grief was caused by His intense desire to pour it forth for our sakes.   So great was the longing of His Sacred Heart, that the blood of life-giving could no longer be contained within the narrow channels of His veins.   Forced by His great love, it burst through the pores of His skin and flowed even to the ground. With the visible sign of His oblation in that shedding of His blood was associated intense prayerfulness. " Being in agony he prayed the longer " (ibid. 43).   He further manifested the perfect dispositions of His soul by using the worship of the body.   " He fell flat upon the ground " (Mark xiv. 15).   Though as God He was equal to the Father, yet as man, and with man's iniquity laid upon Him, He must humble Himself in the most abject way.   " He humbled Himself " (Phil. xxvii. 8).   By His abject prostration in the garden He set Himself on the way of the awful humiliation of His Passion and death, that He might satisfy for our pride.

Having endured the fierce trial of His agony, and strengthened by prayer in His resolute desire of sacrifice, He went forward to meet His enemies, and to deliver Himself into their hands. "Jesus, therefore, knowing all the things which should come upon Him, went forth, and said to them: whom seek ye?" (John xviii. 4). He said to His Apostles: "Rise: let us go. Behold he is at hand that will betray me" (Matt. xxvi. 46). The betraying kiss of Judas was the signal which let loose upon Him the pent-up hatred of the Scribes and Pharisees with the mob at their control. He declared openly to them whence they were: "This is your hour and of the powers of darkness" (Luke xxii. 53). Once again He made manifest His Divine power over all evil, and made clear to them that it was solely by His free consent that He had delivered Himself into their hands. The words which later He addressed to Pilate were true also for them: "Thou shouldst not have any power against me, unless it were given thee from above" (John xix. 11). As they surrounded Him with their lanterns and their weapons and shouted His name insultingly—"Jesus of Nazareth"—He calmly replied: "I am He." "As soon therefore as He said to them: I am He; they went backward and fell to the ground" (John xviii. 6). Blinded to all instincts except that of revenge, these agents of darkness were undeterred from their crime, and, rising again, laid rough hands upon Him and, binding Him with their ropes, brought Him back triumphantly into the Holy City. From that moment the flood-tide of evil was let loose against Him.

Throughout that first Holy Thursday night until daybreak on the following day, the chief priests and magistrates of the Temple, with their henchmen, vented their hatred against Him. They struck Him; they spat upon Him. They mocked and derided Him. They finally declared Him "guilty of death" because

He dared to assert the truth, which many times before
He had both declared and proved by miracles, of which
they had been unwilling witnesses. As the legal in-
heritors of the Promise, they should have been the
first to welcome that truth. Instead, they brought forward all kinds of witnesses to give testimony against
Him. But the charges were so manifestly false that
not even those who thirsted for His blood could admit
them as true. Jesus held His peace, except when there
was question of His Mission or His teaching. "I have
spoken openly to the world. I have always taught in
the synagogue whither all the Jews resort: and in
secret I have spoken nothing" (John xviii. 20). When
one of the servants struck Him for so replying to the
High Priest, Jesus answered him: "If I have spoken
evil, give testimony of the evil; but if well, why strikest
thou me?" (ibid.). The closing act of this mock trial
made it quite clear that the sole reason of His condem-
nation was His claim to be the Messiah. "The high
priest asked him and said to him: art thou the Christ,
the Son of the Blessed God? And Jesus said to him:
I am. And you shall see the Son of man sitting on the
right hand of the power of God and coming with the
clouds of heaven. Then the high priest rending his
garments, saith: What need we any further witnesses?
You have heard the blasphemy. What think you?
Who all condemned him to be guilty of death" (Mark
xiv. 61-4).

The early morning of Good Friday saw Him dragged
through the streets of Jerusalem to the court of Pilate,
who alone had power to pass sentence of death by
crucifixion, which they desired for Him, and which
was reserved only for the worst of malefactors. In
front of Pilate's palace the pent-up hatred of three

years found its expression in a frenzy of shouting—
"Crucify Him!" Pilate was at a loss what to do with
one so obviously innocent of plotting against any tem-
poral power. He tried to evade the issue by sending
Him to Herod, who judged Him to be a fool because
of His silence, and "with his army set him at nought
and mocked him, putting on him a white garment,
and sent him back to Pilate" (Luke xxiii. 11). In
spite of all the urging of His enemies, Pilate could find
no cause in Him. Yet, he ordered Him to be cruelly
scourged. After the scourging, Jesus was made to
suffer the infamy of Roman mockery. Clothed in
purple rags, with a reed for a sceptre, and thorns for a
crown, he was displayed to the mob by Pilate; "Behold
the Man" (John xix. 5). "Behold your king." But
they cried out: "Away with him, crucify him. Pilate
saith to them: Shall I crucify your king? The chief
priests answered: We have no king but Caesar"
(ibid. 14, 15). In one breath they renounced their
Messianic tradition, cast aside the expectation of their
people, and denied their own nationhood.

"Bearing his own cross *he went forth* to that place
which is called Calvary, but in Hebrew Golgotha"
(ibid. 17). The shameful sufferings which Jesus endured, prior to accepting the Cross, formed a prelude
to the final act of sacrifice. The many cruelties and
profanations committed against His sacred Person in
the Body which He had assumed, were part of His preparation as a victim of sacrifice. His body was first
prepared in the garden of His agony by the terrible
sweat of blood, which dyed it red and made it acutely
sensitive to pain. It was prepared by the scourges
which tore His flesh asunder and bathed Him again in
His own blood. His sacred head and face were also

G

covered with His blood from the thorns which formed a fitting crown for Him, Whose kingdom was not of this world.   The Prophet saluted long before this blood-stained figure of the Messiah, "walking in the greatness of his strength"; "Why then is thy apparel red, and thy garments like theirs that tread in the winepress" (Isa. lxiii. 1, 2).   By these sufferings, His body was most perfectly adapted to the shameful death which He was to undergo.   The Cross which He bore on His shoulders was the most ignominious of all burdens in the eyes of Jews and Romans.   It required a victim who was already humiliated.   There was no contradiction in Christ.   He had longed for that Cross all His life, but His privilege of accepting it and carrying it for the love of men came through the tortuous testing of anguish and suffering.   The terrible preparation which preceded His bearing of it had for its purpose to show forth the sanctity and the wisdom of the Cross unto all His followers.   He had already repeatedly announced the law of Christian living as identified with this holy carrying of the Cross.   "He said to all: If any man will come after me, let him deny himself and take up his cross daily, and follow me" (Luke ix. 23).   "The word of the cross, to them indeed that perish, is foolishness; but to them that are saved, that is, to us, it is the power of God' (1 Cor. i. 18).

After three successive falls on the way, He at length reached the place of sacrifice, which was outside the walls of the City.   The ancient Jewish ceremonial had special prescriptions for sacrifices for sin.   "For the bodies of those beasts, whose blood is brought into the Holies by the high priest for sin, are burned without the camp. Wherefore Jesus also, that he might sanctify the people by his own blood, suffered without the gate. Let us go forth therefore to him without the camp; bearing his reproach" (Heb. xiii. 11, 13). As we reverently and prayerfully become witnesses of the final sorrow of the Crucifixion, the thought uppermost in our minds must be that of the converted Centurion: "Indeed this man was the Son of God" (Mark xv. 39). What was accomplished on Calvary was the work of the entire Trinity. It was the work of the Eternal Father, "That spared not even his own Son: but delivered him up for us all" (Rom. viii. 32). It was the work of the Son, who as man offered Himself as a victim. That offering was animated by the fulness of love which is the spirit: "Who by the Holy Ghost offered himself unspotted unto God" (Heb. ix .14).

5

THE CRUCIFIXION

The actual nailing of the body of Christ to the Cross was quickly completed. The suffering which followed it was of long duration. The Divine Saviour willingly submitted to the orders of His executioners and cast Himself upon the ground. At their command, He, their God, extended His arms on the rough wood of the Cross. "They have dug my hands and my feet." One of the Holy Nails is still preserved as a precious relic of the Passion, and speaks eloquently of the suffering which it inflicted. It is a thick square nail of about six inches in length, furnished with a large dome-shaped head, which, when driven home, held hands and feet firmly in position and pressed hard on the flesh surrounding the wound. The blunt points of these nails entered the upper part of the Divine hands, and with repeated blows were driven fast into the wood. A third nail which pierced the insteps of both feet completed the awful punishment of crucifixion. The bones of hands and feet, though not broken, were rudely dislocated by the width of these three nails.

Medical experts who have carefully examined the Holy Shroud of Turin, which bears a photographic image of the dead Christ, have been able to describe the horror of suffering which accompanied death by crucifixion. According to their evidence, the nails which transfixed the hands to the Cross lacerated the main trunk nerve which passes down the arm to the hands. Excruciating pain from this injured nerve would be transmitted with ever-recurring violent shocks to the nerve-centre of the brain. The bare and injured nerve must continue to press on the iron nail. The worst form of this torture came when the cross was raised. Most pitiable then was the suffering of the Saviour. The entire weight of His body pulled downwards from the nailed hands, pressing the great brachial nerve against the rough surface of the nail. Great waves of pain thus surged through the entire body of Jesus. There was only one way of relieving this pressure on the lacerated nerves of the hands. He must lift Himself upwards by downward pressure on the nailed feet. This in turn caused a new agony. Every slightest movement brought its own agonizing effect. No wonder that the Prophet compared the sufferings of the Passion to a great sea, which would overwhelm the Messiah. Yet Christ bore all without a murmur during the three long hours He willed to remain alive on the Cross. "All you that pass by the way, come and see if there be any sorrow like unto my sorrow" (Lam. i. 12).

"As Moses lifted up the serpent in the desert, so must the Son of Man be lifted up" (John iii. 14). "I, if I be lifted up from the earth, will draw all things to myself" (ibid. xii. 32). The raising of the quivering, pain-racked body of Christ on the Cross seemed to mark the final and absolute triumph of His enemies. They quickly forgot their unwilling prostration before Him in the Garden. They could afford to mock Him in the apparent certainty of His final destruction. "They that passed by, blasphemed Him wagging their heads, and saying: Vah, thou that destroyest the temple of God and in three days dost rebuild it, save thy own self: if thou be the Son of God, come down from the cross" (Matt. xxvii. 39, 40). Such insults and blasphemies from His own people, for whom He willed to die, increased the sorrow of the Saviour. His mighty prayer ascended for them even then; "Father, forgive them, for they know not what they do" (Luke xxiii. 34). During the three supreme hours of His life on the Cross His entire being was concentrated on the work on which He was solemnly engaged. His sacrificial work continued. During these three hours He completed what had been in part accomplished in the physical sufferings which He had already endured at the hands of His enemies. The oblation of His body and blood to the Father demanded the internal act of His will as well as the external immolation of His flesh. His sufferings were accompanied with fervent prayer. On the Cross He reached the most sublime moment of His Eternal Priesthood as intermediary between man and God. Earth not merely touched, but was linked with heaven. With outstretched arms, and raised between heaven and earth, He embraced the whole earth and lifted it in the offering of Himself by way of adoration, satisfaction, thanksgiving and petition. The power of His supplication on the Cross was beyond all reckoning. Against that power all the evil which was massed against Him was rendered impotent. Death itself was conquered and sin was taken away. The symbol and source of new life was lifted over the world.

6

CHRIST ON THE CROSS

The Divine Saviour on the Cross tasted every form of bitterness of soul as well as of body. For these three hours the entire weight of His body hung from the transfixed hands. There was no rest from pain. Breathing was wellnigh impossible. The walls of the chest were so extended by the strained, outstretched arms that the breath which filled the lungs could only with the greatest difficulty be again released. To breathe out again required the transferring of the weight of His body from the nailed hands by pressing downwards with His feet on the nail which held them to the Cross. Only by this means could He avoid suffocation. With every breath He drew there was a fresh surging of pain from the wounds. From such suffering death alone could bring relief. He must await the appointed hour for the completion of His work of Redemption.

His seven words on the Cross broke the silence of

His secret and continual prayer. He paused, as the crescendo of hate arose from beneath Him, to pray for His enemies. He was aware of the needs of those around Him, especially of the unfortunates whose wickedness was intended to add to His disgrace. He promised salvation to the penitent thief. "Amen I say to thee, this day thou shalt be with me in paradise " (Luke xxiii. 43). Beneath the Cross stood the few friends who never abandoned Him. His Beloved Mother was there by reason of her office as Co-Redemptrix. With her was John, the beloved disciple, the only one of the Twelve that had not deserted Him in His last hour. He spoke first to Mary, the new Eve, addressing her by her official title of woman, the new woman, and mother of the new generation : "Woman, behold thy son " (John xix. 26). Then He addressed Himself to John, and in him to all the children of men, to tell of the world's debt to this new woman, who became in a far truer sense than the first Eve, "the mother of all the living " (Gen. iii. 20). "He saith to the disciple : Behold thy mother " (John xix. 27). The sufferings of the Passion, which won for Him many brethren, gained for both His Eternal Father and His Beloved Mother a vast progeny of spiritual children.

Jesus spoke yet another time that He might declare to all men the deep mystery of His Passion : "Afterwards Jesus knowing that all things were now accomplished, that the scripture might be fulfilled, said: I thirst " (John xix. 28). To extreme physical weakness, which increased as His precious blood gradually drained from His body, was added another dread torture associated with death by crucifixion. The Royal Prophet had foretold this additional suffering of the Messiah; " My tongue hath adhered to my jaws " (Psalm

xxi. 16). On hearing His cry, one of His executioners, moved by compassion, presented Him with vinegar and gall, which fulfilled yet another prophecy; "In my thirst they gave me vinegar to drink ' (Psalm lxviii. 22). Jesus welcomed that thirst of the body as part of His atonement for the sins of Man's intemperance. "They gave him wine mingled with gall. And when he had tasted he would not drink" (Matt. xxvii. 34). There is a mystery in that Divine thirst which can neither be understood nor relieved by His enemies. There is a longing in the Divine Heart of the Saviour for the souls of men. The assuaging of such a thirst can be the privilege only of His friends.

"About the ninth hour Jesus cried with a loud voice, saying: Eli, Eli, lamma sabacthani? that is, My God, My God, why hast thou forsaken me?" (Matt. xxvii: 46). This cry of desolation which broke from His lips revealed the depth of the sorrow of the Son of God on the Cross. All the sufferings of the Saviour were in satisfaction for sin. He endured the torture of His crucified body, that He might show forth the enormity of offending God. "For the wickedness of my people have I struck him" (Isa. liii. 8). The external affliction of His body was but little when compared with the fearful anguish of His soul. He bore the consequences of man's sin even to the extreme penalty of dereliction. Truly in Him the wages of sin became death.

How mysterious is the voice of the Saviour in the awful hour of His abandonment on the Cross. St. Thomas emphasizes that there is in it no distaste or repugnance of death, which He so willingly endured. It is a declaration of the great mystery of Redemption. The Eternal Father, Who would willingly have given

Him twelve legions of angels, if He had but asked, has abandoned His Beloved Son to the cruelty of His enemies in accordance with His divine decree. Jesus had said to Peter in the garden: "How then shall the Scriptures be fulfilled, that so it must be done" (Matt. xxvi. 54). His cry from the Cross leads us into the mystery of this fulfilment. It is best understood in conjunction with the entire psalm of which His loud voice may well have made the first intoning. This psalm (xxi) speaks graphically of the Saviour's sufferings and dereliction, of His death by crucifixion, of the insults and opprobrium heaped upon Him, of the dreadful blasphemies which even then were being uttered against Him beneath the Cross. Yet even in the depth of His abandonment, there is the certainty of being heard, the assurance of immense benefits from His death, and the new hope of the glorious Church which will arise. "Neither hath he turned away his face from me: and when I cried to him he heard me. With thee is my praise in a great church" (V. 25). The Psalmist's prophetic words were admirably fulfilled in the institution of the Most Blessed Eucharist on the night before He suffered: "The poor shall eat and shall be filled: and they shall praise the Lord that seek him: their hearts shall live for ever and ever" (V. 27). Finally, the fruits of the Passion shall be made manifest in the perfect and world-wide religion which is to follow: "All the ends of the earth shall remember, and shall be converted to the Lord, and all the kindreds of the Gentiles shall adore in his sight" (V. 28).

As the hours went slowly by, the Saviour's sufferings increased. There was no rest for the torn and mangled body on the Cross. Held so rigidly by the nails, every muscle experienced a separate torture. Violent cramps added their horror to His affliction. His back, rent by the cruel scourges, was pressed hard against the rough wood of the Cross. These gaping wounds, which had been filled with the filth of the streets, on which He had fallen along the way to Calvary, and which were so long exposed to the air, showed signs of infection and became still more hideous. This was also foretold by the Prophet: "My sores are putrified and corrupted" (Psalm xxxvii. 6). Every member of His sacred body endured its proper and separate punishment for the corruption of sin, that we, through His Passion and death, might be made healthy members of the Mystic Body, which continues Him on earth. "By his bruises we are healed" (Isa. liii. 5).

As we contemplate the Saviour during these last hours, we must not allow ourselves to forget the actual horror of the sight which He presented to the eyes of God and men. "There is no beauty in him, nor comliness: and we have seen him, and there was no sightliness in him, that we should be desirous of him: despised and the most abject of men, a man of sorrows and acquainted with infirmity: and his look was as it were hidden and despised, whereupon we esteemed him not . . . and we have thought him as it were a leper, and as one struck by God and afflicted" (Isa. liii. 3, 4). Looking down once again on His Beloved Son, Who was made the innocent victim of sin, the Eternal Father was pleased with His sacrifice: "This is my beloved Son in whom I am well pleased" (Matt. iii. 17). We may well ask what manner of Father is He, Who was pleased at the sight of so much sorrow and degradation, Who demanded of His Son so horrible a death? The Father was pleased, because in the willing obedience of His Son Divine justice was satisfied. He was pleased, because a new and everlasting priesthood and priestly covenant was firmly established in the blood of His Son. He was pleased for our sakes that, through the consummation of the Cross the gates of heaven were opened once again, and His Fatherhood over men perfectly established. He was pleased because, in that sacrifice, He was greatly glorified. "The Father also seeketh such to adore him" (John iv. 23). But the principal reason of the Father's pleasure was found in the evidence, so strikingly provided by the death of His Only Begotten, to His own innermost goodness and infinite love. "God is love" (1 John iv. 8). That is the supreme lesson of the Cross. "By this hath the charity of God appeared towards us, because God hath sent his only begotten Son into the world, that we might be saved by him" (ibid. 9).

Jesus declared that the things written of Him had an end. When the three hours of sacrificial suffering and prayer were accomplished, there remained for Him but to make the final and, for us, the most comforting declaration that the work was done, that He had fulfilled all things which the Father had sent Him to do; "Consummatum est"—"It is finished" (John xix. 30). Then, gathering all the strength of His tortured and bloodless body, with Divine and miraculous energy of His great soul, and with a loud voice, He made the final rendering of Himself to His Father in the words of the Psalm: "Father, into thy hands I commend my spirit" (Luke xxii. 46). "And bowing his head, he gave up the ghost" (John xix. 30). The bowing of His head was that of the victor, not of the vanquished. In death He had conquered death, and brought new life to the world. Jesus, God and man, was dead. Nature itself was convulsed at the enormity of the event. "The earth quaked, and the rocks were rent, and the graves were opened" (Matt. xxvii. 51). His enemies ran in terror from the scene of their outrage. He was left alone with His few faithful friends. Those who understand the mystery of the Cross do not run away from it. It removes the fear of death, since on it the Saviour, as the loving physician of our souls, has tasted for our sakes, and in tasting removed its bitterness. "Because the children are partakers of flesh and blood, he also in like manner hath been partaker of the same: that, through death he might destroy him who had empire of death, that is to say the devil: and might deliver them, who through fear of death were all their life-time subject to servitude" (Heb. ii. 14, 15). If we are faithful to Him, and abide in His love, those strong arms, so mercifully extended on the Cross, will bear us, when our hour comes, to the Father: "Come, ye blessed of my Father" (Matt. xxv. 34). "Death is swallowed up in victory. O death, where is thy victory? O death, where is thy sting? . . . Thanks be to God, who has given us the victory through Our Lord Jesus Christ" (1 Cor. xv. 54, 57).

7

THE PIERCED HEART

The reality of Christ's death on the Cross received confirmation, which placed it beyond all doubt. We have the evidence of the soldiers who were sent to break the bones of the crucified, and found that Jesus was already dead. For them the sight of the mani-

festly lifeless body of Jesus made further action un-
necessary, and they thereby unconsciously fulfilled yet
another prophecy: "For these things were done that
the scripture might be fulfilled: You shall not break
a bone of him" (John xix. 26). But there still remained a final prediction: "They shall look upon
him whom they pierced" (Zach. xii. 10). St. John
stresses both the fulfilling of the prophecy, and the importance of the event. "One of the soldiers with a
spear opened his side, and immediately there came out
blood and water. And he that saw it, hath given testimony; and his testimony is true. And he knoweth that
he saith true; that you also may believe" (John xix.
34, 35). The fifth sacred wound was made by the
lance, which, with an upward diagonal thrust, pierced
the heart of the dead Christ. The wound was so large
that, after the Resurrection, Thomas was able to place
his hand within it. St. Augustine emphasizes the
significant word used by the Evangelist: "He would
not say, he struck his side, or wounded it; but that he
opened it, that the door of life might stand open."

This last act of the drama of Calvary revealed yet
another, though hidden, suffering of the Saviour. The
water which flowed so copiously with the blood has
been noted by medical experts, who declare that it was
located in the pericardium or outer envelope of the
heart. This physical phenomenon was caused by the
nervous strain of His sufferings. The water which had
thus collected held the heart bound as in a vice, so that
every beat of His Sacred Heart caused its own excruciating pain. That was yet another part of the great
price which Jesus paid in His excess of love for each
one of us. It is no wonder that St. Catherine of Siena,
when contemplating the Passion and in the greatness

of her own love, should address Him with the words:
"O Thou fool of love."

This fifth wound is the most sacred of all five, and
from the earliest times has been held in special veneration in the Church. That veneration has been the
foundation of our present-day devotion to the Sacred
Heart. The Fathers of the Church emphasize the
splendid efficacy of this fifth wound. According to
St. John Chrysostom, the water and blood were figures
of the new life, which comes through water and the
Holy Ghost, and of the Mystic Body of Christ, which
is His Church. "From these the Holy Church was
founded, through the regeneration of water and reno-
vation in the Holy Spirit. . . ." From His side, therefore, Christ built His Church, as from Adam's side
came Eve, his spouse. "This is he," says St. John,
"that came by water and blood, Jesus Christ: not by
water only, but by water and blood" (1 John v. 6). St.
Paul emphasizes the mystic identity of Christ with His
Church: "No man ever hated his own flesh: but
nourisheth and cherisheth it, as also Christ doth the
Church: because we are members of his body, of his
flesh and of his bones" (Eph. iii. 29, 30). "In one
Spirit were we all baptised into one body" (1 Cor. xii.
13). St. Leo declares the same doctrine: "The body
of one baptised becomes the flesh of the Crucified
Christ."

In His Passion and death Jesus is truly the "author
and finisher" of man's Redemption. "Without the
shedding of blood, there is no remission" (Heb. ix. 22).
"You were redeemed with the precious blood of
Christ, as of a lamb unspotted and undefiled" (1 Pet.
i. 18, 19). "Let us go therefore with confidence to this
throne of grace, that we may obtain mercy and find

grace in seasonable aid" (Heb. iv. 16). From the Agony in the Garden until the final piercing of His Divine Heart, Jesus found efficacious ways of shedding that precious blood in His infinite generosity of a loving God. "How much more shall the blood of Christ, who by the Holy Ghost offered himself unspotted unto God, cleanse our conscience from dead works to serve the living God" (ibid. ix. 14). Our eyes, and, with our eyes, our hearts must be ever turned towards the redeeming sign of the Crucified Christ. The Crucifix presents us with the perfect symbol of our eternal salvation. On our knees before it, we must, like St. Thomas and other Saints, learn all wisdom. We sign ourselves with the Cross in confession of our Christian faith. It is a holy sign, which commemorates the death of the Saviour and renews our confidence in its salutary fruits. But, through the Divine goodness of Jesus, we have a sign which not only commemorates, but in a manner renews that death. This is the sign of Consecration which places the Victim once again living upon our Catholic Altars, and presents Him on our behalf to the Eternal Father as "the Lamb standing as it were slain" (Apoc. v. 6). Meditation on the Passion should above all else stir up in our hearts an ever greater love for Jesus in the adorable Eucharist, "in which the memory of His Passion is renewed, the mind is filled with grace, and there is given to us a pledge of everlasting glory" (St. Thomas). When we are present at Holy Mass, we assist, like Mary His Mother, and St. John the Beloved Disciple at the Holocaust of Calvary, in which all the efficacy of the original sacrifice is poured out upon us. The Mass and Calvary are one and the same act of infinite worship of God, differing only in the manner of their offering.

As we come out from our churches, where we have witnessed once again the raising of the Sacred Host, the Victim of our everlasting Christian sacrifice, we truly say, like the Centurion who looked with new light on the face of the Crucified Christ: " Indeed, this was the Son of God " (Mark xv. 39).

Fourth Chapter

THE WAY INTO THE HOLIES

(Heb. ix. 8)

1

LIVING STONES BUILT UP

A N outstanding, though external, testimony to the vitality of our Catholic faith and religion is provided by the crowd of worshippers to be seen entering and leaving our church on a Sunday morning or, indeed, any morning during the week, as well as at various other times. It is clear that the church, as a sacred edifice, plays a very important part in the lives of the faithful. Non-Catholics, at least those who are willing to give some consideration to the matter, are unfailingly impressed by this phenomenon of Catholic life. Some have tried to explain it away by attributing it to the splendid externals—vestments, lights, incense, etc.—all of which give a certain comfort, which at best would be only some form of religious emotionalism. They should venture within the building, and probe the meaning of the external ritual, to find the real secret of this drawing power. Whilst not denying the value of externals, nor the splendour, on occasions, of the Catholic ritual, since it is man's nature to be drawn by the aid of such things to the knowledge of things spiritual, it must be admitted that such externals play but a small part in ordinary and everyday Catholic services. In the Low Mass of a Sunday, for example, there is little to appeal to the sense faculties beyond the essential visible rite of the Mass itself. There is no singing, nothing is heard but the voice in Latin of the Priest and server, and that only occasionally; yet each worshipper, through association with the sacrificial act taking place on the altar, is intent on fulfilling the most serious obligation of his religion, namely, the worship of God through Jesus Christ. Mere religious emotion or priest-craft will not explain the presence of high and low, of rich and poor, of educated and ignorant, not only at Sunday Mass, when attendance is of obligation, but at daily Mass during the week at the cost of no little sacrifice of time and comfort.

From out the centuries that have passed there springs a similar, though not more glorious, evidence to this truth. The world-famous Cathedrals of the Middle Ages, which made ecclesiastical architecture one of the noblest of the arts, confront us with a splendour which bespeaks the living faith of these centuries, and which architects to-day may seek to imitate, but can never rival. In those medieval temples of God we behold, enraptured, against a background of perfect architectural form, a profusion of adornment, of sculpture and of painting, raised over, and emphasizing an altar of sacrifice. Those who devoted their talents and their labour to the building of these sacred edifices wished through the splendour and order of construction to focus attention on that centre-piece which inspired their design and work. In these Cathedrals we do not find beauty or art merely for art's sake. The medieval architects and artists desired above all else to emphasize the glory of the treasure hidden in their tabernacles. The building of these temples of God was not due to the genius of their constructors alone, but to the faith of a believing people, for whom the Mass and the Real Presence were the foundation of human life, social as well as individual.

Without the innermost treasure of the Blessed Eucharist and its sacrificial Rite, the rest, no matter how splendid, becomes meaningless and empty. This is particularly evident to-day in the ancient Cathedrals of England, which Catholic faith conceived and fashioned long before the Reformation. In them one finds a like exterior splendour, but the centre-piece is now missing. There comes a feeling of desolation at seeing them deprived of what so long ago inspired their construction. " To-day," wrote Cardinal Gasquet, " we look merely upon the setting which the piety and devotion of Catholic Englishmen had fashioned to be somewhat less unworthy of the precious jewel of the Holy Sacrament. The very beauty of the setting only emphasizes the absence of the jewel. . . . Now the light is gone, the jewel torn from its place, and even the setting shows patent proof of the violence of the means employed, and seems to proclaim aloud that the glory of God which enlightened it and the lamp thereof is departed." The history of the Church in England and Ireland, following so sad a tragedy, shows how relatively unimportant was the exterior grandeur or setting for the treasure of our Catholic faith. Amidst the fury of persecution the faithful found all they needed on some Mass Rock in the lonely mountains, and gathered around their altar of sacrifice, securely confident as in the shelter of some great Cathedral. Over altars such as these there was no dome except the canopy of heaven, no splendour other than the green of the surrounding hills. The plain truth is that the Mass contains within itself—within its own sacred Rite—all the essentials of adornment. Jesus gave Himself to His people to be their sanctuary, their Holy of Holies. Wherever the Altar Stone of His Sacrifice is found, there is His Temple, great or small, there is the House of God and of His people. "We have such a high priest, who is set on the right hand of the throne of majesty in the heavens, a minister of the Holies, and of the true tabernacle, which the Lord hath pitched, and not man" (Heb. viii. 1, 2). By His omnipotence God pitched this most perfect tabernacle on earth, not confined to Jerusalem, nor to any one place, but wherever and whenever His ordained priest pronounces the words of Consecration: "For as often as you shall eat the bread and drink the chalice, you shall shew forth the death of the Lord, until he come" (1 Cor. xi. 26).

To appreciate what a Catholic church means to a devout Christian, whether it be cathedral or catacomb, we must see it against the vast design of God through Jesus Christ for the sanctification of all men. It is not the external fabric, be it noble or be it poor, that makes the church, which is "built upon the foundation of the Apostles, Jesus Christ himself being the chief corner-stone: in whom all the building, being framed together, groweth up into a holy temple in the Lord. In whom you also are built together into an habitation of God in the Spirit" (Eph. ii. 21, 22). The outer fabric which we call a church is but a symbol of that great spiritual temple fashioned by Christ to the glory of His Father, which He Himself likened to a city built upon a hill. Jesus is the living eternal corner-stone of this spiritual edifice. "The rock was Christ"

(1 Cor. x. 4). Just as the great Cathedrals of old were inspired by, and built around the holy altar-stone of the altar of sacrifice, so each living stone, inspired by faith in Christ, rests solidly on Him who is the Head of grace and becomes a vital part in the spiritual temple of God. Of such Our Lord said: "Every one that cometh to me and heareth my words, and doth them, I will shew you to whom he is like. He is like to a man building a house, who diggeth deep, and laid the foundation upon a rock" (Luke vi. 47, 48). St. Paul declares to the early Christians: "You are God's building," of which the foundation can be none other than Jesus Christ (1 Cor. iii. 9). St. Peter very beautifully emphasizes the same idea: "If yet you have tasted that the Lord is sweet. Unto whom coming, as to a living stone, rejected indeed by men, but chosen and made honourable by God: Be you as living stones built up, a spiritual house, a holy priesthood, to offer up spiritual sacrifices acceptable to God by Jesus Christ" (1 Pet. ii. 3-5). This is the secret of Catholic church-going. "Faith is the substance of things to be hoped for" (Heb. xi. 1). That substance which is at once truth and life is sought for and assuredly found in the life-giving activity of the Catholic Church.

2

THE PATTERNS OF HEAVENLY THINGS

As has been already emphasized, the Christian religion was not a break with the past but, rather, a continuation of it into its perfect phase of fulfilment through the coming of the Messiah. So, likewise, our

Catholic churches of to-day are the outcome of that primitive and providentially designed development which brought the infant Christian Church out from the Jewish Temple into the service of the entire human race. It alone had to give what all men needed, namely, a religion of perfect adoration of the Father of all, "in spirit and in truth" (John iv. 23). Yet the Temple of the Jews held already within itself the germ and figure of what was to come, and what we now possess. In the ancient building of the Chosen People of God we find what St. Paul describes as "a parable of things present" (Heb. ix. 9), which helps us to appreciate more fully the abundance bestowed on us by God through our Catholic religion.

Almighty God ordered the people of Israel through His servant Moses to set up a place of worship to the One True God: "They shall make me a sanctuary, and I will dwell in the midst of them: according to the likeness of the tabernacle which I will show thee, and of all the vessels for the service thereof" (Exodus xxv. 8, 9). Moses received the minutest details for every part of this tabernacle and for all that was to pertain to the worship of God. Moses' brother Aaron and his sons were solemnly consecrated by a special ritual to the service of the altar. "Thou shalt consecrate the hands of them all, and shalt sanctify them, that they may do the office of priesthood unto me" (ibid. xxviii. 41). In these detailed prescriptions St. Paul discovers "the example and shadow of heavenly things". Moses received his directions on Mount Sinai during the forty days which he spent in close communion with God. The Jewish religion came from on high, whence would come also the new priest of a more perfect tabernacle. God fashioned both Pattern and Perfec-

tion. The importance of the pattern lies in its being
the shape of things to come: "As it was answered to
Moses, when he was to finish the tabernacle: See (says
he) that thou make all things according to the pattern
which was shown thee on the mount" (Heb. viii. 5).
When everything was prepared, the temple and all that
it contained, as well as the people, were cleansed and
dedicated in the blood of sacrificial victims, of which
Moses declared to the Children of Israel: "This is the
blood of the testament which God hath enjoined upon
you" (ibid. ix. 20; Exod. xxiv. 8). In this mosaic ritual
was found a foreshadowing of the more perfect testament yet to come. The ancient consecration, being but
a figure, was inferior to the perfect consecration of
the New Testament which was to be made, not in the
blood of animals, but in the most precious blood of the
Redeemer. "It was necessary therefore that the patterns of the heavenly things should be cleansed with
these: but the heavenly things themselves with better
sacrifices than these: For Jesus is not entered into the
Holies made with hands, the patterns of the true: but
into heaven, itself, that he may appear now in the
presence of God for us" (ibid. xxiii. 24).

Jewish worship, being by way of preparation, manifested definite limitations in its ritual, which are in
contrast with the wider scope and more accessible
character of the perfect religion of Jesus Christ. This
difference was apparent even in the construction of the
Tabernacle of Moses, and later of the Temple of Solo-
mon. It was still more evident in the ritual restrictions
of the Jewish priestly ministry, to which the building
was itself adapted. Within the Temple, but walled
off from the main part of it by what was called the Veil,
was found the Holy of Holies. St. Paul, who in his

early days was well acquainted with the Jewish religion, gives us a minute description of the inner and outer parts of the Temple, as well as the ritual uses to which they were put. " The former (testament) had also the justification of divine service, and a worldly sanctuary. For there was a tabernacle made the first, wherein were the candlesticks, and the table, and the setting forth of loaves, which is called the Holy. And after the second veil, the tabernacle, which is called the Holy of Holies, having a golden censer, and the ark of the testament, covered about on every part with gold, in which was a golden pot that had manna, and the rod of Aaron that had blossomed, and the tables of the testament, and over it were the cherubims of glory overshadowing the propitiatory: of which it is not needful to speak now particularly. Now these things were thus ordered: into the first tabernacle the priests indeed always entered, accomplishing the offices of sacrifices. But into the second, the high priest alone, once a year: not without blood, which he offereth for his own, and the people's ignorance: the Holy Ghost signifying this, that the way into the Holies was not yet made manifest, whilst the former tabernacle was standing " (ibid. 1-8). The Holy of Holies was rightly regarded by the Jews as the holiest place on earth. It held all the sacred emblems of their religion and of God's covenant with His people. Yet its use was extremely restricted. Neither the people nor the priests were allowed to enter or take part in any religious service in that innermost sanctuary. The High Priest alone had the right to enter, and that only once a year. Preparation for this annual entry was made in the shedding of blood, that he might be worthy to go in on behalf of the people. It was one of

the most solemn of Jewish festivities, and was filled
with Divine portent. Heaven was closed to mankind
after the sin of our First Parents. It could be opened
only through the merits of the Messiah who was promised. The first and limited tabernacle of the promise
had to pass away in favour of the second and perfect
tabernacle of the fulfilment, before the true way into
the Holies could be opened for all—for people and for
priests. That opening was accomplished by Jesus
Christ in the shedding of His "blood of the New
Testament". Of this fulfilment St. Paul quotes from
the prophecies: "Behold, the days shall come, saith
the Lord: and I will perfect unto the house of Israel,
and unto the house of Juda, a new testament" (Jer.
xxxi. 31).

3

THE TABERNACLE OF CHRIST'S BODY

With the coming of the Incarnate Word the time
of the old Temple's dissolution was near at hand.
"That which decayeth and groweth old is near its end"
(Heb. viii. 13). The death of the Divine Saviour on
the Cross was followed by a most significant event
within the innermost sanctuary of the Temple, which
marked its ending as a place of worship. "Behold the
veil of the temple was rent in two from the top even
to the bottom" (Matt. xxvii. 51). With the consummation of the Cross the new religion was established,
and the old temple ceded place to the new temple of
Christ's crucified body. The new Holy of Holies was
established on Calvary, whence it must spread over the

world.   By His death Christ established the new and perfect tabernacle which was opened wide to all men through the efficacy of the shedding of His blood. "Christ being come a high priest of the good things to come, by a greater and more perfect tabernacle not made with hand, that is not of this creation: neither by the blood of goats and calves, but by his own blood, entered once into the Holies, having obtained eternal redemption" (Heb. ix. 11, 12).   Mysterious and grandiose as was the ancient Temple of the Jews, it was but a symbol of the Christian temple—the Holy of Holies of the New Testament.   "Jesus is made a surety of a better testament" (ibid. vii. 22).   Through His sacrifice on the Cross Jesus removed the veil which barred the way into God's innermost sanctuary.   Instead of the old veil, there is nothing now between us and God but the veil of His body which, though it hides the glory of the Divinity Who assumed it, is the perfect instrument of the Divine communication.   In the body of Christ the fulness of the Godhead dwells substantially.   Through His Humanity we have access to the innermost sanctuary of that Divinity.   This way of approach to God is called by St. Paul: "A new and living way which he hath dedicated for us through the veil, that is to say, his flesh; and a high priest over the house of God" (ibid. x. 20, 21).

The body of Christ is not only the veil, it is the temple, the sanctuary, the covenant, the tabernacle. Jesus said: "Destroy this temple, and in three days I will raise it up. . . . He spoke of the temple of his body" (John ii. 19, 20).   The entire Christian religion, the entire Christian Church is mysteriously centred in this body of Christ.   Through the institution of the Most Holy Eucharist, He assured to us the everlasting presence of this centre of life and holiness. Through the mystical renewal of His death in the Mass He established a permanence of the new sanctuary in the blood which He once poured out from that body on Calvary. Jesus said again: "I am the door. By me, if any man enter in, he shall be saved: and he shall go in, and go out, and shall find pastures" (John x. 9). He became that door principally through His Passion and death. But that door of His sacrifice remains ever present—ever open. He is for ever the "High priest over the house of God". The doors of our Catholic Churches are but symbols of that Living Door which they contain, and which admits all, not only the priests, but the laity, into the closest communication through the body of Christ with God. The most sacred recesses of this new Temple of God are open to all men. Herein lies the profound secret of the drawing power of Catholic worship—the drawing power of Christ Crucified. "And I, if I be lifted up, will draw all things unto myself."

4

ENTERING INTO THE SANCTUARY

It does not require any deep knowledge of the Rite of the Most Holy Sacrifice of the Mass to realize that those who are present in the Church are not meant to be merely onlookers at a sacred function, which takes place within the sanctuary. The ceremonial and prayers are a constant reminder to the faithful to enter into close union with the priest on the altar, who offers the sacrifice on their behalf in virtue of his ministerial power. We have, unfortunately, in great measure lost the sense of our corporate union with Christ through His ordained minister. For far too many the Mass is but a half-understood Sunday obligation at which they must assist under pain of mortal sin. These mere Mass-going Catholics may get within the sanctuary, but they are not part of it, or at least not as vitally part of it, as they should be. It must be remembered that the responses, which are now made by the altar-servers, originally formed part of a sacred dialogue between the people and the priest. Through this dialogue the priest, as another Christ, gradually leads the faithful by prayer and supplication, made in their name, into the heart of the great Christian act of worship. With the power of the seal of Ordination, the divinely appointed minister, representing the people, becomes increasingly identified with Christ, until at the moment of Consecration the mysterious affinity is complete, and his priestly words are spoken in the very Person of the Incarnate Word—"This is my body." Through the sacrament of Holy Orders, and the power it bestows at that most solemn moment, Christ, as it were, appropriates His ministers and charges their words with His own omnipotence. Once the Saviour and High Priest is present on the altar, the priest continues the solemn Rite of sacrifice in the name of all the people. Having partaken of the body and blood of the Victim, he communicates the self-same Victim to the faithful, that they also may be really and truly united to Him, Who is the life of their souls. Following the Communion, the sacred dialogue continues with prayers, until he finally dismisses them with the "Ita Missa est", to which they all answer: "Thanks be to God."

The evidence from the external ritual of the Mass of such intimate association of the people with the priest, and through him with Christ, clearly indicates the presence of some inner disposition, or power of the soul, whereby each of the faithful can be vitally knitted to the personal redeeming act of the Incarnate Word. The juridically appointed minister at the altar has this power by reason of his priestly ordination. This is called the active power of the priesthood (cf. Discourse 2). In the ordinary faithful there must also reside what enables them to participate in the act of sacrifice, and to enter with the priest into the innermost sanctuary of the New Testament in His blood. The voice of the people which rises in such harmonious consent with the voice of the ordained minister, presupposes some form of Divine acceptance—some relation in them also to the priesthood of Christ. To enter so intimately into the Divine action on the altar demands something more than mere bodily and passive presence in the place of sacrifice—something more intimate and vital than a mere external denomination which includes them in some religious sect. Without a realization of what this vitalizing principle is, there can be no complete appreciation of the depth of our Catholic religion. The Mass does not stand alone. It is an essential part of the whole scheme of Divine salvation and sanctification which flows from the God-Man, "of whose fulness we all have received".

Jesus Christ is the prototype of every Christian. He is the "Pattern on the Mount", in which all things are made new. Through the mystery of the Incarnation He not only identified Himself with the human race but, in a true sense, made the human body which He thereby assumed to be a living temple of God. That body became substantially united to the Word of God in an all-holy hypostatic union. With the Son made Man was the Father in the unity of the Holy Ghost. Through the Incarnation the Son of God became also the Son of Man, and "the First-Born of many brethren". He thereby established a new generation of the children of His Father on the earth. St. Peter dares to say that, by the grace of Christ, we are "made partakers of the divine nature" (2 Pet. i. 4). Jesus is the Head and source of sanctifying grace, which establishes a conformity with Himself within the soul through the sanctifying power of the Spirit, so that Christians become the sons of the same Father by adoption: "Made comformable to the image of his Son" (Rom. viii. 29). This new life makes each Christian also a temple of God. The indwelling of God in a special way through grace is one of the most consoling mysteries of our Christian religion. God is Himself directly the Divine agent of our sanctification. "Know you not that you are the temple of God: and that the spirit of God dwelleth in you. . . . The temple of God is holy which you are" (1 Cor. iii. 16, 17). "Know you not that your members are the temple of the Holy Ghost, who is in you, whom you have from God" (ibid. vi. 19). "You are the temple of the living God" (2 Cor. vi. 16). St. Ignatius the martyr called all Christians *Theophoroi*; the "Carriers of God".

5

THE MYSTIC BODY

From the multitude of living members of Christ's mystical body the Church is formed: "Now you are the body of Christ, and members of member" (1 Cor. xii. 27). The head of this body is Christ: "From whom the whole body, being compacted and fitly joined together, by what every joint supplieth, according to the operation in the measure of every part, maketh increase of the body unto the edifying of itself in charity" (Eph. iv. 16). Christian meeting-places are called churches because of their relation to the entire society of the faithful. St. Paul develops that idea by comparing the society of the faithful to a great and solid building: "Now therefore you are no more strangers and foreigners: but you are fellow citizens with the saints and the domestics of God, built upon the foundation of the apostles and prophets, Jesus Christ himself being the chief corner-stone: in whom all the building, being framed together, groweth up into a holy temple in the Lord" (Eph. ii. 20, 21). St. Peter regards each Christian as a stone in this temple of God in Christ; "Be you also as living stones built up, a spiritual house" (1 Pet. ii. 4).

The union of members in Christ's mystic body goes far deeper than any mere gathering in a material building. The church in which they meet is, indeed, the House of God by reason of the Head, Who dwells bodily in the Tabernacle. But the members of the faithful, linked to Him by sanctifying grace together with Him form the living temple of God or the

"Whole Christ". The word Church means called of Christ—the "chosen generation", to whom His kingdom has been promised. The day will come when the mystic body of Christ on earth shall have attained to the fulness of its growth; "Until we all meet into the unity of faith, and of the knowledge of the Son of God, unto a perfect man, unto the age of the fulness of Christ" (Eph. iv. 13). Then there will be no need of any material edifice; for the living temple of God—of Christ, the Head, and all His members—will then have been everlastingly and perfectly established. "I saw," says St. John, "no temple therein. For the Lord Almighty is the temple thereof, and the Lamb" (Apoc. xxi. 22).

Baptism is the doorway into this living temple or society of the Church. Jesus said to Nicodemus: "Amen, amen I say to thee, unless a man be born again of water and the Holy Ghost, he cannot enter into the kingdom of God" (John iii. 5). Baptism constitutes the first union of Christ with the members of His Mystic Body. This sacrament assimilates the Christian to death of Christ on the Cross. "Know you not that all we, who are baptised in Christ Jesus, are baptised in his death" (Rom. vi. 3). Regenerating waters make us members of Christ's body. "In one spirit were we all baptised into one body" (1 Cor. xii. 13). Herein also is the source of our likeness and conformity to Christ, the Only Begotten of the Father. "As many of you as have been baptised in Christ, have put on Christ" (Gal. iii. 27). The Baptismal ceremonial preserves the symbolism of entrance into the Church, when, having placed the extremity of his stole on the child, the priest commands: "Enter into the temple of God, that thou mayest have part with Christ

in eternal life." The division of the Mass into that of
the Catechumens and the faithful is a relic of the early
observance of the Church, when those awaiting Baptism were not allowed into the church proper. They
were permitted to remain for the preparatory prayers
of the Mass, but only in the Narthex or porch, as a
sign that only by Baptism could they be linked with
the death of Christ on the Cross, renewed on the altar.
Only through union with the Head can the members
of the body benefit by the sacerdotal power which
resides in Christ in its fulness.

6

SHARING IN THE PRIESTHOOD OF CHRIST

Too little consideration is given by Christians to the
fact that, apart from the sanctifying grace, which
makes them members of Christ's Mystic Body, Baptism also impresses on their souls a spiritual mark,
which is called the sacramental character. Too frequently the doctrine of this additional effect of the
sacrament, even if learned in school, is quickly dismissed as having little or no practical bearing on
Christian life. This spiritual mark is in a special way
associated with what St. Paul calls "Baptism in
Christ's death". It associates the Christian with the
great sacrificial act of the High Priest on the Cross.
For it is through the sacramental character that the
Christian receives the right of entry not only into the
Church, but into its innermost sanctuary of the body
and blood of Christ Jesus in sacrifice upon the altar.
Baptism is not only the door into the Church, but the

I

door into the Mass. · "The sacramental character," declares St. Thomas Aquinas, " is especially the character of Christ, to whose character the faithful are likened by reason of the sacramental characters, which are nothing else than the participations of Christ's priesthood flowing from Christ Himself." This participation which is common to all Christians is called passive, as distinct from the active sharing of Orders, because it enables the laity to enter into the worship of the Father instituted by Christ. It permits them to be lifted up to God in the renewed offering of the body and blood of the Divine Saviour, and to share in the fruits of His immolation of Calvary.

The High-priesthood of Christ began at the moment of His conception. His life from the Crib to the Cross was a most holy offering of obedience to His Eternal Father. The character of Baptism associates the Christian with this priestly life and death of the Incarnate Word. The Christian life is thus endowed with what St. Thomas calls "the character of Christ". By reason of that association each member of the Mystic Body in sanctifying grace may say with St. Paul: "I live, now not I; but Christ liveth in me" (Gal. ii. 20). The sacramental character opens the soul to a direct participation in those acts of the Man-God which belong essentially to His Priesthood, especially in His most sublime act of self-immolation to His Eternal Father. The Priesthood of Christ is unceasing. "He is always living to make intercession for us" (Heb. vii. 26). The strength of intercession goes forth in a particular way from the altar of sacrifice which He instituted on earth. Through the character of Baptism every Christian is enabled to do with Christ, through His ordained minister, what Christ Himself does. By this sharing in the Priesthood of Christ, Christians enter the Holy of Holies, and are made "Heirs of the promise" (Heb. vi. 17), which God swore to Abraham: "That by two immutable things, in which it is impossible for God to lie, we may have the strongest comfort, who have fled for refuge to hold fast the hope set before us, which we have as an anchor of the soul, sure and firm, and which endureth even within the veil; where the forerunner Jesus is entered for us, made a high priest for ever according to the order of Melchisedech" (Heb. vi. 18-20).

St. Peter, who describes the faithful as "living stones" of our great "spiritual house" which is the Church of God, exhorts them also to appreciate their sharing in the priesthood of Christ. "Be you a holy priesthood, to offer up spiritual sacrifices, acceptable to God by Jesus Christ" (1 Pet. ii. 5). Again he declares: "You are a chosen generation, a kingly priesthood" (ibid. 9). The new priestliness of life bestowed by Jesus Christ is far more perfect than that which was lost by the first Adam. It reaches the summit of its perfection, when the faithful are gathered around the altar in the supreme "spiritual sacrifice" of the Mass. Seeing the nature of this sacrifice, and the declared desire of the Father, "Who seeketh such to adore him" (John iv. 23), it is necessary that some character should mark off those who belong to Christ, and have a vital part in the offering. "I know mine, and mine know me" (John x. 14). Without this sharing in the power of offering, the faithful at Mass would be but external witnesses of a religious ceremony, which would belong exclusively, as a sacrificial act, to a priestly caste. The Rite of the Holy Mass itself proclaims how false would be such an idea. The

doctrine of Christian unity in the living Christ revolts
against such a misunderstanding.

7

WITH JESUS ON THE ALTAR

In every Mass, Christ, as Head of the Church, is
always the principal minister and offerer, just as His
body is the centre of the Mystic Body, which is the
whole temple of God.   The ordained priest at the
altar is the juridically appointed and visible minister,
who takes the place of the invisible High Priest, Who
through the priestly active power of His minister becomes really present once again at the moment of Consecration.   By means of his priestly association, each
Christian, physically present and devoutly associating
himself with the Divine action of Christ and His priest
at the altar, is swept into the might and power of the
One Priest and the One Victim, Who, in offering Himself, offers also all men to the Father.   In the Mass,
Jesus, the Head, raises the entire Mystic Body as a
pleasing offering to the Divine majesty of God.   As a
great Captain, He leads His army of the faithful before the throne of God.

Every Christian is enabled by his personal co-operation to enter into this Divine action of the Saviour,
and, clothed in the merits of His Passion and death, to
participate in the sacrificial act, and to offer himself
together with the All-Holy Victim of God.   As a result
of this co-operative offering with Christ, the abyss between ourselves and God is bridged, and all the fruits
of His Passion and death are poured out upon us.

When we assist devoutly at Holy Mass, we ascend the heights of the mysteries of God, until we arrive at a point nearest to heaven itself.   Nothing on earth, though it be the work of God Himself, can be holier or more efficacious than this union with Christ in the renewal of His sacrifice.   It is the never-failing miracle of Divine omnipotence and love.   St. Augustine boldly declares: "All wise though He be, God knows nothing better; all powerful though He be, He can do nothing more excellent; infinitely rich though He be, He has nothing more precious to give, than the Most Holy Eucharist."

St. John in his Apocalypse was lifted up to heaven and beheld the Ancients before the throne of God.   In the midst of the Ancients, he saw the "Lamb standing as it were slain", and he heard sung a splendid new canticle: "Thou art worthy, O Lord, to take the book, and to open the seals thereof, because thou wast slain, and hast redeemed us to God in thy blood, out of every tribe, and tongue, and people, and nation, and hast made us to our God a kingdom and priests, and we shall reign upon the earth" (Apoc. v. 9, 10).   The beloved Disciple presents us with a picture of the glory of the Church, whether triumphant in heaven, or militant upon the earth.   The All-Holy Lamb of God is ever in the midst of this temple of God, ever presented, "as it were slain", and ever renewing the power and glory of His sacrifice upon the Cross. Gathered around Him is His kingdom of the "kingly priesthood"—the ordained ministers and the entire body of the faithful—all permeated with His priestliness, and sharing in His Glory of body and soul, whether in hope or actual possession.   "Our conversation is in heaven: from whence also we look for the

Saviour, our Lord Jesus Christ, Who will reform the body of our lowness, made like the body of his Glory, according to the operation whereby also he is able to subdue all things unto himself " (Phil. iii. 20, 21).

This splendour of association with the Lamb of God is not the privilege of just a chosen few, but is the inheritance of every Catholic. Once grasped, this ideal lifts the Christian way of life above the drabness and uncertainty of human things. It gives that " anchor of the soul " in the strength of its assurance of vital union with Christ, through the pivotal point of that association in the Mass. From this point of view, the ministerial priesthood is ordained to the priesthood of the laity, though it surpasses it in honour and dignity. The purpose of the ministry of the priests of the Church is to supply the laity with the immense treasure of good things, to which their passive priesthood gives them a right. Priestly Ordination is a social sacrament for the good of the Church. Its primary purpose is not the personal sanctification of the priest himself, though it presupposes it, but the building up of the Mystic Body of Christ, the feeding of the sheep, the saving and sanctification of souls, purchased in the blood of Christ. Priests and people form one body in Christ, one great organism, comprised, like the human body, of a variety of members with different functions, unto "the supplying of every want", and the good of the whole.

8

MY SACRIFICE AND YOURS

The reality of every Christian's participation in the Mass, as well as his right to appropriate to himself what is being accomplished on the altar, is stressed in the words of the celebrating priest, who seeks the prayerful co-operation of all the faithful. "Pray, brethren, that my sacrifice and yours be made acceptable to God, the Father Almighty." Of special significance in this respect is the drop of water which the celebrant mixes with the wine when preparing the chalice. Most probably this rubric goes back to the ceremony of the Last Supper, which was a pre-celebration of the sacrifice of Calvary, and bore resemblance to it in external signs. The commingling of water with the wine, which is to be changed in the blood of Christ, is commemorative of the water and blood which flowed from the open side of the Crucified, and which the holy Doctors say was a figure of the Church. In the Roman Rite a very beautiful prayer emphasizes the mysterious significance of this drop of water in relation to the entire sacrifice: "O God, Who, in creating human nature, didst wonderfully dignify it, and hast still more wonderfully renewed it; grant that, by the mystery of this water and wine, we may be partakers of His Divinity, Who vouchsafed to become partaker of our humanity, Jesus Christ, Thy Son, our Lord." The "mystery of the water and wine" is the gateway through Consecration into the mystery of the Incarnation. "God became man," declares St Augustine, "that man might become God." The Mass works out this mighty design of God in His Beloved Son. He assumed our human nature in the Incarnation, and we pray in the Mass that the symbolism of the mixing of water and wine may reach its fulfilment in the Holy Sacrifice, namely, that our poor human nature, which is signified by the water, may, by association with the Divinity, which is signified by the wine, be found worthy to partake of the grace of adoption through the mystic shedding of the blood on the altar of our sacrifice. St. Cyprian declares: "When the water is mingled with wine in the chalice, the people are united with Christ, and the multitude of the faithful are joined with Him in Whom they believe." In the Mass the misery and nothingness of each one of us is borne away into the Bosom of the Trinity, and the fruits of Redemption are again made actual in us through the Eucharistic renewal of His sacrifice; "For by one oblation he hath perfected for ever them that are sanctified" (Heb. x. 14).

Through consideration of realities such as these we must judge individually of our startling privilege of intimate association through the Mass with the "High Priest of the good things to come". The Church has commanded us to assist at the Holy Sacrifice at least once a week in order that we may observe the Lord's Day, which has taken the place of the ancient Sabbath, and sanctify ourselves in the sight of God. So essential is the act of sacrifice to the Christian Religion that this Sunday Mass is the minimum required of all who would live in the friendship of Jesus Christ. So grave an obligation cannot be neglected with impunity. God is dishonoured by its neglect in the measure in which He is honoured by its fulfilment. It is not sufficient merely to attend, as some do who are merely listless and

thoughtless onlookers at a ceremony, which they wish
only to have finished as speedily as possible.   Such a
lack of fitting disposition is a sign of exceedingly
shallow faith.

The Mass is the great Christian act of public worship.   As we form members of the one body, which is
the Church, so we should enter into the sanctuary of
our common worship as a united body in the one
Head.   The strength of this united entry must depend
on the personal union, through intelligent appreciation of the mystery of the altar, of each one with the
Victim of sacrifice.   The closer our sentiments of heart
and mind approach those of Jesus Christ, the more
fully will the fruits of His Passion and death descend
into our souls.   "Let this mind be in you, which was
also in Christ Jesus" (Phil. ii. 6).   St. Albert the
Great declares that the faithful do by desire what the
priest does by Consecration.   We desire Him to come
on the altar that He may continue the work of His
Redemption; "For the perfecting of the saints, for the
work of the ministry, for the edifying of the body of
Christ" (Eph. iv. 12).   There can be no better way
of accomplishing this desired end than by following
the prayers of the Missal.   There is nothing wanting
to the perfection of the Priest and Victim.   There is
nothing wanting to His own desire of union with the
members of His Mystic Body.   Failure to reap the
fruits of the Mass comes from ourselves alone.   God
does not force Himself upon us without desire on our
part.   In no ceremony or ritual of the Church, and
certainly not in the Mass, can we behave as mere auto-
matons.   Jesus Christ on the Cross not only presented
to His Eternal Father the visible offering of His body,
but with it lifted His soul in prayer.   We must like-

wise remember that our religion, our sacrifice, our priestliness, our prayerfulness do not consist merely in externals, but demand that inner raising of the heart and mind in a sincere conversion unto God. " But if the oblation whereby the faithful in this sacrifice offer the Divine Victim to the Heavenly Father is to produce its full effect they must do something further; they must also offer themselves as victims " (P. Pius XII; *Mediator Dei*).

The Sacred Heart beats with the same intensity of love on the altar, as on the Cross. " Greater love than this no man hath, that a man lay down his life for his friend " (John xv. 13). He continues the sublime principle of His friendship in the Mass as on Calvary. Friendship, however, cannot be merely one-sided. His love must find a corresponding activity in our own hearts in mutual surrender of ourselves, not merely during the short time of our assistance at Holy Mass, but, through the strength given to us in His sacrifice, in frequently renewed acts during the day. Returning from the sanctuary of our Church, we will go back to our daily work, to our trials, to the sadness, as well as to the joys of life. These things will still be the same, but, washed in His precious blood, we will in God's abundant grace be different. The ordinary things of life will take on a new meaning. The various happenings of life will no longer be mere human adventures: they will become charged with the fulness of grace in Christ and lead us to God.

The idea of sacrifice can never be disassociated from the idea of the priesthood. The Mass provides for both priest and people the highest form of priestly association with the great High Priest in His supreme sacrificial act. Our likeness to the character of Christ through Baptism must permeate the whole of life. The life of Christ was one great act of sacrifice, which ended only on the Cross. In the Mass we are made one with His spirit of sacrifice. There we learn the law of Christian living. "He said to all: If any man will come after me, let him deny himself and take up his cross daily, and follow me" (Luke ix. 23). "Always bearing about in our body the mortification of Jesus, that the life also of Jesus may be made manifest in our bodies" (2 Cor. iv. 10). There should be no contradiction between the Christian's manner of worship and his way of living. Religion and sanctity are the same thing. In the Cross and in the Mass there is complete opposition to the world. Through that source of all holiness we can overcome the world. "Have confidence, I have overcome the world" (John xvi. 33). Through the Mass, life becomes united to Christ suffering; death becomes the final and joyous entering into the sanctuary of His sacrifice, Who tasted death for all (Heb. ii. 9): In both life and death there is a new, living, and priestly way of passing from the earthly to the eternal Sanctus which is yet to come.

Fifth Chapter

THE LORD'S SUPPER

(1 Cor. xi. 20)

1

MY GUEST CHAMBER

THE prophetic rays, which shine out from the Old Testament as from stars at divers distances, seem to converge with special brilliance on the Upper Room, whither on the last night of His visible presence on earth Jesus led His Apostles. That is not surprising, seeing that the importance of that night can never be fully appreciated. On that night in the Upper Room He established what was the culmination of thousands of years of expectation. On that night He fashioned the new Christian religion until the end of time. On that night in His last will He left to the sons of men the new and everlasting testament in His blood. That night was the appointed night of His leave-taking—"The same night on which He was betrayed" (1 Cor. xi. 23). He had already assured His Apostles that He would not leave them orphans. His last testament was intended to secure them against the spiritual destitution which would otherwise have been their lot after His departure. The sheep were not to be deprived of their shepherd. He made them heirs on that night to Himself. His last Testament was by

way of gift to them under the appearance of bread and
wine of His sacrificial flesh and blood, hypostatically
and inseparably united to His Divinity. Of that night
we may cry out with St. Paul: "O the depth of the
riches of the wisdom and of the knowledge of God!
How incomprehensible are his judgments, and how
unsearchable His ways" (Rom. xi. 33).

A few simple words spoken in the omnipotent power
of the Incarnate Word at once wrought the mystery of
that night and transferred the power of its making for
all time to the Church. So tremendous are these words
of the Institution of the Most Holy Eucharist that it
is impossible for anyone to grasp their full import
without allegiance to Christian truth. There must be
a foreknowledge and acceptance of Jesus the Saviour
of men. He must be acknowledged as the Divine
Second Person of the Most Holy Trinity. The purpose
of His coming must be recognized, in that He came to
translate into terms of flesh and blood the splendour
of Divine diffusion of good by God, Who is love. The
Beloved Disciple epitomized both the cause and the
immensity of the gift: "Jesus, knowing that his hour
was come, that he should pass out of this world to the
Father; having loved his own who were in the world,
he loved them unto the end" (John xiii. 1).

To understand the mystery of the Eucharist we must
accept the mysterious attachment of God to His
creature through Christ, "Whose delights are to be
with the children of men" (Prov. viii. 31). We must
view what was accomplished on that night against the
background of God's marvellous design, foreshadowed
in ritual and foretold in prophecy down the ages which
prepared for it. The Apostles did not enter the new
Holy of Holies of the Upper Room without such pre-

paration. Their knowledge of the Old Testament had been added to during the three years of their apostolic preparation by Christ. Their intimacy with their Divine Master had acquainted them with His generosity. They had already heard and accepted the promise of a new and miraculous food. "Labour not for the meat which perisheth, but for that which endureth unto life everlasting, which the Son of man will give you" (John vi. 27).

The scene of Holy Thursday's dramatic events opened with the selection of the place of their celebration. There was something mysterious in the choice of the cenacle, or "furnished guest room". Jesus referred to it as "my guest chamber". It would seem to have been the gift to Him of the man to whom He directed His Apostles. He, Who declared before that the Son of man had not whereon to lay His head, then appropriated this large furnished dining-room. He, Whose kingdom was not of this world, claimed ownership of the Upper Room, because it was to be the Temple of the new sacrificial worship of God—the first of countless Christian churches to be raised the world over, so that, once established by Him, that same worship might be continued for ever.

To-day venerable and ancient traditions surround this primitive sanctuary. The house and room of the Last Supper became one of the most hallowed places in Christian memory. It was there that Our Lord appeared to His Apostles after the Resurrection. There the first Christians assembled with the Apostles and persevered in prayer with Mary the Mother of Jesus, awaiting the birth of the Mystic Body of Christ in the glorious manifestation of the promised Paraclete. Tradition also asserts that the "Dormition" or

death of the Mother of God occurred in the same place.
St. Epiphanius, writing at the close of the fourth century, mentions that the Emperor Hadrian in A.D. 117
found the City of Jerusalem as it had been devastated
by Titus—"With not a stone left upon a stone". All
he found intact were only a few houses, together with
a "small church of God, which had been erected on the
spot where after the Ascension the Disciples went up
into an upper room". St. Cyril of Jerusalem also
refers to the miraculous preservation of this hallowed
place amidst the surrounding ruins. "To-day the
traveller coming toward Jerusalem from the south des-
cries a minaret which still marks the location of that
Guest Chamber. It towers over a vast hall, which, al-
though much altered during the Middle Ages, is still
the same which St. Cyril venerated in the fourth Century" (Fouard).

2

MOUNT SION

"Jesus suffered without the gate" (Heb. xiii. 12).
The actual sacrifice of Calvary took place outside the
walls of the Holy City. In contrast, its pre-celebration
as a new sacrificial rite at the Last Supper took place in
Jerusalem itself. The site of the Upper Room formed
part of the renowned Mount Sion, which King David,
who was a figure of Christ, captured and made his own
city. For this reason it was called by the early
Christians: "Holy Sion." It was fitting that the everlasting testament in the sacrifice of the body and blood
of Christ should be proclaimed from the Holy Mount,

which occupied so prominent a place in the prophecies of the Messiah. In the Psalm of Christ's eternal priesthood Sion is mentioned as the source of the new priestly power. "The Lord will send forth the sceptre of thy power out of Sion" (Psalm cix. 2). The Upper Room was destined to become the mother of all Christian churches throughout the world. There the sacrifice of the Mass was first celebrated, which was to become by Divine command the unique sacrifice of all peoples. The Prophet foresaw this honour for the City of David. "In the last days the mountain of the house of the Lord shall be prepared on the top of the mountain, and it shall be exalted above the hills, and all the nations shall flow into it . . . for the law shall come forth from Sion, and the word of the Lord from Jerusalem" (Isa. ii. 2, 3).

Through the institution of the Blessed Eucharist, which established His real and permanent presence in the midst of men, Christ became in a very real way the corner-stone of His Church. St. Peter, the first Pope, had no hesitation in applying to Christ the words of Isaias: "Behold I lay in Sion a chief corner-stone, elect precious, and he that shall believe in him, shall not be confounded" (1 Pet. ii. 5). The important rôle to be played by King David's city was also acknowledged by St. Paul. He contrasts Christ's loving invitation to all men from Mount Sion to the sacrifice and banquet of His love with the dread which the forbidding thunders and lightnings of Mount Sinai engendered in those of a stiff-necked race, who were warned not to approach the barriers under the pain of death. "But you are come to Mount Sion, and to the city of the living God, the heavenly Jerusalem . . . and to the Church of the first-born . . . and to Jesus the mediator of the new testament, and to the sprinkling of blood which speaketh better than that of Abel" (Heb. xii. 22-4). St. John, the Beloved Disciple, who was privileged to recline on the breast of the Saviour at the Last Supper, beheld in vision "The Lamb standing as if it were slain", which was significant of Christ's mystic death in the Holy Sacrifice of the Mass. Later, he saw the Lamb return in triumph to that same Holy Mount where He had instituted His ritual sacrifice. "And I beheld: and lo a lamb stood upon Mount Sion, and with him a hundred and forty four thousand having his name, and the name of His Father written upon their foreheads" (Apoc. xiv. 1).

3

IMMEDIATE PREPARATIONS

The Gospel texts reveal the exactness of design followed by the Divine Saviour in every detail preceding the celebration of the Last Supper within the hallowed walls of the new house of God. Events moved swiftly from Palm Sunday to the Friday of His death. On that Sunday He claimed possession of the Holy City of David, from whom He had descended according to the flesh. The City was His by right of inheritance. The great crowd acknowledged His claim by their hosannas of welcome to the Son of David. "Blessed is he that cometh in the name of the Lord, the King of Israel" (John xii. 13). The Prophet Zachary, we are reminded by the Evangelist, had long before foretold the return of this new King, who would rule over Sion in place of David, and from Sion extend His

K

kingdom over the whole earth. "Fear not, daughter of Sion, behold thy king cometh sitting on an ass's colt"—"His power shall be from sea to sea, and from the rivers even to the end of the earth" (John xii. 15; Zach. ix. 9). Jesus entered the City of Jerusalem that from there He might proclaim the new religion of mankind—the worship of the Father in spirit and in truth. The honouring of the Son was the honouring of the Father Who had sent Him. In His triumph He emphasized the tremendous necessity that lies on all men, and on the whole of creation, of giving this glory to God. When the Pharisees, confounded by His triumph, asked that He should rebuke the disciples who chanted the praise of the Messiah, He declared: "I say to you if these hold their peace the stones will cry out" (Luke xix. 40).

On that Sunday, following His entry into the city of Sion, the Eternal Father gave outward testimony to the great achievement of His Beloved Son, as He had already done at His Baptism and on Mount Thabor. But this time it was with reference to the glory which would shortly ascend to God from the immolation of Himself. Jesus again proclaimed His obedience to the will of His Father and in that obedience the establishing of God's glory. "For this cause I came unto this hour. Father, glorify thy name. A voice therefore came from heaven: I have glorified it, and will glorify it again" (John xii. 28). It was of this same hour that He spoke three years before to the woman of Samaria at Jacob's well. "The hour cometh, and now is, when true adorers shall adore the Father in spirit and in truth. For the Father seeketh such to adore Him" (John iv. 23).

Later in that Passion Week Jesus significantly re-

minded His Apostles of the approaching festivity of
the Passover, and plainly associated His death on the
Cross with the observance of that ancient ritual. "You
know that after two days shall be the pasch, and the
Son of man shall be delivered up to be crucified"
(Matt. xxvi. 2). He Who was the supreme master of
His own life willed that His death on the Cross should
coincide, not only in the spirit and the power of His
offering, but even according to time with the ancient
ritual. On the Friday of that final paschal festivity
the "Lamb that was slain" fulfilled in actual death
the most essential demand of the paschal prophecy.
His institution of the Eucharist by way of ritual sacrifice, on the night before He suffered, was not less intimately linked with that fulfilment. Though its sacrificial character depended totally on the actual shedding
of His precious blood in the bitter Passion of Good
Friday, the Last Supper had a likeness proper to itself
to the paschal lamb whose flesh was eaten by the
children of Israel before setting out for the Promised
Land. By providing under the forms of bread and
wine for a consuming of the Victim of sacrifice, the
Eucharist still further exhausted the mysterious possi-
bilities which the ancient Jewish ritual had foreshadowed. "It was necessary," declares St. Thomas,
"that there should be at all times among men something to show forth the Passion, the chief sacrament of
which in the Old Law was the Paschal Lamb."

"The day of the unleavened bread came, on which
it was necessary that the pasch should be killed, and he
sent Peter and John, saying: go and prepare for us the
pasch, that we may eat" (Luke xxii. 7, 8). The command and detailed directions of Jesus in regard to
the finding of the guest chamber emphasize again that

it was precisely the pasch according to Jewish ritual which they intended to celebrate. For this the two Apostles whom He had commissioned made all the usual preparations. Jesus observed the prescriptions of the ancient ceremonial. He came not to destroy, but to fulfil. Knowledge of the ancient Jewish ritual helps to understand the procedure described by the Evangelists. There were four distinct courses, as we might term them to-day. At each course wine was passed around either in one cup or in separate cups for each. With the first wine herbs dipped in a special sauce were served. With the second wine the paschal lamb was served, and an address was given by the head of the family on the mercies of God. The third wine cup was passed around in token of thanksgiving to God for the deliverance of His people. The fourth and last cup coincided with the singing of the Hallel or psalms which, though directly concerned with God's merciful dealings with His Chosen People, were Messianic in character, and particularly suited to the greater Pasch which Jesus instituted on that night. The first psalm refers to the power of sacrifice in obtaining the mercy of God. Its verses are familiar to-day in the celebration of Holy Mass. "What shall I render to the Lord for all the things that he hath rendered to me? I will take the chalice of salvation; and I will call upon the name of the Lord" (Psalm cxv. 12, 13). The next psalm is an invitation to all to join in the worship of God, which finds its wonderful fulfilment in the Most Holy Eucharist. The third psalm (117) foretells the coming of the Messiah in words which were used by Christ and the Apostles. "The stone which the builders rejected: the same is become the head of the corner. This is the Lord's doing: and is won-

derful in our eyes." Holy Thursday most assuredly
witnessed the coming of the joyous day foretold by
the Psalmist: "This is the day which the Lord hath
made: let us be glad and rejoice therein" (ibid.).
Christ's dramatic words of sad farewell to His native
City were also taken from that third psalm, and found
their fulfilment on Palm Sunday, when He returned
to take triumphant possession: "For I say to you, you
shall not see me henceforth till you say: Blessed is he
that cometh in the name of the Lord" (Matt. xxiii. 39).
The final psalm of the Hallel (118) was in praise of the
observance of God's law, which was so perfectly fulfilled by Him Who became obedient unto death. This
psalm emphasizes in particular the persecution of the
Just One because of His keeping of the law of God:
"The wicked have waited for me to destroy me; but
I have understood thy testimonies."

Whilst it is quite evident that the Evangelists in
their account of the Last Supper are describing the
ordinary Jewish ritual, the memory of the less important parts of that paschal feast faded in the light of the
tremendous fulfilment which the ritual received towards its close. What most concerned them and the
early Christians, for whom they wrote, was the institution of the Lord's Supper which had taken the place of
the old. They emphasized the new rather than the
old.

> In hac mensa novi regis,
> Novum Pacha novae legis
> Phase vetus terminat:
> Vetustatem novitas,
> Umbram fugat veritas,
> Noctem lux eliminat.

(Within our new king's banquet-hall
They meet to keep the festival
That closed the ancient paschal rite:
The old by the new replaced,
The substance hath the shadow chased,
And rising day dispel the night.)

4

BEGINNINGS OF THE NEW PASCH

"When the hour was come, he sat down and the twelve apostles with him.   And he said to them: with desire have I desired to eat this pasch with you before I suffer.   For I say to you, that from this time I will not eat it, till it be fulfilled in the Kingdom of God" (Luke xxii. 14-16).   In these solemn words He declared the particular paschal celebration, in which they were engaged, to be associated with His sufferings and death, and to be His final token to them of His love.   He promised at the same time a still more triumphant fulfilment of the new redeeming Pasch, which would take place in His second coming.   When its daily renewal on Christian altars had accomplished its purpose of salvation of all His followers in the promised land of His Father's kingdom, the great final Passover would take place in the glorification of the Lamb and of all who received life from His death.   "The Lamb that was slain is worthy to receive power, and divinity, and wisdom, and strength, and honour, and glory, and benediction" (Apoc. v. 12).   He used similar words at the first serving of wine with the same significance. "Take it and divide it among you.   For I say to you that I shall not drink of the fruit of the vine, till the kingdom of God come" (Luke xxii. 17, 18).

We are indebted to St. John for a more minute description of what took place in the Upper Room immediately preceding the Institution. He not only speaks of the external events, but seems to enter into the mind of the Saviour and tell more intimately the secrets of His Heart, on which he was privileged to lean his head at the Last Supper. "When the supper was done;"—thus St. John opens an entirely new development in the usual proceedings of the Pasch. This was probably immediately after the eating of the paschal lamb, and before partaking of the third serving of wine which was in thanksgiving for the goodness of God to His people. When the solemn moment arrived Jesus arose from the supper. St. John adds to the solemnity by giving us a glimpse of the soul of Christ at this moment of His rising from the table. "Knowing that the Father had given him all things into his hands, and that he came from God, and goeth to God, He riseth from the supper" (John xiii. 3). These sentiments of His relation with the Father may have been uttered in prayer, and even perhaps heard by the Beloved Disciple leaning on His bosom. We do know that He was accustomed to pray aloud at the most critical moments in His life, as when He raised Lazarus to life. The words used by the Evangelist bring to mind the prophetic prayer of the psalm: "Thou hast set him over the works of thy hands, thou hast subjected all things under his feet." It was in the full consciousness of His omnipotent power as the Son of God that He set Himself to perform the greatest miracle of His love. What He was about to do in instituting the new Pasch was the Father's will as it was also His own. " My Father giveth you the true bread from heaven " (John vi. 32).

"He riseth from supper, and layeth aside his garments, and having taken a towel girded himself. And after that, he putteth water into a basin, and began to wash the feet of the disciples, and to wipe them with the towel, wherewith he was girded " (John xiii. 4, 5). The Apostles were amazed at this new development. Their eyes followed his movements as He prepared all that was necessary for the washing of their feet. He approached Peter first as the head of the Church. Only then did they realize what He intended to do. Peter's question shows how great was the surprise of them all. "Lord, dost thou wash my feet? " Christ's reply reveals how deep was the mystery into which they were entering. "What I do, thou knowest not now, but thou shalt know hereafter." The mystery is part of the Institution. When Peter continued to resist, Our Lord clearly indicated how necessary it was to be washed to enter into the Holy of Holies He was about to establish: "If I wash thee not, thou shalt have no part with me." With so grave an issue involved Peter sought a still greater cleansing: "Lord, not only my feet, but also my hands and my head."

By this menial service rendered to His Apostles Jesus sought to teach them and us how great should be the cleanliness of body and soul to approach the Holy Banquet of His love. In the washing of the body, He would teach them the importance of sinlessness of the soul. He knew the soul of Judas, blackened with his treachery—"Therefore He said: you are not all clean." Having reseated Himself He drove home the lesson which He wished to teach His Apostles. Hitherto they had been too preoccupied with their own selfish ambitions. Even in the Upper Room they carried on the old tiresome debate regarding their positions in the Kingdom to be established by Christ. Jesus drew their attention to the tremendous contrast beween what He was as God, and what He had done for them. His insistence on that contrast shows how important the lesson is for proper appreciation of the Blessed Eucharist and Holy Communion. The humility of Christ in washing their feet was little in comparison with His humility in taking the form of bread for our sakes. "Know you what I have done to You? You call me Lord and Master: and you say well for so I am. If then I, being your Lord and Master, have washed your feet; you also ought to wash one another's feet." The Eucharist is the sacrament of peace, and in peace of humility, without which there can be no true fraternal charity. Like the Disciples at Emmaus, we know Christ best in the Breaking of Bread. In the Blessed Sacrament He appears to the eyes of our faith as One meek and humble of heart.

During these immediate preparations for the Institution of the Blessed Eucharist a great sorrow was in the heart of the Saviour. There was a traitor in their midst. When He sat down after the washing of their feet there was evidence of that sorrow in His countenance. "He was troubled in spirit: and he testified, and said: Amen, amen, I say to you, one of you shall betray me." He had already told them, and Judas in particular, that they were not all clean. By His humble service He would have drawn the traitor to repentance. He quoted the prophecy and solemnly declared His Divine foreknowledge of the treachery already committed for thirty pieces of silver. "At present I tell you, before it come to pass: that when it shall come to pass, you may believe that I am he." He said these things that He might continue to warn Judas to the end, and that He might protect the faith of the Apostles from the dreadful scandal of a betrayer amongst the chosen Twelve. To John alone did He reveal the actual identity. To the former's whispered question Jesus replied: " He it is to whom I shall reach bread dipped." It was customary amongst the Jews at such banquets for the head of the family to pass some choice piece of food to his honoured guest as a special mark of friendship. This was Christ's final appeal to the hardened heart of Judas. The sign of friendship was scorned. That final refusal of grace marked the traitor's complete surrender to the powers of darkness whose hour was fast approaching. "After the morsel, Satan entered him." Jesus dismissed him with a final word, the full and horrible significance of which was known to Judas only. "That which thou dost, do quickly." The Evangelist describes in one graphic sentence the ending of this scene in the great drama of the Passion: " He therefore having received the morsel, went out immediately, and it was night."

Though it is commonly accepted that the morsel given to Judas was the consecrated Bread of the Holy Communion, it is quite possible, not to say probable, that he was dismissed before the actual Institution. The dismissal of Judas seems to follow immediately the washing of the feet without any break of sequence. Our Lord's emphasis on the need of being clean to have a part with Him may be taken as a reason of his being dismissed before the Consecration. The handing of a morsel dipped had its own special significance and is not necessarily connected with the Eucharistic species. It should also be borne in mind that the Last Supper included the entire ritual of the ancient Pasch, which had not yet been fully completed at the washing of the feet. The crime of Judas was so heinous in itself that it would seem fitter that he should be excluded from the august ceremony which followed. But whether or not he received Holy Communion, the entire incident fills one with dread of approaching unworthily this holy table of Jesus Christ, lest, like Judas, who betrayed Him to his enemies, one be "guilty of the body and blood of Jesus Christ".

5

THE INSTITUTION

"And taking the bread, he gave thanks, and brake: and gave to them, saying: This is my body which is given for you. Do this for a commemoration of me. In like manner the chalice also, after he had supped, saying: This is the chalice, the new testament in my blood, which shall be shed for you."

(Luke xxii. 19, 20).

The words of the Institution are amongst the most sacred in Holy Scripture. Pronounced by the God-Man, and presenting in sacrificial form the living memory in body and blood of His Passion and death, they mark the term of God's love, the final phase of Christ's redeeming achievement. It was final because love could do no more. St. Augustine declares: "In order to commend more earnestly the depth of this mystery, Our Saviour willed this last act to be fixed in the hearts and memories of His disciples whom He was about to quit for the Passion." The Word Who came forth from the Father and became man that He might be the servant of men, on this His last night on earth, changed bread into His body and wine into His blood, that He might become their very food. He fulfilled His promise of some twelve months before: "The bread that I will give, is my flesh for the life of the world" (John vi. 52).

On that night there was no doubt or discussion, as there had been previously by the Lake of Galilee: "How can this man give us his flesh to eat?" (ibid. 53). The mystery which was there announced received its solution on that night. Since the first announcement of the Divine Master's intention, the Apostles, who, with Peter at their head, had proclaimed their faith in His omnipotent power, must have wondered and discussed amongst themselves how and when He would honour His promise. The simple words of the first Consecration of bread and wine in His own Divine hands on that night of the Pasch revealed the secret to them. In them Peter saw verified to the full his own splendid declaration of faith when all had abandoned the Saviour, because His was to many "a hard word, and who could believe it". "Lord," Peter cried out on that occasion ," to whom shall we go? Thou hast the words of eternal life" (John ibid. 69). Jesus had already described His promise of giving them His flesh to eat and His blood to drink as words which were "spirit and life". In the Last Supper the great secret of Divine love was told in words which gave the source of life itself to men as their spiritual food.

The Apostles received the new revelation of His love with joyous and grateful hearts. The motive of credibility was the same as when they consented to His promise, namely faith in His Divinity. Peter had then cried out on behalf of them all: "We have believed and have known that thou art the Christ the Son of God" (ibid. 70). With all reverence they accepted the gift from His sacred hands, and divided it among themselves, as they were later to divide it among the faithful, and in dividing multiply the sacramental presence throughout the Church of God. That first Holy Communion rendered their Divine friend more intimate to each one in sacramental union than He had ever been or could ever have been during the years of His association with them. With the gift Jesus gave also a special grace to appreciate the mystery. From within them He worked out the effects of His own sacrament.

From the moment of that first Consecration of bread and wine the ancient Paschal sacrifice passed into the chalice of the New Testament in His blood. Jesus gave sacrificial virtue to His body, present sacramentally in His Divine hands, by speaking of it as given, and to His blood in the chalice by joining it to the shedding of the Passion. By thus directing the purpose of His new sacrificial rite, Jesus in the Mass became "the Lamb of God, Who taketh away the sins of the world". Thus the ancient Pasch was absorbed into the new. All the ceremonial, all the sacrificial ritual which had preceded, thereby became completely abrogated in favour of the Christian sacrifice. In the hidden splendour of His real presence, and in the utter simplicity of this new rite, Christ willed to provide a means, whereby, for all time, all men might be incorporated into the Victim Who had satisfied the justice of God on their behalf. Mere spiritual union with His Passion and death could not satisfy the generosity of the Incarnate Word. He desired an indwelling in the souls of men through the real presence of His body and blood, His human soul, and His infinite Divinity.

6

THE EUCHARIST AND CALVARY

Without minimizing the faith of the Apostles in accepting the truth of the Most Holy Eucharist, one may legitimately wonder to what extent the full significance of what was done on that night was then perceived by them. The Last Supper spoke to them of death, of separation of body from blood by shedding— but all that was still in the future. In spite of what Jesus had foretold them, that future was as yet only vaguely known, and with difficulty accepted. Their flight after His arrest showed how little they were attuned to the mind of the Divine Master, or grasped the full meaning of His words: " The Son of man must be crucified." They could not realize until after the Passion how terrible was the tragedy which the words of the Institution entailed. In the Upper Room they were still comforted by the accustomed presence of their loving friend. St. John speaks of certain events which the "disciples did not know at first", but which they remembered after Jesus was glorified. Our Lord promised that the Holy Ghost would bring all things to their mind whatsoever He had taught them. Our Lord Himself certainly enlightened them in the understanding of the mystery which He shared with them, but the full understanding of it had to await the completion of the Passion and Resurrection, and His manifest triumph over death.

Though having to await for the full appreciation of the mystery of the Eucharist, the Apostles were not without some understanding of the sacrificial character of the new rite. They had met to offer sacrifice—to perform an act of religion according to an ancient ritual. They knew from their early association with the Precursor that Jesus was called by St. John the Lamb of God. The prophetic portent of the paschal lamb was not lost on them. The old feast had a sacrificial character. The new one which He commanded them to substitute spoke of a more perfect testament in His own blood. It spoke of eating and drinking of flesh and blood under the unchanged appearances of the original bread and wine. The two separate formulae of consecration, in so far as words went, spoke of separation. They knew by reason of His visible presence amongst them that no real separation had as yet taken place. But the significance of His words and actions was perceived by them. He assured them at the same time that what was here so realistically represented would in its due time receive the required fulfilment. They were overwhelmed with the generosity of their loving Lord. It was as if He said to them: "Here is my gift to you of my body and blood. Take ye and eat, that you may receive within yourselves the undying testimony of my love, which sends me forth to die for you. What I now give you will be an everlasting and powerful memory of all I have done for men. It contains the fulness of my love and obedience to my Father even unto the death of the Cross. Here is miraculously represented what will take place to-morrow in my actual death on the Cross. Before this

comes to pass, whilst I am still with you, I give myself
to you in a new and most wonderful way. Yours is the
gift. It will be for me to pay the price of it. To-
morrow it will be paid. I will tread the wine-press of
my sorrow alone."

As we lovingly think of and mentally reconstruct
the scene in the Upper Room, we are in the privileged
position in which the Apostles only later found themselves. We can view it now in the full light of complete accomplishment. We have moreover the advantage of the guiding hand of the unerring Church, which
has declared in its teaching the glories of the Mass.
The Church has surrounded her inherited sacrificial
act with the splendour of its ceremonial, which has
for its purpose to emphasize the innermost beauty of
the act itself, all of which comes directly from Christ.
He offered the first Mass, and in that offering willed
the offering of countless Masses until the end of time.
That is the reason why it is so necessary to recur to the
source, and by meditating on the Saviour in the Last
Supper, on His declared intentions, on His words, His
actions, realize more and more what He continues to
do through the agency of His ordained minister. In
the Last Supper He was visibly present before the
Apostles; they beheld His outward actions, and knew
something of His intention and dispositions in His
prayer of thanks. Though invisible, He is not less
really present to-day in each Mass, as He continues the
offering which He once made of Himself. He conse-
crates the bread and wine, and in so consecrating continues the religious worship which He established on
the first Holy Thursday night. That is the marvel of
the Mass.

7

SACRIFICIAL WORSHIP

There are two essential truths concerning the Mass
which every Catholic must believe. The Mass is a
sacrifice. It is the same sacrifice as that of the Cross.
A sacrifice entails some external act of religion. The
word sacrifice, as St. Thomas reminds us, means to
perform something sacred. "Properly speaking, it
requires that something be done to the thing which is
offered to God; for instance, animals were slain, the
bread was broken, eaten, blessed." The Angelic
Doctor gives three essential elements of this act of worship. It must be offered by a priest, that is by one
appointed by God, and representative of the people.
It must be offered to God, since it is an act of adoration.
"God alone is the Creator, and in Him alone the
beatitude of the soul consists." What is offered to God
must be representative of the interior disposition of
the soul. This is the most essential element in an act
of sacrifice. "The sacrifice that is offered outwardly
represents the inward spiritual sacrifice whereby the
soul offers itself to God" (II-II. 85, 2). "External
things are offered to God, not as though He had need
of them, according to Psalm 49. 13, 'Shall I eat the
flesh of bullocks? or shall I drink the blood of goats?'
but as signs of the internal and spiritual works, which
are themselves acceptable to God. Hence Augustine
says: The visible sacrifice is the sacrament or sacred
sign of the invisible sacrifice" (ibid. 81, 7, ad 2).

The most essential parts of sacrifice are the oblation,
or the interior offering of priest for and on behalf of

L

the people, in which the people voluntarily join, and the immolation, which is the external act whereby the victim is slain. The slaying of the victim had for its primary purpose the acknowledging of God's supreme dominion by the complete surrender of what God gave for man's use and benefit. It was at the same time an acknowledgment by man of his own nothingness, in so far as the holocaust reduced the thing offered to nothingness, at least in so far as man was capable of so doing. Prayer was the natural accompaniment of sacrifice, since it was necessary that man expressed in the act of immolating the victim what he intended in regard to the worship of God. The oblation was a raising of the mind to God in worship, thanksgiving, petition, and in repentance. In other words, it directed the external rite into the intended channels or purposes of each particular sacrifice.

It is clear that the victim offered had value only in proportion to its being representative of the mind of priest and people towards God. Only in that way could the victim become one with the priest, and those for whom he offered it. In the sacrifices of the old law oblation and immolation were always distinct, since the priest was not himself the victim. The victim, however, was something which belonged to man, and therefore through sacrifice marked man's surrender of his dominion to the supreme dominion of God. By earnest prayer he placed in it something of himself, and it became representative. The victim was always by way of substitution. Man considered his own nothingness, and God's infinite Being, and endeavoured to express what he knew to be inexpressible, by the surrender of life to God in another creature which he substituted for himself.

From this doctrine on the nature of sacrifice we may judge how excellent was the sacrifice of Christ in the sight of His Father. The Passion and death of Christ is the one supreme act of sacrifice. There is no need of any other, since it is infinitely satisfying of its very nature. It possesses the highest possible perfection of oblation, since the offering is the prayerful act of the Son of God made man. It possesses a completeness of immolation in a fulness of sorrow and of suffering to the shedding of the last drop of the precious redeeming blood (cf. Third Discourse). But in the sacrifice of Christ there is no substitution. The two essential parts of the religious act are joined together. "He was offered because it was His own will." The one Person is both priest and victim.

Good Friday was filled with every conceivable horror, betrayal, perfidy, cruelty, hatred, blasphemy, deicide. All these abominations were necessary that His immolation might be complete. The awfulness of Hell was let loose against Him, bcause He was the appointed victim of sin. His enemies who heaped opprobrium on Him were blind, hate-driven instruments of evil, who unwittingly became agents of the Divine Justice. But the essential element in the sacrifice of Christ was found in His own will, wherewith He submitted Himself to the powers of evil. He most willingly surrendered Himself to the external cruelties of His bitter Passion and death, that He might show forth to His Father the perfection of His obedience. He most willingly laid Himself on the hard wood of the Cross. Most willingly was He lifted up on high. Most willingly did He pour out His blood for man's redemption. In every phase of His immense sorrow and suffering His conduct bore witness to His interior sacrificial disposition. . His sacrifice consisted essentially in the perfect freedom of His will, wherewith He offered up His life, and endured the shame of the Cross on our behalf.

In Christ there were not many separate acts of sacrifice, with a certain cumulative effect. " By one sacrifice he hath perfected for ever them that are sanctified " (Heb. x. 14). The essential sanctifying efficacy of that one sacrifice lay in His will to suffer. "In the which will, we are sanctified by the oblation of the body of Jesus Christ once " (ibid. 10). Christ's one offering of Himself is infinitely good and meritorious, because it is the act of the Divine Person of the Son of God through the conjoined instrument of His Sacred Humanity. That same offering can be ceaselessly renewed in God's sight for man's benefit, because it is ever present to the human mind of the Saviour, together with all those for whom it was offered, by reason of the beatific vision. This is what He intended on the night before He suffered, when at the Last Supper He willed that particular consecration and all the consecrations which He ordained to follow, and in so willing presented Himself before His Eternal Father in the guise of His Passion and death, and showed forth His unceasing redemptive desire on our behalf.

8

MYSTIC DEATH

The Last Supper was separated from the beginning of the Passion by but a few hours. We may say that it

was even part of the Passion at least in the fervour
of its intent.   There He anticipated the betraying kiss
of Judas.   There He foresaw, and in foreseeing
accepted, the torture and mangling of His flesh, the
pouring forth of His precious blood.   In the first Consecration on that Holy Thursday night He offered His
body and blood in His own all-pure hands to the
Father, before delivering Himself into the sacrilegious
hands of His enemies.   In His infinite wisdom He did
not allow our Christian religion and its sacrificial act
to appear as arising out of the crime of His own people,
out of the hypocrisy and hatred of the Sanhedrim, out
of the savagery and cruelty of the Roman soldiery.   For
that reason He celebrated His sacrifice of the new and
perfect worship before enduring the actual violence of
His Passion and Crucifixion.   Our Eucharistic sacrifice comes to us directly from the hands of the Lamb of
God.   It is all His making.   It renews the strength and
efficacy of His interior offering of Himself, without the
awfulness and horror of its actual price becoming
apparent, except in a most consoling and pleasing sign.

The sacred ritual inaugurated in the Upper Room,
and by His command continued, contains the two
essential elements of sacrifice, and the sacrifice is none
other than that of Calvary itself.   " As often as you shall
eat this bread and drink the chalice, you shall show
forth the death of the Lord until he come " (1 Cor.
xi. 26).   It contains in reality all the perfect dispositions of the Divine and human will of Christ,
which were the essential part of His oblation of the
Cross.   It contains all the reality of the immolation of
His Passion, though in an unbloody manner, and in
the guise only of death.

By way of oblation Jesus poured into that first consecration of bread and wine all the intensity of His desire for justice. He thirsted for the baptism of blood which would establish the glory of His Father on the earth in the new religion of the sons of God. St. John, whose intimate account of that night has already been noticed, seems to indicate this desire of His Father's glory as a prelude to the Institution. "When he (Judas) therefore had gone out, Jesus said: Now is the Son of man glorified, and God is glorified in him. If God be glorified in him, God also will glorify him in himself: and immediately will he glorify him" (John xiii. 30-2). No words could more emphatically express the religious fervour of the soul of Christ in this saying of the First Mass. The will of Christ which was so lovingly and devotedly turned to the Father was in the same Father turned towards us. He willed to save us in His Passion and death. But what He willed on the Cross on which He surrendered His body, He willed also in the Upper Room where He gave His "flesh for the life of the world". By the Institution of the Last Supper He brought that redemptive will into close contact with all men unto the end of time. He so arranged in His Divine love that every man might through union in His sacrifice raise himself into that redeeming will in which he was eternally contained according to the Divine purpose of Redemption. The will to redeem of Christ never ceases before the throne of God, Where "He is always living to make intercession for us" (Heb. vii. 25).

Our linking with the will of Christ turned to His Father and to us is not dependent on mere verbal assurance to be accepted in faith. In the Sacrifice of the Mass the inner disposition of the Great High-Priest is supported and made evident by a sign which by intimate commemoration gives a true character of immolation to the ritual. By two separate consecrations at the Last Supper Jesus presented Himself in the guise of death which would follow on the morrow. "In virtue of the consecration," declares St. Thomas, "the body of Christ is under the species of bread, while His blood is under the species of wine." Neither at the Last Supper, nor now, is it possible to have body actually separated from the blood. That happened only once in the Passion. But the words of two separate consecrations which make Him present on the altar speak for themselves. Their consecrating virtue extends only and separately to body and blood. The fact that now, after consecration, where the body is, there also must be found the blood, does not follow from the words or consecrating form, but from what St. Thomas calls *natural concomitance*. That is to say, that, since in Christ's glorified state body and blood are no longer separable, He must be in the sacrament as He is in reality. St. Thomas points out that, were the sacrament consecrated at the time when Christ suffered, when His blood was really separated from His body, then the body only would have been present under the species of bread, and the blood only under the species of wine.

Our Lord called the new ritual sacrifice a memory of Himself. It is a memory of His Passion and death. It is not just a mere memory, a mere social function to keep Him in mind. The memory is itself representative of what He suffered for us. It places Him in the guise of death, and so links us with His redemptive will on the Cross. For that reason the Last Supper and every repetition of it on our altars contains a real immolation. He immolated Himself in its institution on that night, since by consecrating bread and wine He placed Himself before the Father in the sign of the one supreme sacrifice which would follow on the morrow.   Thus He poured into it all the efficacy of His actual sacrifice in suffering and death.   By commanding it to be done unto the end of the world, He but transposed the efficacy of the new Pasch to the time after He had suffered.   All the virtue that was in it before continues to be in it after the Passion.   The same redeeming will remains in the same sign which continues to present Him "as if He were slain".   St. Thomas declares: "The celebration of this sacrament is a certain image representative of the Passion of Christ, which is His true immolation.   And therefore the celebration of this sacrament is called Christ's immolation" (III. Q. 83, Art. 1).

Mystic death is all-sufficient for this sacrifice of the New Law.   In the Old Law, because it "brought nothing to perfection", there was need of a multiplying and constant repetition of sacrifices to represent the various dispositions and needs of the priest and people.   But the sacrifice of Christ is one and all sufficient.   What is so utterly perfect in one act cannot be repeated—only shown forth.   Christ is the life-giving head and centre of the entire Church.   Virtue goes out from His Sacred Humanity.   The Mystic body and each individual member of it lives in Christ, and Christ lives in it, pouring out through His divinely appointed channels of the sacraments the abundance of life.   In the working of each sacrament He speaks indeed, authoritatively as God, but through His human nature which voices that authority, and is empowered by the Divinity which assumed it.   So likewise in the Mass, through the agency of His ordained minister,

who is linked in power to that same humanity, He
continues to speak in His blood the efficacy of His
Passion. There is found in the sign of consecration
the new pact between God and man of His death
for our sakes. The once Crucified Christ in the Elevation of the Mass unceasingly lifts the world to God
as long ago He lifted it by being raised on the Cross.
"I, if I be lifted up from the earth, will draw all things
to myself" (John xii. 32). As the vivifying centre of
His mystic body, He works through the sacramental
signs which cause in the soul within what they signify
without. So also in the Mass He has instituted the
sign of His immolation on Calvary. What is so signified without is in a certain manner wrought within,
and the soul joined with Him on the Altar receives the
efficacious grace of the one sacrifice, of the one Priest,
of the one victim, of the one Christ. The purpose of
the Mass is not only that He may be made present on
our altars, or that we may receive Him in Holy Communion, but that, by His presence, He may renew us
in His own most splendid act of sacrificial worship.
The sacred wounds which Jesus received in hands, feet
and side, which by Divine design were retained in His
glorified body, are marks of His triumph over sin, and
an everlasting reminder to the Eternal Father of His
unceasing intercession for us. On earth these wounds
are no longer visible, but in their stead there is the
visible memorial of His Passion and death in unceasing offering.

Looking down over the ages to come Jesus saw the
immensity of human need. Men would forget His
death for them unless it had some form of visible
renewal. Men to whom He gave a new religion would
also require a new and perfect sacrifice. Amidst the

sufferings and stress of earthly life they would need a visible altar and a visible victim. Doubtless they could recall the story of His Passion and death, as the one oblation and the centre of all salvation. But Christ knew the weakness of our nature, our need of seeing and touching, of being drawn by the visible into the knowledge and love of the invisible. All down the ages of human history man has experienced that need, and has found comfort in the offering of visible sacrifices. The Jews had faith also and hope in the Divine promise, but God prescribed for them as well a splendid ceremonial. Looking back over that splendour which preceded, we have been led to expect some far more grandiose expression of Divine worship. We have not been disappointed. The liturgy given to us is the work of the Incarnate Word in the continued exercise of His priestly office as the Head of His Mystic Body which is the whole Christ, as St. Augustine says, "He the Head and we the members."

The Angelic Doctor describes this work of the ever-abiding Christ in the Mass as both mighty and universal in its effect. "Mighty . . . because this is the sacrament of the Passion of Christ, since it contains within itself the crucified Christ. Therefore whatsoever belongs to the effect of Christ's Passion pertains also in all its entirety to the effect of this sacrament. For that reason this sacrament is nothing else than the applying to us of the Passion of Christ. It was not seemly that Christ should remain always visibly present amongst us, and He wished to compensate for that loss by means of this sacrament. It is therefore evident that the destruction of death which Christ wrought in dying, and the renewal of life which He established in His Resurrection, are the effects of this sacrament.

It is universal because the life which it bestows is not the life of one man only, but in keeping with what it contains, of the entire world, for which Christ's death suffices. *He is the propitiation for our sins; and not for ours only, but for those of the whole world* (1 John ii. 2). It should also be observed that He is present in this sacrament otherwise than in the other sacraments, because the other sacraments have only an individual effect, as for example in Baptism only the baptised receives grace. But in the immolation of this sacrament there is a universal effect, because not only the priest receives that effect, but all those for whom he prays, and the entire Church both of the living and of the dead" (*Comment. St. John*; Cap. 6, Lect. 6).

9

OUR INHERITANCE

For wellnigh two thousand years this solemn act of worship has been maintained unceasingly in the true Church of Christ. For well-nigh two thousand years Christ has consecrated countless times through the agency of countless other Christs as He did in the Upper Room. The Apostles who first received His command, "Do this for a commemoration of me," transmitted their power in unbroken line down the centuries to the present day. What is now celebrated on every Christian altar goes back in perfect continuity to the night of the Last Supper. Christ is as truly present as the offerer and consecrator of the Mass with His ordained minister, as He was in the Upper Room.

In the solemn moment of the sacrificial rite Christ makes His own of the priestly activity. He appropriates the human personality by identifying the priest with Himself, when through the power of the word which is granted him the priest speaks again as Christ spoke: "This is my body"—"This is the chalice of my blood." "The priest," says St. Thomas, "bears the image of Christ in Whose person and by Whose power he pronounces the words of consecration" (III. Q. 83, 1, ad 3).

It is not surprising, seeing what the Holy Sacrifice of the Mass is in itself, that it should become the centre of life and holiness within the Church from the very beginning. It immediately distinguished Jew from Christian. It shaped Christian living. It gave characteristic form to Christian spirituality. The Acts of the Apostles provides the earliest history of the predominating part it played in the early Church. Each century that followed left its own record in one form or another of Christian observance of the Lord's command on the night before He suffered. In the "Didache", for instance, which most probably belongs to the first century, we find a striking witness to the observance of the Sunday precept as well as to the reverence due to the Mass. "On the Lord's Day," it ordains all, "to gather together and break bread, and offer the Eucharist, having first confessed our transgressions, that our sacrifice may be pure; for this is the word spoken by the Lord." To St. Andrew the Apostle is attributed a magnificent apologia in favour of the sacrificial character of the Mass, addressed to the Roman Consul. "I sacrifice every day on the altar to the All-powerful, the one and only God, not the flesh of bulls, nor the blood of goats, but the Immaculate Lamb, always whole and entire, always living after the faithful have eaten his flesh." The Roman Catacombs bear witness in primitive Christian art to the glory of the Most Blessed Eucharist. Such testimonies might be multiplied into volumes. Such records are there for all to see. It is quite clear that we had not to await the sixteenth century, or to depend on the words of an apostate monk to know what Jesus really intended when He instituted His Last Supper. The continued teaching of the Church, its art, its monuments, its literature, point inexorably to the reality of sacrifice and sacrament, which was received by the Apostles and handed down from age to age in the Church of Christ.

External evidence to the truth of the Mass is most helpful in convincing us of the credibility of this dogma of Christian worship. But to accept, as one should, this sublime mystery of the Eucharist, grace is absolutely necessary. Only God's gift of faith can make this truth become a living, transforming force within the soul. This mystery surpasses all human understanding, though it does no violence to it. It depends in its last analysis on the word of our omnipotent and loving Christ. Only by faith can we see in the Mass the mystery of Calvary renewed. By faith "the eyes of our hearts" behold more than the externals. We witness again the death of Our Saviour. We touch Him, and are touched by Him. Faith draws us confidently to the new "Tabernacle of God with men" in His ever-abiding presence. From His altar there is poured out the same compassion and love which long ago He manifested to the multitude. He is there to heal, and give us life more and more abundantly. Long ago, a woman touched merely the hem of His garment, and was healed. She had gone to Him in faith. So also does our own faith, and in faith confidence, draw His attention to our misery. "Who is it that touched me? . . . Thy faith hath made thee whole, go thy way in peace" (Luke viii. 45, 48).

Sixth Chapter

PARTAKING OF THE BODY OF THE LORD

(1 Cor. x. 16)

1

CONSUMING THE VICTIM

LOOKING back over the ancient ritual of God's chosen people, which foreshadowed the great things which were to come, we see that in nearly all these typical sacrifices there took place a consuming of the victim. This was apart from the act of sacrifice properly so called which consisted in the oblation and immolation. The ritual closed with the dividing of the flesh according to detailed instructions, first for the priest and his sons and then for the people. The consuming was an integral part of the old sacrificial worship. The prayer of priest and people had, as it were, penetrated the flesh and made it holy in the sight of God. Thus the flesh or whatever else had been offered in sacrifice was called even in the Old Testament " consecrated ", or " sanctified to the Lord ". The eating of the flesh that had been sacrificed by way of substitution, and which had become expressive of their interior disposition, brought priest and people into closer union with the victim. What had been immolated thus became part of themselves, and seemed,

171

once eaten, to bring with it something of its own contact with God, and to share more intimately the sacrificial virtue which it contained.   "The offering of a
victim suffices for the essence of sacrifice: at the same
time the religious instinct is not completely satisfied,
and the sacrifice itself would not seem to be entirely
consummated, except by an act which unites us more
intimately to the oblation. . . . That act is the eating
of the victim.   Tradition shows it to us in the greater
number of ancient sacrifices.   We see man drawing
near to God by participation in the same sacred banquet.   The incense, the clouds, the bitter savour of
blood, the smoke of the whole burnt offering—these
are God's share; the sanctified flesh of the victim, that
is man's share" (Monsabré).

"Take ye and eat: this is my body" (Matt. xxvi. 26).
The ritual sacrifice instituted by Christ at the Last
Supper presents a further essential fulfilment of its
splendid foreshadowing.   What was instinctive in the
old, we are not to be deprived of in the new.   Even
without the invitation of the Saviour, the very elements
which He used in consecration, and wherein the Divine
Victim lies concealed, clearly dictate His intention of
providing a banquet for men.   Jesus chose two substances normally associated with hunger and thirst,
which appeal to the natural appetite, that He might
share with us more intimately the virtue that proceeds
from His sacrifice.   By changing bread into His body,
and wine into His blood, yet preserving the outward
appearances of the original substances—the appearances of common food and drink—He fulfilled what
He had foretold: "My flesh is meat indeed; and my
blood is drink indeed" (John vi. 56).   Had all sacrifice
ended with the one actual sacrifice of the Cross, were

there no Last Supper—no institution of the Most Holy
Eucharist, not only would we have been deprived of a
splendid form of sacrificial worship, but the prophetic
words of Christ would have been meaningless: "The
bread that I will give is my flesh for the life of the
world. . . . Except you eat the flesh of the Son of man
and drink his blood, you shall not have life in you"
(ibid. 52, 54).

Jesus gave Himself for the whole human race upon
the Cross.   From out of His sacrifice comes the
efficacy of His sacraments.   But the greatest of all
these is the Blessed Eucharist, which is not only sacrament, but sacrifice—the one unique sacrifice in the
renewal of Calvary in the Holy Mass.   This sacrament
is whereby we are joined in the worshipful act of
Christ in oblation and immolation, and whereby,
through the Holy Communion, each one is brought
into a still more perfect and more personal union with
the Victim of the altar.   In the Mass we receive, not
only the virtue of Christ, but Christ Himself, the source
of all life.   As a sacrifice the Mass is Calvary—it depends totally upon Calvary.   But in a manner it completes Calvary, or rather completes the desire of Christ
on Calvary to bring the fruits of His Passion and death
into each individual soul.   The ritual sacrifice makes
possible a desired intimacy whch would be entirely
repugnant in the actual sacrifice of the Cross.   Had
we not known the manner of Christ's Institution, we
would have cried out at His first announcement of the
mystery, if not in doubt, at least in our anxiety for
fuller information: "How can this man give us his
flesh to eat and his blood to drink?" (ibid. 52).   What
love foretold in the slaying and eating of the paschal
lamb, love fulfilled in the celebration of the new

M

Pasch, in which the Lamb of God gives His immolated flesh and blood to be the life of each soul.

The ancient consuming of the victim was an integral part of the sacrifice; such is it also in the new. The all-holy body and blood of Christ was offered for a redemption, whereby it became still more sacred in the sight of God. Priest and people, who gather around the altar, approach that table and receive that flesh and blood, that has become present by consecration, and has therein renewed the pact between God and man. By means of a Holy Communion, the immolated victim becomes part of the worshippers, or, more accurately, the worshippers become part with Him, and are, in a manner, integrated into the victim. Thus, in the new sacrifice, which sweeps into its mighty perfection all that went before, Christ shares with each communicated soul in a most intimate way the virtue and holiness of His sacrificial act. St. Thomas declares: "The effect which the Passion of Christ produced in the world this sacrament produces in each one." In one short antiphon the same Doctor sets the mystery before us: "O Sacred banquet in which Christ is received, in which the memory of His Passion is renewed, in which the mind is filled with grace, and there is given to us a pledge of eternal glory."

2

MY FATHER GIVETH TRUE BREAD

The amazing generosity of the Saviour in establishing so wonderful an intimacy with His fellow men is in perfect accord with the expectation of the Chosen People. The coming of the Messiah was associated with the provision of bread from the beginning of their nationhood. The chief priests and scribes, who answered Herod's question: "Where Christ should be born," should have known how significant of that association was His birthplace. "They said to him: In Bethlehem of Juda. For so it is written by the prophet; and thou Bethlehem of Juda art not the least among the princes of Juda: for out of thee shall come forth the captain that shall rule my people Israel" (Matt. ii. 5, 6). Nothing in the Divine arrangement of man's redemption happened by chance. Bethlehem —the City of Bread—was known, if not named by Jacob. There Rachel his wife was buried. Later in direct line of descent, and still closer to Christ, came David who was born and went forth from Bethlehem to challenge Goliath. King David, who was one of the greatest heroes of sacred history, was a figure of Christ, and sang, as did no other prophet, the glories of the Messiah and His kingdom. From him Christ descended according to the flesh. From the city of David, Christ also came forth to engage the powers of evil in the work of man's redemption. When the order of enrol-ment—"every one in his own city"—was issued by Caesar Augustus, Joseph "went to the city of David, which is called Bethlehem, because he was of the house and family of David" (Luke ii. 4). Bethlehem, so called because it was fertile of wheat, became truly the City of Bread when it housed the Incarnate Word —"The living bread that cometh down from heaven" (John vi. 41).

From the time of the Passover which, by the com-mand of God became an "everlasting observance", the Jewish Pasch became known as "the days of un-leavened bread". The significance of that title, and the ordinances of God in its regard, have been touched on before (cf. First Chapter). Bread was eaten with the paschal lamb. Both lamb and bread in diverse ways signified the same gift in perfect combination, since the new Lamb of God is presented to us in the changing of unleavened bread into His flesh through the power of Consecration. In the worship of the Temple the chief priests were also well acquainted with the use of bread in the various sacrifices and oblations. The twelve loaves of Proposition, which were placed before the altar of God and renewed weekly, were a reminder of God's goodness, and sig-nificant of the abundance which was to come from Christ's gift to the Apostles. St. Paul speaks of "the golden pot which had manna", which was preserved in the Holy of Holies. This relic of the past held one of the most precious memories of the Chosen People. It enshrined outstanding evidence of God's providential care over them in the desert at the time of Moses and their wanderings. Though material bread, it had mysterious qualities not associated with ordinary bread, which made it truly representative of the Bread of Life which it foreshadowed. "Thou didst feed thy people with the food of angels, and thou gavest them bread from heaven, prepared without labour; having in itself all that is delicious, and the sweetness of every taste" (Wis. xvi. 20).

In the preparation of the minds of the Apostles and of the multitude that had followed Him into the desert, Our Divine Lord took the prophetic sign of the Manna as the starting point in the revelation of the new mystery, which was to provide a food infinitely superior to what had gone before. The multiplication of bread and the feeding of the multitude was a challenge to those who refused to accept Him as the Messiah. The superabundant supplying of their need in the desert, whither He had led them, was strongly reminiscent of what God had done for His Chosen People in the desert of their wanderings towards the Promised Land. The Gospel account reveals how the memory of that favour was uppermost in the minds of those who challenged Him on that occasion. Their disbelief opened the way to His announcement of the Most Blessed Eucharist. "They said therefore to Him: What sign therefore dost thou shew that we may see, and may believe thee? What dost thou work? Our Fathers did eat Manna in the desert, as it is written; He gave them bread from heaven to eat" (John vi. 30, 31). It is evident that the pharisaical element among the crowd sought to minimize the effect of His miracle, and kill the enthusiasm of the people, by lauding the greater miracle which Moses had already worked on their behalf. He had claimed to be greater than Moses. Let Him then do greater work than Moses. That was the test. Jesus met the test—how well the Scribes and Pharisees refused to believe.

The argument which followed reveals Christ as the "author and finisher of our faith", before Whom all foreshadowing passes away, in Whom all that was prophetic was splendidly fulfilled. Jesus immediately contrasted the wonderful work of Moses with what He intended to do on their behalf. Moses indeed gave them bread from heaven, but not the bread of heaven itself. He alone was that bread. "I am the bread of life." He was Himself the gift of bread which came down directly from the Father. "My Father giveth you the true bread from heaven." This is the very bread for which He told His Apostles to pray on a previous occasion: "Give us this day our daily bread" (Luke xi. 3). "The bread of God is that which cometh down from heaven and giveth life to the world" (John vi. 33). Thus He identified Himself with the bread which His Father gave to the world. It could never be anything else than Himself. He was the bread of truth, giving His new doctrine to the world. The Father willed that they should nourish themselves on that bread by believing. But the new dispensation does not end there. Jesus continued to contrast the bread of Moses with His own. What Moses gave was a purely material bread. It, at best, and only for a short time, sustained the life of the body. Moreover, it was a bread that perished, if kept for more than a day. At first the Jews were satisfied that He meant to continue some form of the Mosaic bounty. They thought only in terms of material bread—that was the sole reason of their following Him. "Lord," they cried out, "give us always of this bread." But He had already warned them: "Labour not for the meat which perisheth, but for that which endureth unto life everlasting, which the Son of man will give you" (John vi. 34). His bread was to be "supersubstantial" (Matt. vi. 11), that is to say, imperishable. It is not merely for the body, but for the soul. "If any man eat of it, he may not die." On the other hand, those who had eaten of the bread of Moses were all dead.

Before making the final tremendous announcement of His purpose, Jesus again stressed the necessity of faith. Only those who believe could enter with Him into the mystery of this new food of the soul. "I am the bread of life. He that cometh to me shall not hunger; and he that believeth in me shall never thirst . . . because I am come down from heaven" (ibid.). He concluded the first part of His discourse with the strong words: "Amen, amen, I say to you, he that believeth in me hath everlasting life." Faith alone unlocks the door of the great mystery which, despite their unbelief, He must propose to them all, whether they will accept or not. Its truth will not depend on their acceptance, but solely on His own word. Again He repeated: "I am the bread of life." But now it is no longer a question of spiritual union by faith in His Divinity, but of a real eating and drinking. Once again He emphasized the contrast between His bread and that of Moses. "Your Fathers did eat manna in the desert and are dead. . . . If any man eat of this bread, he shall live for ever." Then followed the astounding declaration: "The bread that I will give, is my flesh for the life of the world." This announcement caused an angry commotion in the crowd—"They strove amongst themselves, saying: How can this man give us his flesh to eat?" Jesus made no defence of His statement, other than to drive home His teaching in regard to the necessity of receiving the adorable Eucharist. They must accept the entire mystery of His Divinity, and therefore of His omnipotent power to provide what He had promised. There is no question of choice. Only those who believe, and in believing make one with Him in the banquet of His love, can save their souls. Holy Communion is necessary for eternal salvation. "Amen, amen, I say unto you: except you eat the flesh of the Son of man, and drink his blood, you shall not have life in you. He that eateth my flesh, and drinketh my blood, hath everlasting life; and I will raise him up on the last day." The Jews who were so disappointed and angered by the type of food which He proposed to give, knew well that He spoke of His real flesh and blood. No truth could be put more clearly. The amazement of His hearers is ample proof that our faith in the Eucharist corresponds accurately with His revelation on that day. It is the same faith which brought forth Peter's splendid confession: "Lord to whom shall we go? thou hast the words of eternal life. And we have believed and have known that thou art the Christ the Son of God" (John ibid.).

From the Adorable Trinity, whence He came through His Incarnation, He reaches us in the Eucharist through the Institution of His Last Supper. This, we may say, is the ideal and ultimate existence which He chose for our sakes, that He might live with us, not for a span of time, as when He was visible on earth, but for all time "until He come again". How well He fulfilled what He promised! "Behold I am with you all days even unto the end of the world" (Matt. xxviii. 20). Contemplating this prodigy of Divine love, St. Augustine boldly declared: "I dare to say that God in His omnipotence could not give more, in His wisdom He knew not how to give more, in His riches he had no more to give." Truly this Divine communication exhausts God's benevolence in our regard. He truly loved us unto the end. He gave until there was nothing left to give.

3.

MYSTERIOUS INCORPORATION

Christ's purpose in instituting the Blessed Eucharist is identical with that of all His redeeming work, namely the salvation of souls through personal sanctification. According to His own words, the union of the soul in the eating of His flesh and drinking of His blood is necessary for eternal life. Holy Communion is the central point—an intense phase in God's design of Divine living. In our knowledge of what is contained in the Blessed Sacrament, we can appreciate the more the wonder of our interior life of grace. On the other hand, seeing that grace is itself the close union of a member of the Mystic Body with Christ Who is the Head, we realize how perfectly in accord is the Eucharist with the gift of supernatural life. The Church is an organic whole, composed of many members and a Head, Who is entirely in the whole and in every part. "For as the body is one and hath many members; and all the members of the body, whereas they are many, yet are one body. So also is Christ" (1 Cor. xii. 12). As the everlasting Head, Christ's work never ceases for this Mystic Body which He has joined unto Himself. Though now working through the various agencies of sanctification which He has appointed, it is always He Who vitalizes the whole and each part. Virtue goes out from Him unceasingly. "From whom the whole body, being compactly and fitly joined together, by what every joint supplieth, according to the operation in the measure of every part, maketh increase of the body unto the edifying of itself in charity" (Eph. iv. 16).

Because of what it does in the soul, sanctifying grace is called an incorporation in Christ. The word implies an entering into a corporate union with other members in one headship. We speak of local governments as corporations because they form a public body engaged in working for the good of the whole city. So the Church is a body or spiritual corporation, into which we are received and thereby become incorporated. Membership entails vital union with the Head, in Whose merit we are admitted, and in Whose grace we are maintained and perfected. Baptism is the gateway into this incorporation in Christ and in His Church. "In one Spirit we are all baptised in one body" (ibid. 13). From that moment Jesus, Who is the Head of the whole body, becomes the particular Head of my new life in me. I am personally in vital contact with the whole Christ, and He in me. Speaking of this grace, St. Paul could affirm: "I live, now not I, but Christ liveth in me" (Gal. ii. 10). Obviously Holy Communion is an intensifying of this incorporation, since it brings us the very body of Christ to become the nourishment of our souls. Through the grace of the sacrament we become more intimately incorporated, more deeply rooted in the Mystic Body because of our vital contact with the body and soul of Christ, which is the conjoined instrument of Redemption and the living source of all grace.

The association of Eucharistic and Baptismal grace is emphasized in the teaching of St. Augustine. "No one should doubt that each one of the faithful is made a partaker of the body and blood of the Lord at the very time when, in Baptism, he becomes a member of Christ's body, nor is he deprived of that intimacy with the Bread and the Chalice, even though he depart this life without eating the Bread or drinking the Chalice, because he has entered into Christ's body." Again the same Holy Doctor declared: "One Bread; Who is this one Bread?—the body of Christ. Remember that this bread is not made of one grain but of many grains. When the exorcism was pronounced over you, you were ground, and when baptised, sprinkled with water, and when you received the Holy Ghost, you were baked. Therefore be what you receive, and receive what you are." St. Thomas teaches the same truth: "We partake in Baptism, at least by implicit desire, to be incorporated, to be made one with Him."

This perfect suitability of the Eucharist to the interior life of the soul is further emphasized by considering the innermost nature of sanctifying grace. Grace is first of all the gift of God to His Incarnate Son made man. By reason of the Hypostatic union the sanctifying grace of Christ was the most excellent that could be conceived. "It hath well pleased the Father that in Him all fulness should dwell" (Col. i. xix). It is that selfsame holiness which He pours out into the soul, a sharing in His own vitality. "For them do I sanctify myself: that they also may be holy" (John xvii. 19). Our grace is in likeness of Christ, "that we may be made conformable to the image of His Son". By giving us grace He shares with us His own sonship in the Father; by maintaining that grace in us He works out the perfection of our resemblance to Himself, "the first born of many brethen". It was significant that He spoke on the night of the Last Supper, after the Institution of the Eucharist of the nature of

His union with the soul, which, though applicable to the life of grace in general, was intended to illustrate in particular the effect of the Holy Communion which the Apostles had just received. He selected the simple metaphor of the tree of the vine, from which came the wine which He had just changed into His precious blood. " I am the vine, you are the branches. As the branch cannot bear fruit of itself, unless it abide in the vine, so neither can you, unless you abide in me. He that abideth in me and I in him, the same beareth much fruit, for without me you can do nothing " (John xv. 5). Rooted in the Godhead whence He came in the mystery of the Incarnation, the Humanity of Christ is the new trunk of the vine, which represents the human race. From that trunk there flows the Divine sap of supernatural life and holiness into the entire tree. The goodness and fruitfulness of the branches is the same goodness which is found in the trunk, since it is His own vitality which flows into them. In the Blessed Eucharist the soul becomes more embedded in that trunk and the fruit of His precious blood flows into it more perfectly.

4

UNION IN THE VICTIM

To appreciate the precise and principal effect of Holy Communion in the intensifying of this process of incorporation in Christ, the association of the consuming of the victim with the prior sacrificial act must again be stressed. At the Last Supper that consuming was emphasized more than the act of sacrifice. It

was the ultimate desire of the Saviour, once He had
offered Himself to the Father in the guise of death
through the Consecration, to reach in that same guise
into the hearts of the Apostles, and in a manner to
complete His immolation within them. The essential
strength and efficacy of Holy Communion springs from
the sacrificial act which called it forth and made it
possible. In Holy Communion Christ is the "living
bread that cometh down from heaven", but in coming
He had to pass through the renewal of His Passion and
death. He enters into the Communicant as the victim,
fresh, as it were, from His act of sacrifice in the sight
of the Father. By so doing He draws that soul into His
loving embrace, and links it firmly with the efficacy
of His act.

No one can be saved without passing into the
Passion and death of Christ. "He that will come after
me, let him deny himself and take up his cross daily,
and follow me" (Luke ix. 23). By Holy Communion
Jesus desires to set up His Cross in the heart of each
one, to impregnate it with its wisdom, and stamp the
soul with the seal of His self-sacrifice. St. Paul declares: "All we who have been baptised in Christ
Jesus, are baptised in His death" (Rom. vi. 3). So,
again by association in His sacrifice, the Holy Communion intensifies what was first done in Baptism.
By receiving His immolated body and blood "we are
planted in the likeness of His death", since it retains
that likeness within us in its real presence. "The
chalice of benediction which we bless, is it not the
communion of the blood of Christ, and the bread
which we break, is it not a partaking of the body of
the Lord" (1 Cor. x. 16). Again St. Paul lays down
the principle of association in sacrifice by means of

the consuming of the victim, which is as true of Christian sacrifice as it is for other sacrifices. "Are not they that eat of the sacrifices partakers of the altar" (ibid. 18). Through Holy Communion we become partakers of the Christian altar—of Calvary itself. The fruits of Holy Communion come to us directly from the Crucified Christ. There is no more efficacious way of sharing in the merits of His Passion and death.

From all this we may judge how great is the error of those who regard Holy Communion as something apart from the Mass—as an act of devotion complete in itself, or still worse, merely as a duty of our religion to be fulfilled at least once a year. The Holy Communion belongs to the Mass, even when it is received outside of it, as in the case of the sick. He always comes into the soul as both priest and victim, bringing with Him the strength and comfort of His own immolation.

The words of St. Gregory the Great leave no doubt about the intimate relation of the Holy Communion with the sacrifice. "The Victim in a wonderful way saves the soul from eternal death, who through this mystery renews in us the death of the Only Begotten. Though 'rising from the dead, he dieth now no more, and death shall have no more dominion over Him' (Rom. vi. 9), nevertheless, He is immolated again for us in this mystery of His holy oblation. For there His body is consumed, His flesh is divided for the salvation of the people. His blood is poured out, not as heretofore in the hands of infidels, but into the mouths of the faithful. Let us therefore consider what this sacrifice means to us, which for our salvation ever assumes the guise of the Passion of the Only Begotten Son. Who amongst the faithful can doubt, that at the hour of His immolation at the voice of the priest, the heavens are opened, the choirs of angels are present in that mystery of Jesus Christ, all that is below is lifted up above, what is of earth is joined to what is of heaven, and the visible is made one with the invisible? "

5

UNION IN LOVE

Our Lord in His first announcement of the mystery of the Eucharist took pains also to set down the effect of this union in the soul. His words scale the unapproachable heights of the mystery of life in God Himself. It is that mystery which is intimately though invisibly shared in by those who receive Him worthily in the sacrament of His love. "He that eateth my flesh and drinketh my blood hath everlasting life" (John vi. 55). He immediately gives the reason of this effect: "He that eateth my flesh and drinketh my blood, abideth in me and I in him." Holy Communion, because of its intimate union with the body and blood of Christ, and in that humanity with the entire Christ, God and man, is the nearest approach to heaven itself. His abiding means a setting up of His kingdom within the soul—the kingdom of His grace which is a prelude to the kingdom of His glory.

In a still more precise way on the same occasion He proceeds to tell the secret of this newness of life within the soul. His words convey a mystery which soars above the power of human comprehension, but which, since we rely on His assurance, we cannot doubt becomes a reality within the soul. "As the living Father hath sent me, and I live by the Father: so he that eateth me, the same also shall live by me " (ibid. 58). Here there is a question of living by a human being, but not of merely human living. The life shared is the eternal life of the Son in the bosom of the Father in the mutual love which is the Holy Ghost. There is question in these words of the innermost life of God in the adorable mystery of the Trinity. In the Blessed Sacrament, as when He lived visibly as man on earth, Jesus lives His eternal life as the Only Begotten of the Father, returning the Father's love which is in the mutual breathing of love which is the Holy Spirit. But when we receive Him in Holy Communion He lives this same life within the soul, and draws the soul in close union with Himself into that same Divine cycle of life. He thus fulfils the desire of His heart, which He so beautifully expressed in prayer to His Father in the Upper Room after the first Communion of the Apostles. That prayer is His sacerdotal prayer —His Eucharistic prayer of thanksgiving for the Twelve. "I in them, and thou in me: that they may be made perfect in one: and the world may know that thou hast sent me, and hast loved them, as thou hast loved me " (John xvii. 23). Grace, we know from St. Peter, is a sharing in the Divine Nature of God. (2 Pet. i. 4). The Holy Communion is the culminating point of that grace of earth, in which Jesus lives His adorable life in the verity of His Humanity within the soul.

St. Thomas calls the Incarnate Son of God "the Word breathing love". He is eternally breathing forth that love to the Father. He breathed out that same love whilst He lived on earth. He breathed it out on mankind visibly, as if even His human breath had become charged with love. "He breathed on

them; and He said to them: Receive ye the Holy
Ghost" (John xx. 22). So by becoming really present
in the soul does He breathe His love of the Father in
the soul, that it may be joined as He is to the Father
in the strong love of the Spirit, Who for us is the Spirit
of adoption, "whereby we cry: *Abba*; Father" (Rom.
viii. 15). His prayer after the first Holy Communion
also included that request on our behalf to the Father:
"That the love wherewith thou hast loved me, may
be in them, and I in them" (John xvii. 26). In the
Holy Communion "the charity of God is poured forth
into our hearts" (Rom. v. 5).

Long ago, in the Temple, Jesus declared that He
must be about His Father's business. By means of the
Blessed Eucharist He sets up His temple within the
heart of man, and continues the work which His Father
sent Him to do. "By this hath the charity of God
appeared towards us, because God hath sent His Son
into the world, that we may live by him" (1 John iv. 9).
This is also the will of the Son, namely to give evidence
of His own and the Father's love. "I am come to
cast fire on the earth, and what will I but that it be
kindled" (Luke xii. 49). Every Holy Communion is
an earnest of this love of God. Jesus associated that
fire He came down to cast on the earth with His intense desire to undergo the baptism of His sufferings.
For that very reason the fire of His love in the soul
of the communicant is most intense by being coupled
with that desire in the renewal of His sacrificial will
and the sign of His immolation which placed Him living on the altar. What is true of the charity of grace is
especially true when the Incarnate Word is sacramentally present in the soul: "If any man love me, he will
keep my word, and my Father will love him, and we

N

will come to him, and will take up our abode in him"
(John xiv. 23). To receive the Blessed Eucharist one
must already possess love in the state of grace; one
must believe by accepting the word of the Institution.
In return for this loving faith we become the tabernacle of God. "Behold the tabernacle of God with
men, and he will dwell with them. And they shall
be his people; and God himself with them shall be
their God" (Apoc. xxi. 3). Conscious of the Immensity within the soul, we may cry out with St. John:
"We have heard, we have seen with our eyes, we have
looked upon, and our hands have handled the word
of life" (1 John i. 1).

The saints, benefiting by their own experience, have
been able to tell us the splendour of this union of the
soul in God through Holy Communion. St. Cyril of
Jerusalem thus described it: "Throw melted wax into
melted wax, and the one interpenetrates the other perfectly. In like manner when the body and blood of
Christ are received, the union is such that Christ is in
the recipient, and he in Christ. We have the same
body and the same blood." St. Catherine in her Dialogues wrote what she was privileged to hear in her
ecstasies from the Eternal Father concerning His
sacramental presence in the soul. "See in what an
excellent state is the soul who receives as she should
the bread of life, this food of angels. By receiving
this sacrament she dwells in me and I in her. As the
fish is in the sea and the sea in the fish—thus do I dwell
in the soul and the soul in me—the sea pacific." Later,
the Eternal Father speaks of the permanence of His
effect in the soul even after His real presence has
ceased. "I leave you the imprint of my grace, as does
a seal, which when lifted from the hot wax upon which

it has been impressed, leaves behind it its imprint, so the virtue of the sacrament remains in the soul, that is to say the heat of my Divine Charity, and the clemency of the Holy Ghost."

6

THE BREAD OF LIFE

St. Thomas is said to have laid his treatise on the Blessed Sacrament at the feet of the Crucifix, and to have heard a voice from heaven in praise of his doctrine: "Well hast thou written of me, Thomas." The Universal Doctor is certainly a sure guide, and we may turn to him to understand in greater detail the wonderful effects of Holy Communion on the soul. In common with other Doctors of the Church, he draws a parallel between the natural order of bodily life and the supernatural life of the soul in God. The natural order helps us to appreciate the laws of the spiritual, since, as the Angelic Doctor points out, God did not do less for the soul than He did for the body, and it is clear also that Our Lord Himself used material things to help us to realize the immensity of His invisible working in the soul through grace.

This use of the natural to explain the supernatural was particularly apparent in Christ's first teaching regarding the Most Holy Eucharist. He fed the multitude with material bread to teach them the spiritually nutritive power of His supersubstantial bread. Nourishment is a fundamental law of the life of the body. Without it there can neither be growth nor a healthy condition of the body. This law, moreover, demands that the material nourishment contain within itself the chemical elements of which the body is itself composed. Eating releases a certain digestive process whereby food is absorbed and becomes its bone, its flesh, its blood, its sinews. By comparison with this law of nature we can admire God's admirable provision of nourishment for the soul. Seeing that the law of supernatural life entails conformity with Christ through incorporation into His Mystic Body, it is evident that our spiritual food of the Eucharist contains within itself the essential element of our supernatural living. But it may be added that the process of absorption in this supernatural food is the reverse of the process of ordinary bread. Christ is not absorbed into us, but we are into Christ, as St. Augustine has expressed it in words of Christ: " I shall not be changed into thee, but thou shalt be changed into me."

Continuing the comparison, St. Thomas places the effect of material bread under four headings, which he proceeds to apply also to the effect of Holy Communion. Ordinary bread sustains, increases, repairs and delights the body; so does the heavenly bread for the soul.

Just as man needs energy to make his way along the road of life, to overcome the obstacles, face the dangers, and persevere until he reaches his journey's end, so, in the way of life from God back to God, there are many obstacles; man himself is weak, he is exposed to the pitfalls of sin, and he lacks the energy required to maintain his progress from day to day. Our return to God is made through Jesus Christ. He came to give life and to give it abundantly. In the Blessed Eucharist He provides for a healthy measure of that life in a vigour which helps man to overcome himself.

THE BODY OF THE LORD

" The kingdom of heaven suffereth violence," said our Lord, "and only the violent shall bear it away." Christian living requires self-denial. Man must go against the current of his fallen nature. This needs vigour. He is beset by his own inherent weakness, but he is made strong to overcome through the bread of life. St. Thomas says that this sacrament preserves the soul from mortal sin, because it joins the soul to Christ, who strengthens its spiritual life. Because of this sustaining effect of the Eucharist it has been associated with the bread divinely given to the Prophet Elias, who in the strength of it walked for forty days and nights even to the mountain of God.

Growth is a normal law of the body, at least until it arrives at its perfection of stature. For this food is also necessary. In the spiritual life also there must be growth. The beginning of that life is bestowed in Baptism. But the soul so baptised should advance in grace and holiness. What is bestowed in spiritual birth should be developed and brought to perfection. So St. Paul speaks of our growing up in Him Who is the Head, Jesus. He also lays down the term of that perfection: "Until we all meet . . . unto a perfect man, unto the measure of the age of fulness of Christ" (Eph. iv. 13). Growth of the soul is caused by grace, and particularly through the increase of charity, which is the principal effect of Holy Communion. Jesus feeds His lambs and feeds His sheep. He adapts His work to the needs of every soul. Every soul is loved by Him with a particular and most personal love. His supreme desire is to make it love Him in return. That is His desire especially in the Sacrament of His love. " Behold, I stand at the gate, and knock. If any man shall hear my voice, and open to me the door, I will come into him, and will sup with, and he with me" (Apoc. iii. 20). If miracles of grace are worked through the relics of the saints, how much greater is the effect of vital contact with the body and blood of Jesus Christ! This is the law of the spiritual vine: "He that abideth in me, and I in him, the same beareth much fruit" (John xv. 5).

Were we sinless—as Our Blessed Lady was—the effect of Holy Communion would be irresistible. From each Communion would come a steady and unbroken increase of charity. But our nature is a fallen one, and full of all kinds of imperfection and sin. Jesus does not come into an ideal heart, but to one in which the love of Him is mixed with affections which are foreign to His love. Nourishment of the body is necessary, declares St. Thomas, to repair the loss which it sustains daily. So also in ourselves there is a daily wasting of our spiritual fabric from the effect of concupiscence and venial sins, which lessen the fervour of our charity. So it belongs to this sacrament to forgive venial sins. "This daily bread," says St. Ambrose, "is taken as remedy for our daily infirmity." This bread of life is at once food and medicine. It heals as well as sanctifies. The Angelic Doctor adds that the charity which is found in this sacrament is stronger than our venial sins and imperfections. His prayer by way of preparation for Holy Communion makes an ideal way of approach to the Holy Table. "As one weak and infirm, I draw near to the Physician of life; as one unclean to the fountain of mercy, as one blind to the light of eternal brightness; as one needy to the Lord of heaven and earth." Our Lord's own invitation is particularly pressing: "Come to me all ye that labour and are burdened, and I will refresh you."

Almighty God attached a sensible pleasure to eating whereby the good of the body is promoted. Hunger creates an appetite or desire to eat which is satisfied by taking food. So by comparison St. Thomas speaks of a final effect of the Most Holy Sacrament. It delights the soul. From the presence of God in the soul through grace, the Angelic Doctor declares that we have an almost experimental knowledge of the known in the one who knows and the beloved in one who loves. The Apostles knew Christ in the external ceremony of the breaking of bread. We by faith in approaching the Holy Table move into an intimacy of knowledge of this infinitely good God, Who comes to us under the appearance of bread. But this Bread of Life gives us possession of the One we love. He becomes totally ours—totally mine. Nothing is closer to me than the bread I eat, because it becomes mine—it becomes me. So by no other means are the body and blood, soul and Divinity of Christ closer to me than at the moment of Holy Communion. To one who loves there is natural concomitant of joy in the close and intimate companionship of Jesus, though His abiding is known only through the eyes of faith. The livelier is our faith, the better is He seen and enjoyed. This delight of Holy Communion is not in any sense perception, nor in any sense emotion. It is a joy in the innermost soul that perceives and in perceiving loves. Joy was the purpose of Christ's coming. "Behold," said the angels to the shepherds of Bethlehem, "we bring you tidings of great joy. . . . This day is born to you a Saviour who is Christ the Lord." Each Holy Communion is a renewal of His coming and of the joy which he came to give. Jesus gave the word of His Father, which He was, for the purpose of giving joy to mankind. "I have given them thy word. . . . These things I speak in the world, that they may have my joy filled in themselves" (John xvii. 14, 13). He stressed the effect of His word to the Apostles: "These things I have spoken to you, that my joy may be in you, and your joy may be filled" (ibid. xv. 11). In Holy Communion Jesus becomes the Word Incarnate within us. In the secrecy and quiet of our own hearts He can speak His very personal message to the soul, and increase its delight in His transforming truth. St. Thomas declares that the effect of the Eucharist is to transform and inebriate with God.

7

HOLY DISPOSITIONS

It is true that the effects of Holy Communion come directly from Christ Himself. It is all His work within the soul. Grace is received "*ex opere operato*". But the working of the Sacrament is not an automatic thing. It undoubtedly gives some grace to every soul, because the soul must be in the state of grace to receive it worthily, and is therefore capable of receiving an increase of life. But the Eucharist is a sacrament of the living, and the more it becomes a living thing in us by our co-operation, the greater is its power of sanctification. We must speak therefore of our good dispositions before we receive, in the moment of reception, and during His time of real physical presence in the soul. The importance of such considerations is easily seen. The principal effect of the Sacrament is an increase of charity, but charity is something between two. It cannot be one-sided, since of its nature it is mutual. If it is to increase, it must do so in both. The Charity of Christ cannot increase in our regard, since it is infinite love. But its measure in us must be measured by a corresponding love in ourselves. The more we love the more is the Heart of Jesus opened to us. He will not force His love on us. We must open our own hearts, that He may take possession more fully in an increase of His love. If we come to Holy Communion, more or less mechanically, with cold hearts untouched by the magnitude of our privilege, with hearts attached to our faults, with bitterness in them, or full of pre-occupations about worldly things, we cannot expect to receive the full effects of this sacrament. It is true that it gives grace to all, but it gives this grace in proportion to our own dispositions.

In the Dialogues already referred to, St. Catherine of Siena describes in a significant metaphor the different dispositions of communicants and the variety of effect of the Sacrament. She continues to speak in the voice of the Eternal Father. "If thou hast a light, and the whole world should come to thee in order to take a light from it, the light itself does not diminish, and yet each person has it all. It is true that every one participates more or less in this light, according to the substance into which each one receives the fire. Suppose there are many who bring their candles, one weighing an ounce, others two or six ounces, or a pound, or even more, and light them in the flame; in each candle whether large or small is the whole light, that is to say the heat, the colour and the flame. Nevertheless you would judge that he whose candle weighed an ounce has less light than he whose candle weighed a pound. Now the same thing happens to those who receive this sacrament. Each one carries his own candle, that is the holy desire with which he receives this sacrament, which of itself is without light, and lights it by receiving this sacrament."

The keynote of devotion St. Thomas declares to be thoughtfulness. To receive Holy Communion with a devout soul must depend on how much and how lovingly we think on the nature of this act of our religion. The thought uppermost in our minds must be that the Lord God of infinite majesty desires to be united with His creature—with the nothingness which we are. Who would dare to approach were it not for that desire of Him who is love. Because He does desire it infinitely in the tenderness of His love for us, "let us go with confidence to the throne of grace; that we may obtain mercy, and find grace in seasonable aid" (Heb. iv. 16). But before approaching I would wish to prepare His temple of my soul, and make it a little less unworthy of His abiding. But even that we cannot do of ourselves; so we ask for grace to receive Him in some way befitting His dignity. We have recourse especially to His Most Holy Mother, asking her to prepare us for the coming into our hearts of her own Son, as she in her immaculate purity was privileged to receive Him. We prepare best by looking forward to His coming, and knowing what He would most desire to see in us when He comes. Jesus seeks above all else our own love through the Eucharist. By our thoughtful preparation we endeavour to give Him signs of it before He comes. Just as a great personage is met with many banners bearing words of welcome before he arrives in the heart of the city, so should we wish to show Our Lord how welcome He will be

THE BODY OF THE LORD 199

by our expression of faith, confidence and love before
He enters our hearts. Outside the city of Jerusalem
they met Him with the waving of palm-leaves, strew-
ing their garments on the ground, and the singing of
their hosannas—so ought we to demonstrate the sincerity of our reception. We must detach ourselves from
the love of creatures, strip ourselves of self-love, repent
of our offences, not only by a good confession, but by
rooting out all that in any way displeases Him by the
amendment of our lives. An intense Christian living
is the best and only really sincere preparation for
Holy Communion. As already stressed, that act is not
an exercise of religion apart. It is life. It is itself
a more intense moment of Christian living in closer
union with Christ. So the preparation for it is in
living—the actual reception in intensifying, and the
thanksgiving in endeavouring to make fast the increase
of that life.

In the moment of reception of Holy Communion
all else is forgotten, except the one thing that is necessary—a welcoming in words, deep in the heart of love.
A Gaelic prayer taken down from a native speaker
expresses something of that idea of a loving welcome,
without in any way standardizing it, or demanding
that it should assume any formality of expression:
" Hail to Thee, O Body of Christ—Hail to Thee O
King of Hosts. Hail to Thee O Glorious Godhead.
Hail to Thee O true manhood. As Thou wert pleased,
O Christ to come under the cover of bread, Thy
whole body, heal my soul from every evil that is upon
me now. Hail to Thee, Blood and Flesh—Hail to
Thee, Food of grace—wash my sins in the blood of
Thy grace. Hail to Thee both man and God—guard
me from him that goeth about. May I receive Thee

at the hour of my death. O Trinity without end,
without beginning—neither let thy anger fall upon
me. Hail to Thee True Body, born of Mary Virgin—
By Thy being pierced, shedding waves of blood, Holy
Trinity grant us Thy sacraments—to-day and at our
death, and Amen."

That there should be a period of thanksgiving
follows from the nature of the act. The Encyclical
"*Immortale Dei*" on the Liturgy condemns those who
say that both Mass and Holy Communion end with the
dismissal of the "*Ita Missa Est*". Such people honour
the letter but not the spirit of the Sacrament and Sacrifice. It is true that the Post-Communion prayers are
acts of thanksgiving, and very appropriate. But the
Church wishes those who have received to spend some
time after the Mass in recollection and thanksgiving.
The allotted time of the real presence of Jesus Christ
in the soul occupies, according to St. Thomas Aquinas,
the most precious moments of our spiritual life. Then
He is all ours. The Holy Communion endures as long
as He is present sacramentally. Its act is the act of
eating, but the union caused by that act endures. It
would indeed be a strange mentality to leave Him all
alone in the house with no thought of entertaining the
"Sweet Guest of the soul". During the time at our
disposal we may have what St. Teresa calls a "heart to
heart talk with one Whom we know loves us". Love
is a very personal thing, especially the love of friendship which Our Lord desires for us, and from us.
"You are my friends." At no time is He so personally
ours as at Holy Communion, since it is that Divine
Person Who comes to us through His sacred Humanity.
During the precious moments of His presence we become closely united to Him in faith, though not in

vision either of His Divinity or of His Humanity, but love which is the perfection of that union knows no limitations, and can move beyond the veils of the sacrament and the obscurity of faith itself to attach ourselves to Him as He really is in Himself.   He comes to abide in us for a short while. It is for us to abide in Him.   "He that eateth my flesh and drinketh my blood, abideth in me and I in Him" (John vi. 57).

Seventh Chapter

COMMUNICATION OF THE BREAKING
OF BREAD

(Acts ii. 52)

1

BIRTH OF THE CHURCH

THE Upper Room that witnessed the last loving
testimony in His body and blood of the Saviour
was also the chosen place of the great fulfilment of
His promise of the Spirit. The Church was to take
the place of the visible Humanity of Christ, and, like
that assumed Humanity, it had first to be sanctified by
the Holy Ghost. That was the law of the Incarnation.
The angel said to Mary by way of elucidation of the
mystery—" The Holy Ghost shall come upon thee and
the power of the Most High shall overshadow thee.
And therefore also the Holy which shall be born of
thee shall be called the Son of God " (Luke i. 35). Just
as the Beloved Son assumed human nature from the
Father who created it in the womb of the Virgin
Mother, and in the Holy Ghost Who sanctified it and
fitted it for union in the Second Person, so also the
Church, which is the Mystic Body of Christ, had in a
manner to be assumed by God. The Eternal Father
ratified the mandate and power given it by His
Beloved Son as a continuation of His own mission

entrusted by Him to the Word Whom He had sent.
"As thou hast sent me into the world, I also have sent
them into the world" (John xvii. 18). The Holy
Ghost Who launched the Incarnate Word upon His
way in the fulness of grace and holiness, was also to
be the launching power of the Mystic Body which
was to succeed Him. This sanctifying of the Church
could not take place until Christ had ascended to His
Father (cf. John vii. 39). Once glorified and en-
throned as man on the Right Hand of His Father in
the triumph of His accomplishment, He merited the
sending of that mutual breathing of love between
Himself and the Father into the appointed agency
of His salvation of mankind unto the end of the
world. From the Upper Room the new agency of the
Church issued forth on its redeeming and sanctifying
mission.

Pentecost was the triumph of the Sacred Humanity
of Jesus Christ. The Mystic Body, "endued with
power from on high", had extended the efficacy of
Christ's Humanity, as the instrument of His Divinity,
unto the whole earth. During His life on earth Jesus
had prepared this society of His Church for the great
day of its Pentecost. He had called His Apostles. He
had organized and instructed them. He gave them
definite powers of transmitting His own life of grace
to men. Finally, He had given them the mandate
unto all nations, and for all time. So established, this
group of believers with Mary His Mother still abiding
with them, and the Apostles at their head, had but to
await the final impulse of the Holy Ghost. The Spirit
was the sealing of the compact between Father and
Son for the salvation of the human race. It was a
confirming of the souls of the Apostles that they might

salt the earth unto a newness of life in Christ. "The Paraclete, the Holy Ghost, whom the Father will send in my name, he will teach you all things, and bring all things to your mind, whatsoever I shall have said to you " (John xiv. 26).

The first witnessing to the truth of this new agency of life which emerged from the Upper Room is of the greatest possible importance, as showing forth proof of the perfect continuity of the Catholic Church of our day with the original apostolic society of the first century of Christianity. It serves also to emphasize the great realities of our religion, and to stir up our devotion to these very realities which conquered the world of long ago, and can conquer it again. From the moment the Apostles issued forth from the Upper Room with their followers, the Church was a perfect society, that is to say, she possessed there and then all that she required for the accomplishment of her purpose, and possessed it abundantly. The Church did not and could not acquire new powers as she proceeded along the course of her history. She was the recipient of the fulness of Christ, Who said: "I am come that they may have life, and may have it more abundantly " (John x. 10). It is evident from the beginning that the "little flock", headed by St. Peter, the first Pope, is conscious of its powers, and in complete agreement on their plan for the work of eternal salvation. It sets out straight away as the appointed mouthpiece of God and of Jesus Christ.

FIRST PREACHING AND PRACTICE

As was to be expected, St. Peter took the initiative on Pentecost Sunday in the launching of the new religion. His first sermon brought conviction and conversion to three thousand souls. This earliest Christian manifesto is of the utmost importance. It proclaimed faith in the Divinity of Jesus Christ, condemned to death by the Jews, but risen again, and showing forth power in the Apostles on whom He had sent His Spirit. "This Jesus hath God raised again, whereof all we are witnesses. Being exalted therefore by the right hand of God, and having received of the Father the promise of the Holy Ghost, he hath poured out this which you see and hear" (Acts ii. 32, 33). The Apostle clearly affirms in whose abiding power they are sent. Jesus is no longer visible, but He is still really present in the agency which He had appointed to carry on His work. The Apostles attribute nothing to themselves. This is obvious a few days later at the healing of the lame man at the porch of the Temple. "Why look upon us, as if by our strength and power we had made this man to walk." St. Peter proceeded to drive home the lesson of the miracle. It is a token to all of the glory of Jesus Who was crucified, but rose again as they were witnesses. "The faith that is by him has given this perfect soundness in the sight of you all." St. Paul later expresses the same truth in calling himself a coadjutor of God. "Neither he that planteth is anything, nor he that watereth; but God that giveth the increase" (1 Cor. iii. 7). The first and most fundamental truth which was evident from the beginning is that Jesus abides in His Church in conformty wth His promise: "Behold I am with you all days, even to the consummation of the world " (Matt. xxviii. 20). Christ clearly remains the centre from which the new life is diffused. Power goes out from Him through the secondary agency of His Church.

There is also unmistakable evidence from the very beginning of a well-defined discipline of Christian observances, which are immediately made a condition of participation in the promise of the Father through Jesus Christ. Peter said to the first converts on Pentecost Sunday: "Do penance, and be baptised every one of you in the name of Jesus for the remission of your sins, and you shall receive the gift of the Holy Ghost" (Acts ii. 38). Faith in the teaching of the Apostles, who spoke in Christ's name, followed by repentance and Baptism, and Confirmation, led the first Christians into the heart of the new religion of the Mass and Holy Communion. Faith demanded accepting Christ as Divine, and the Apostles as His ambassadors in unerring truth. It demanded a reconciling of their lives with Christ's teaching and commands. Thus the Apostles instructed the first converts in the way of Christian living and the Christian practice of the sacraments, of which the Most Holy Eucharist held the dominating position. By the cleansing of Baptism, and the strengthening of their souls in the giving of the Spirit, they received a certain gift of perseverance. Briefly their new life is summed up: "They, therefore, that received his word were baptised. . . . And they were persevering in the doctrine of the Apostles, and in the communication of the breaking of bread, and in prayers " (ibid. 41, 42).

From the outset the Christian Church formed a group apart, distinguished by their most essential act of worship, which had been delivered to the Apostles at the Last Supper. Joy and gladness became characteristic of the members of this new group. "Rejoice in the Lord always," St. Paul admonished them, "again I say to you rejoice" (Phil. iv. 4). In Christ they had found firm anchorage, and a great freedom from the rigidity of the old law, made still worse by their pharisaical masters. "Christ has made us free" (Gal. iv. 31). But that newly found joy arose principally from their consciousness of close union with Jesus Christ in faith and love, and more certainly still in the Most Blessed Eucharist, which brought Him living and entire into their hearts. Sanctifying grace which flowed from the Apostolic power bore its fullest fruits in those first followers of Christ. The instinct of grace in imitation of Christ was strong in them. They sold all their possessions, and lived a life of perfect charity amongst themselves. This ardour of charity found its strongest source in the Mass and Holy Communion. "Continuing daily with one accord in the temple, and breaking bread from house to house, they took their meat with gladness and simplicity of heart" (ibid. 46). The meat here referred to was surely not "the meat that perisheth", but that which "endureth unto life everlasting". In the Breaking of Bread, or the Eucharist, they found fulfilled the promise which many of them had heard by the Lake of Galilee: "My flesh is meat indeed; and my blood is drink indeed. He that eateth my flesh, and drinketh my blood abideth in me: and I in him" (John vi. 47). Clearly from Apostolic times the Mass is the centre and heart of the Church and of Christian living.

THE ABIDING CHRIST

The overwhelming influence of the Blessed Eucharist in forming the life and spirit of the early Church can only be understood in relation to the doctrine, which stands out so prominently in all the early documents, of the abiding presence of Jesus, and of the power of His Sacred humanity within the body of the Church. The certainty of this presence gave the Apostles courage to face death itself, and endowed them with confidence in the power of their word which was the word of Christ. They knew that their labour was not in vain in the Lord (cf. 1 Cor. xv. 58). The Acts tell of them: "They spoke the word of God with confidence." All the Christians prayed in the moment of stress that this confidence might be given to them. They asked God that Christ might exercise His power through them: "By stretching forth thy hand to cures and signs and wonders, to be done by the name of thy holy Son, Jesus" (Acts iv. 30). St. Peter emphasized the effect of that presence in the souls of those who consented to the truth which they were commissioned to preach. "Be penitent therefore, and be converted . . . that when the times of refreshment shall come from the presence of the Lord, and he shall send him who hath been preached unto you, Jesus Christ" (Acts iii. 20). In this reference to "times of refreshment" he may well be alluding in particular to the reception of the Eucharist, whither his word led them. Later in his epistles he speaks of his apostolic mission as a "making known of the power and presence of our

Lord Jesus Christ"(2 Pet. i. 16). Without doubt that "power and presence" was the sustaining factor in the early Church.

St. John speaks of the Apostles remembering that Jesus called His body a temple (John ii. 22). So well did they remember it that the idea formed a central point in their teaching. They availed of it to emphasize how closely knit were Christians to the body of Christ. Constantly each soul in grace is called a temple of God. The whole Church is alluded to as His temple. But that temple is but a continuing of the temple of Christ's own body. That body pervades the entire building by its virtue. Christ is the "living stone" in Whom the entire fabric of mankind is "built up" into "a spiritual house". (1 Pet. ii. 4, 5). St. Paul stresses the same doctrine. Jesus is "Chief corner stone", "in whom all the building, being framed together, groweth up into a holy temple in the Lord. In whom you also are built together into an habitation of God in the Spirit" (Eph. ii. 20-22). "You are God's building. . . . Know you not that you are the temple of God" (1 Cor. iii. 9, 16).

St. Paul further develops this idea of the indwelling Christ, so that there is no longer a question of temple compared with temple, but of identification of body with body. He calls Christ "the saviour of his body" (Eph. v. 23). He became the saviour by dying for it. "Christ loved the Church, and delivered himself up for it; that he might sanctify it, cleansing it by the laver of water in the word of life" (ibid. 25, 26). Christ must love that Church for the very reason that it is His own body. "No man ever hateth his own flesh, but nourisheth and cherisheth it, as also Christ doth the church" (ibid. 29). We cannot but surmise

here again that St. Paul had in mind the nourishing of
the Mystic Body of the Church through Christ's gift
of His body and blood in the Holy Communion.   He
proceeds to push this identity of body with body still
farther by declaring: "We are members of his body,
of his flesh, and of his bones" (ibid. 30).   It is true that
this teaching belongs to the order of mystic theology,
but it is not less real for that reason.   The sanctified,
crucified, and now glorified flesh of the man-God,
which linked the Incarnate Word with the human race
by its assumption, is still the link between man and
God.   The process begun in the Incarnation continues
in all flesh and blood within the Church.   By the virtue
transmitted from it, "the whole body, being compacted and fitly joined together . . . maketh increase
of the body" (Eph. iv. 16).

That the power of Christ's body should still be
operative was not a startling doctrine in the minds of
the Apostles.   They had witnessed virtue going forth
from it during the years of His public life.   He did
not need to be visibly present for the effectiveness of
its power.   They had seen the power of His word go
out to the son of the ruler in Cana.   This man desired Christ to go down to his house to heal his dying
son, believing that His presence there would be necessary.   Jesus said to him: "Go thy way, thy son liveth"
(John iv. 50).   They discovered that the son had re-
covered at the same moment in which Jesus had pronounced these words.   St. Thomas' teaching on the
nature of what is called instrumental causality ampli-
fies and explains this primitive doctrine of the power
of Christ and His Church.   We are dealing with the
question of the giving of grace.   Being entirely supernatural, only God can give grace as of Himself.   Yet

God may employ an agency in this giving.   Such an
agency, and the most perfect of all by its nature, is the
Sacred humanity of Christ.   It is what Aquinas calls
a conjoined instrument of the Divinity, because it is
substantially united to the Divine Person of the Son.
That humanity is an organ of the Divinity according
to St. Damascene.   But the agency of grace does not
stop at Christ's Humanity.   He willed to have other
agencies, namely, the ministers of His Church, in
giving, and all souls in receiving and co-operating.
"The stronger is a conjoined instrument," says the
Angelic Doctor, "the more virtue can it bestow on a
separated instrument, as the hand gives to the stick."
In this way the Divine action of the Divinity, moving
through the Humanity of Christ, moves in turn into
the living body of the Church, and so the order of
causality is completed, but the series of causes moves
always as one.

   It is evident then that the Mystic Body of the Church
is not just a society endued with the vague spirit of
its founder, as are merely human organizations.   It is
imbued with the virtue of Christ's own body.   Stored
up, as it were, in the Humanity of Christ, through His
infinite merits, is the fulness of holiness and of life.
He poured out that fulness into the Church, and ever
continues its outpouring, so that the Church itself is
called the fulness of Christ—"The fulness of him,
who is filled all in all" (Eph. i. 23).   All that Christ
did, especially by His supreme sacrifice of the Cross,
the faithful, in a manner, did also; since He did it for
them, and in time actually works it out in them.   St.
Paul explains this solidarity of the whole body in the
enlivening Head.   "The charity of Christ presseth us,
judging this that one died for all, then all are dead

(died): that they also who live, may not now live unto themselves, but unto him who died for them" (2 Cor. v. 14, 15). Christ's death is made actual in each one at Baptism: "We are baptised in His death" (Rom. vi. 3). From out of that strong and sanctifying death of the body that suffered and died new life was given to the world: "Who in his own self bore our sins in his body upon the tree; that we being dead to sins, should live to justice, by whose stripes you are healed" (1 Pet. ii. 24).

In the newly founded Church where doctrinally such importance was attributed to the presence of Christ, where the Mystic Body is regarded in such close relationship with His physical body, it was only natural that the actual real presence in the Eucharist embodied and in a manner guaranteed the fulness of Christ's indwelling, and gave assurance of the continuance of His holy action in the Church. Through the Sacrament of His love, not only do Christians form one body with Him; they form even one bread. "We being many, are one bread, one body, all that partake of one bread" (1 Cor. x. 17). Devotion in the Church to the Sacred Humanity, and in that Humanity to its supreme redeeming work of the Passion, inevitably riveted attention to the renewal of the sacrifice in the "Breaking of Bread". "The chalice of benediction which we bless, is it not the communion in the blood of Christ" (ibid. 16). What was so doctrinally real concerning the Divine communication of life through the conjoined instrument of the body of Christ, especially in His Passion and death, became also the dynamic centre in the development of life and liturgy. The "Chalice of Benediction" became the natural focus point of Christian ritual, the heart of all Christian assemblies, the living core of its devotional life in prayer and praise. The main purpose of the early Christian meetings was to eat "the Lord's Supper". Around the altar they learned Christian life and prayer, because at these gatherings the Church found its living expression of the truth which was within it. There with the living substance of the Bread of Life, the living word of Christian faith and conduct was also broken to them. The Roman Catacombs bear remarkable testmony to this centralizing of thought and life in the mystery of the Eucharist. These early cemeteries and places of worship are adorned with the earliest Christian art, which concentrates especially on symbolizing the sacred ritual of the *"Fractio Panis"*—the Breaking of Bread. Though in the first centuries of persecution the mystery of the Eucharist was kept concealed under the strict "Discipline of the Secret", to guard against misunderstanding and possible profanation, there existed a very remarkable liberty both in its use and reservation. We know how it was brought secretly, even by laymen, to the Christian martyrs in the Roman prisons to give them strength in their hour of suffering and death. There was also a practice of carrying the Sacred Host in a clean white cloth to be reserved in Christian homes. This practice may well have arisen from the early custom in the times of the Apostles of celebrating the Holy Sacrifice "from house to house". We are not surprised at these primitive practices. In our own days of persecution, such as has been witnessed in Russia, Mexico and Spain, the Adorable Sacrament secretly consecrated became the comfort of many a modern martyr for Christ. Both the ancient observance and the new bespeak the mind of the Church in attaching so essential a part to the Blessed Eucharist in the life and death of every Christian.

4

THE CENTRE OF THE SACRAMENTS

Study of the developments of ritual of the other sacraments in relation to the Blessed Eucharist, both in primitive practice and down the course of centuries to our present day, provides evidence of the importance of the Mass in the complete life-giving sacramental system bestowed on the Church by Christ. We have already seen how, in the earliest days of the Church, repentance, Baptism, and Confirmation led the Christian into the "Communication of the Breaking of Bread". These first assemblies provided the natural opportunity, both as regards place and time, for the conferring of all the sacraments, and much of that practice is retained up to the present day. Later liturgical documents, which have been preserved, and which show the development of Christian ritual life, emphasize what obtained from the beginning and gradually became the set practice of the Church. The first Missals were known as Sacramentaries, because with the Mass Rite were included also the rites of the other sacraments. St. Augustine and some of the Fathers of the early Church refer to the celebration of the Holy Sacrifice as the "Accomplishing of the sacraments".

Such a centring of all things holy in the Mass, which is the holiest of all, was not by any complex arrangement, but through the instinct of a believing and living Church, which shows forth unerringly her deep sense of the fitness of things. All grace is found in the Passion and death of the Divine Saviour, and comes out from it, so also in that death renewed ritually on the altar are all the other sacraments discovered, either as leading into or emerging from it. Each sacrament confers its own particular grace of union, or of reunion in Christ. Taken as a whole, they provide the fulness of life in the individual soul and in the Church as a corporate body. The first five sacraments are directed to the perfection of personal holiness in attachment of the soul to Christ. Baptism is the gateway, the birth of the soul in the likeness of Christ through water and the Holy Ghost. Confirmation further seals that pact with God of the Christian soul, giving it a strength against the external enemies who war on that soul. But the mainstay of the Christian's interior life of grace, and the secret of his spiritual growth and development, come from the Sacrament which more than any other unites his body and soul in God through the Eucharistic presence of Jesus on the Altar. This close union is already eternal life begun. It achieves the purpose of all the sacraments. This sacrament is meant to provide constant nourishment along the way of life. There is nothing worse for the soul than to deprive itself of this food by deliberate mortal sin. Christ in His love and mercy found a way to reopen the door to His Divine sacramental nourishment in the sacrament of Penance, in which sin is blotted out and grace restored. From the Mass Jesus goes out to console the sick and dying. The Holy oils bring their special comfort, and our preparedness to meet God is finally completed by receiving the Viaticum, the Victim of the Sacrifice Who paid the price of our eternal

life.   The remaining two sacraments are concerned
with the good of the whole Church as a society of the
faithful in Christ.   Holy Orders, of its nature, is entirely
ordered to the Blessed Eucharist.   The conferring of
these minor and major Orders brings the priest-to-be
by an ordered ascent ever closer to the altar of God.
The sacrament of Matrimony, which confers a special
grace of family life and love unto the building up of
the Mystic Body, has also a very close association with
the Holy Sacrifice.   The Blessed Eucharist, and because of it the Sacrament of Penance, are the only two
sacraments which are unlimited in their frequency of
reception.   The other sacraments are either received
only once, or are limited to special occasions and neces-
sities.   The Holy Communion, with Penance keeping
open the way to its reception, is the noblest of them
all, because it contains Christ Himself the eternal life
of the soul.   For this reason St. Vincent Ferrer declares: "As the sun is the centre around which the
planets revolve, and is the source from which they
receive their light, so also is the Eucharist the vitalizing
centre of the sacramental system."

In the early Church the externals of worship laid
greater emphasis on the place occupied by the Holy
Mass amidst these appointed sources of grace.   The
exigencies of modern life have made the preservation
of many incidental parts of the Sacramentary difficult
to maintain.   Persecutions which drove the Mass
underground, and later out into the distant hills of the
Mass Rocks, did much to deprive men of the full expression of the Liturgical life of the Church.   Nevertheless, the Ritual of to-day preserves much of the
ancient practice, and it is the want of instruction that
has obscured its deeper meaning, especially in relation

to the Most Holy Sacrifice. A few observations regarding the more salient characteristics in this respect of the Liturgy may help towards a fuller appreciation.

Baptism was always regarded as the gateway to the Mass. The ancient practice of dismissing the Catechumens before the Offertory is now discontinued. But a relic of this primitive practice remains in the ceremony of the Blessing of the Font, which occurs on Holy Saturday and on the Vigil of Pentecost. The Blessing is part of the ceremony of the Holy Sacrifice, and is made after the singing of the prophecies. Normally the two great ceremonial Baptisms of the year occurred at this time, and the ritual still enjoins the officiating priest to baptise if there are present those to be baptised. The place in the ritual still emphasizes that through water and Holy Ghost we have access to the Altar of Christian Sacrifice. Four Sacraments use oil as either essential matter, as in Confirmation, Holy Orders, and Extreme Unction, or as auxiliary to the essential matter as in Baptism. The three oils used in the administration of these sacraments, of Catechumens, of Chrism, and of the Sick, are solemnly consecrated in the Mass of Holy Thursday by the Bishop of each Diocese. This sanctifying of the Holy oils takes place after the Consecration of the Mass, thereby connecting them and giving them the virtue of the sacrificial act of Jesus Christ, which is the source of all sanctification. Thus it is seen that all the tangible matter used in the administration of the sacraments is made ready by association with the Holy Mass, just as all matter was in a manner assumed by Christ in His Incarnation, and rendered holy by the sacrifice of His body and blood on Calvary. The Mass in Christ is a lifting of all creation back to God.

The liturgical prayers of the Mass, especially during the seasons of Lent, Easter and Pentecost, frequently refer to the needs of the faithful in respect of various sacraments, particularly those of Regeneration, Penance and Confirmation. It should be remembered that originally the Baptismal ritual began with Lent, in so far as these weeks were a time of intense preparation of the Catechumens by prayer and instruction. This preparation reached its climax on Holy Saturday, or later on the Vigil of Pentecost, with the actual administration of the sacrament. In the early Church, also, Confirmation followed Baptism without any delay. The present-day anointing of the forehead with Chrism at the end of the ceremony would seem to preserve a record of this older practice. The Missal still preserves in the Mass the fervent prayers of priest and people for these Catechumens. For instance, on Good Friday we still pray: "Increase the faith and understanding of our Catechumens, that, reborn in the Baptismal fountain, they may be numbered among the children of your adoption." At Easter and Pentecost the special addition to the prayer "*Hanc Igitur*" of the Canon directs the special attention of the Sacrifice: "For those whom Thou hast pleased to make to be born again of water and of the Holy Ghost."

The time of Lent is, above all else, a time of repentance. It was customary for many centuries to devote these forty days to rigorous penances, even of a public nature. Penitents dressed in sackcloth, and with ashes on their heads, remained prostrate at the steps of the Church during the Holy Mass in token of their unworthiness to take part. Within the Church special prayers were offered that they might get the grace of true repentance. The great reconciliation through the sacrament of Penance came with Holy Thursday—the day of the Last Supper. On that day they were again admitted to union with the faithful in the Most Holy Sacrifice. Various references to this reconciliation are still to be found in the Missal. These very brief findings may be concluded by a reference to the ceremonies of Holy Saturday in St. John Lateran's, the Mother Church of the world, which still bear witness to more ancient observances. On that morning there is a special ritual in which all the sacraments are administered, before and during the Most Holy Sacrifice, as a full expression of the Liturgical life of the Mystic Body.

5

THE NUPTIAL MASS

The Sacrament of Matrimony, by reason of its special association with the Mass, is deserving of particular attention. Though the Sacrament itself consists in the brief formula of mutual consent in regard to conjugal rights, pronounced by the contracting parties, and can be solemnized outside the Holy Sacrifice, yet there is every reason for believing that the Eucharistic ritual received this sacrament, as it did all the others, into its holy action. The early Christian meetings "in the communication of the breaking of bread" provided also opportunities for receiving what St. Paul calls "the great sacrament" (Eph. v. 32). Tertullian in the early third century speaks of "the oblation which confirms matrimony". All the ancient Roman sacramentaries contain forms of what is now known as the Nuptial Mass, or the "Mass for Bride-groom and Bride".

From the outset, marriage, restored by Christ to its original purity and sanctity, and raised by Him to the dignity of a sacrament, loomed large in the life of the Church. Christ made all things new, including the marital union, which, declares Pope Pius XI, "is the principle and foundation of domestic society, and therefore of all human intercourse". The Epistles of St. Paul bear ample evidence how awful was the cor-ruption of Jew and Gentile, and how great was the task which confronted the early Church of raising the married state to the sacramental dignity conferred on it by Christ. But no effort at instruction could have equalled in effectiveness the placing of that contract of love in the ritual of the Holy Sacrifice. Through the Blessed Sacrament there was imparted a blessing of the High Priest and Victim, Whose Church was called a bride, whose linking with the human race in the mystery of the Incarnation was styled a holy wedlock, and Whose grace was in His own parable compared to a nuptial banquet. For that reason St. Paul could lay down the Christian standard of married love: "Hus-bands love your wives, as Christ also loved the Church, and delivered himself up for it" (Eph. v. 25).

In the beginning God bestowed on man the strong power of the natural love of the married life. It is the strongest of all natural loves, so much so that it induces a man to "leave Father and Mother and cleave to his wife". Because it is the strongest, it should of its nature also be the most enduring. By delivering Himself up unto the death of the Cross, Christ merited a renewal of strength in that love by raising it into the supernatural order, and consecrating it to God in a holy sacrament. No better source of blessing could be imagined for that mutual married love than to bring it back to the source on the altar whence it sprung. To-day, as in the days of ancient Rome, every available spiritual force must be marshalled to stem the tide of corruption which threatens to engulf human civilization by disrupting its foundation in the heart of the family life. Christian marriage and the Christian family are the salt of the earth. By linking both with Holy Sacrifice in their inception, and by maintaining that strong link throughout the years of married life, there is found the surest guarantee of the enduring love which alone can bring success to this great venture of life.

The Nuptial Mass follows the actual administration of the Sacrament. In some respects it is akin to the Mass of priestly Ordination, in so far as the Rite of the Holy Sacrifice is interrupted in its normal procedure in order that a special blessing may be called down through the Victim of the altar on the new life just begun. The entire Proper of the Mass is devoted to instruction and petition on behalf of the newly married. The Introit is taken from the Book of Tobias, and repeats the form used at the marriage, arranged by his good angel, of the young Tobias to the daughter of Raguel: "May the God of Israel join you together; and may he be with you, who was merciful to the two children; and now, O Lord, make them bless Thee more fully." The Prayer petitions that what has been done by the ministry may be abundantly fulfilled with the Divine blessing. The Epistle gives the instruction of St. Paul to the Ephesians comparing love of husband to love of Christ, and his headship in the family to the headship of Christ over the Church. It

P

is followed by a very beautiful Gradual: "Thy wife shall be as a fruitful vine on the sides of thy house. Thy children as olive plants round thy table. May the Lord send you help from the sanctuary, and defend you out of Sion." The Gospel relates Christ's teaching on the indissolubility of marriage. Its closing words emphasize that the marriage union is from God and belongs to God, not to man. "What therefore God has joined together, let no man put asunder." The Offertory places all dependence in the hands of God. The Secret prayer refers to the gifts offered for the sacred law of marriage, asking God to dispose according to His will, that which He instituted in His bounty. The Post Communion asks for the blessing of children. The final prayer petitions for lasting peace for those whom God has joined in lawful union.

The Nuptial blessing proper takes place immediately after the "Our Father". The petitions of the blessing seem to be added to the general petitions of the Lord's prayer. The Celebrant turns towards husband and wife that his prayer may seem more especially for them. "Let us pray: Be appeased, O Lord, by our humble prayers, and do thou please assist this institution of marriage established by Thyself for the increase of mankind; so that what is joined together by Thine authority, may be preserved by Thine aid." The second part of this blessing is for the woman alone—"Thy handmaid about to be joined in wedlock, who pleads for thy defence and protection. May it be to her a yoke of love and peace; faithful and chaste, may she marry in Christ." There follows a list of the great women of the Old Testament who are a true example of perfect marriage. Other strong virtues are asked for her from God, and the blessing concludes with a wish: "May they both see their children's children to the third and fourth generation, and may they thus reach the old age which they desire." Again before the Last Blessing the Celebrant turns to the newly wed, and repeats the blessing of Tobias and concludes with a wish for a long life with happiness of children, and thereafter life everlasting.

What is true of the source of the wedding blessing is also true of its continuance. Matrimony is unique in that it is the only sacrament in which the laity are privileged to enter into the sacramental ministry. The husband and wife are ministers to themselves of the sacrament. That means that in the moment of their mutual consent they are in direct touch as instruments of grace with the Sacred Humanity of Jesus Christ. The Mass and the Holy Communion binds them constantly to that Sacred Humanity, and maintains that first contact in a continuance of the virtue which by their own words they drew from it in the beginning.

Married love spells devotion and self-sacrifice of both parties until death. On these twin virtues the future fabric of the Christian home must rest. They are an indispensable condition of lasting union. In the Mass is the consummation of devotion and self-sacrifice. Jesus prayed on the night of the Institution for the good fruit of His Passion and death: "That they may be made perfect in one." When He declared marriage to be indissoluble, He quoted the words of Genesis which proclaimed to man God's design: "They shall be two in one flesh." In a far higher sense that also is the formula of the Eucharistic Banquet. Through the Holy Communion we are truly joined to His Body, and become what St. Paul declares:

"Flesh of his flesh, and bone of his bone" (Eph. v. 30). The Blessed Sacrament for the married is the constant source of renewed grace in a strengthening of love like unto the love of Christ for His Church. To live with one another "for better, for worse, for richer, for poorer, in sickness and in health", amidst the trials inseparable from human life on earth, the frailties of human nature, the need of constant forgivingness, requires, at least for its perfection, the nourishment of the living Jesus. The ring which symbolizes mutual unending love requires the support of the giving and forgiving Saviour, "Who when he was reviled did not revile, when he suffered threatened not, but delivered himself to him that judged him unjustly" (1 Pet. ii. 23).

The natural end of marriage is the procreation and the education of children. But the Sacrament of Matrimony raises this purpose to a still higher level. The children of a Christian marriage belong not only to their father and mother of earth, but through grace and parental care even to their Father of heaven in Jesus Christ His Son, through the motherhood of His Church, which is symbolized in the Motherhood of Mary. The Eucharistic marriage leads to the Eucharistic family. The love in which children are begotten becomes the love in which they are reared. The influence of the sacrificial action of the Mass and Holy Communion passes on as the most precious inheritance with which parents can enrich their children, by making them "Heirs indeed of God and joint heirs with Christ" (Rom. viii. 17).

6

THE INTERIOR LIFE

It would be a grave error to consider our Catholic religion as a matter of externals only. Religion is a virtue within the soul, consisting in a well-ordered disposition of mind and will in all that pertains to the worship of God. It is this inner force that seeks to express itself, both inwardly in prayer and outwardly in external acts, which it vivifies and directs to God. Jesus condemned the externalism of the Pharisees in the words of the Prophet Isaias: "This people honoureth me with their lips, but their heart is far from me, and in vain do they worship me" (Mark vii. 6, 7). Like all the infused virtues, religion thrives on its own exercise. Its acts merit, according to the progressive disposition of the soul, an increase from God, Who is the author of grace.

Christ's life was filled with an intense virtue of religion, of thirst for justice, which found its complete satisfaction in the holocaust of Himself to the worship of His Father. In the Holy Sacrifice He unites us with that supreme and most perfect act. The more accurately our own inner dispositions harmonize with His, the more perfect becomes our own worship, clothed, as it were, in the merits of His death, and, consequently, the higher are we raised into the perfection of the inner order of the soul to God. In this raising true sanctity and self-perfection consists. "God," declares St. Augustine, "is a kind and not a needy exactor; for He does not grow rich on our payments, but makes them who pay him grow rich in Him."

The first and primary act of religion, which is the motive power of all the others, is an interior disposition of the will in a promptness of its service which is called devotion. This initial motive power is frequently confused with a certain emotionalism or devout feeling which belong rather to the sense faculties. The word is also used for certain precise exercises of piety, as when we speak of evening devotions. On the other hand, we rightly speak of a man devoted to his work or his profession. In this case, the word conveys earnestness, an absorption born of interest, and, consequently, a willing surrender of time and energy to proficiency in himself and perfection in his work. This also is its true meaning in relation to religion, which is the profession of every man, and especially of every Christian. It betrays itself, and becomes active in a like earnestness and solicitude for the glory of God, and makes prompt our attendance to the duties of our State in His Divine sight.

It is this same inner promptness of the will which gives vitality to our appreciation of the Mass. St. Thomas says that devotion is fed by meditation or contemplation, and especially by thinking on Jesus Christ. His Sacred Humanity is the "guiding hand" to the knowledge and love of Divine things. The way into the Holy Sacrifice must be found through consideration of all that it contains. The bare fulfilling of the Sunday precept, and the too evident lack of devotion during its celebration, are due to failure, either through ignorance, or want of faith. The Mass is itself a perfect "guiding hand" into the sanctifying mysteries of God. We are associated with the priest on the altar

in prayer, whereby he draws us onward into its sacrificial centre, in which Christ's own prompt will in His
Passion and death can become ours.   In the Mass
Christ leads us along His own path, and plunges us
into His obedience, that we may emerge with still
readier wills ourselves for the glory of His Father.

It is already evident how well the Holy Sacrifice
deserves its claim to be called the centre of the organic
life of the Church in the living acting headship of
Christ.   What is true of the whole is also true of each
part.   From the altar of Christ's own sacrifice, life
radiates into each member of the Mystic Body in the
form of grace, the infused virtues, and the gifts of the
Holy Ghost.   The virtue of religion is not an independent virtue.   It is powerfully aided by the theological virtues.   It is only by faith that we know what
the Mass contains.   Every access to the altar is a
renewal of that faith, and at least a preparing of our
souls for further increase of that fundamental virtue.
To believe in Jesus Christ raised aloft in the hands
of the priest under the appearance of so humble a
substance as bread, to confess to that living blood in
the chalice under the appearance of wine, requires a
complete denial of the evidence of the external senses.
Faith is all the more perfect because of its so blind
consent.   "By sight, and touch, and taste we fail to
reach Thee.   By hearing alone does faith consent"
("*Adoro Te*").

Hope, being reliance on the word of God's goodness,
also works through religion in the praise of that goodness.   The second theological virtue takes its stand
like the virtue of religion in the thought of the
nothingness which we are.   It delights in our conse-
quent dependence.   Every expression of religion is

an implied act of hope, since it approaches God confident in His Divine goodness. The most outstanding evidence we have of that goodness lies in the Crucifixion. That is the reply of the God of mercy to man's infidelity. He sent His Son to be a redemption for all. The Mass contains the continued evidence of that mercy and love in the same sacrifice of Calvary. "Let us go therefore with confidence to the throne of grace; that we may obtain mercy, and find grace in seasonable aid" (Heb. iv. 16). By the very nature of things, there can be no more acceptable time to ask confidently for all our needs, than when we can join them to the desires of Christ on the altar. Then we truly ask in His name—the name of the anointed High Priest and Victim. The Mass most certainly engenders fresh hope in the souls of all sinners, as being the wide open doorway to His mercy and love.

7

ABOVE ALL CHARITY

"Greater love than this no man hath, that a man lay down his life for his friends" (John xv. 13). The Mass continues that supreme act of Christ's friendship with man. It is called the Sacrament of love, because it is love that makes Him present on the altar—the same love which nailed Him to the Cross. All the love which Jesus poured out on His fellow men during his visible presence on earth is found pent up in His Sacred Heart physically present through Consecration. For those who see with the eyes of their faith, herein is love beyond the power of human intelligence. "That

Christ may dwell by faith in your hearts: that being rooted and founded in charity, you may be able to comprehend with all the saints, what is the breadth, and length, and height, and depth, to know also the charity of Christ which surpasseth all knowledge" (Eph. iii. 17-19). "Abyss calls to abyss," sang the Psalmist. Love opens the gateway to the Holy Sacrifice—only love can understand love, and the more we understand, the more does love tend to increase by desire to understand the more.

Love, St. Thomas teaches, feeds on devotion, and devotion in turn feeds on love. The thought of what Jesus does on the altar for our sakes is the incentive to devotion to, and in, the Mass. In a friend's company we best penetrate the secret of his love. In this company with Jesus on the altar of His sacrifice He pours out His friendship in a visible sign. As we raise our eyes to the Sacred Host and to the chalice of His blood, we must surely be drawn into the infinite depth of that love, unless we are unheeding of what goes on at the altar. By assisting more frequently and with more devotion at Mass we shall better than anywhere else learn the secret of His Heart, and be drawn to a more personal love for Him thereby. If we would but realize that each one of us is very personally in the Sacred Host, and very personally in the chalice, we would stir up in ourselves a more sincere response to His loving invitation to return love for love. "If so be you have tasted that the Lord is sweet" (1 Pet. ii. 3).

The Holy Sacrifice and Communion which bind each member so closely to the Head must inevitably bind them closely also to one another. In Christ, especially as the Living Bread, is found the entire Mystic Body closely compacted together: "We being many, are one bread, one body, all that partake of one bread " (1 Cor. x. 17). Not only does the Eucharist bind together those who are actually part of the Mystic Body; it must bind them in love to all mankind, since the desire of the Head goes out to all. The great fruit of the Mass must be in fraternal charity, without which there is but a mockery of the true religion. The Saviour expressed this as His supreme desire in His prayer of petition and of thanksgiving on Holy Thursday night: " That they all may be one, as Thou, Father, in me, and I in thee: that they also may be one in us " (John xvii. 21). He gave the Apostles and us the symbol of this fraternal love, not only in the washing of their feet, but in the still more complete emptying of Himself in the Institution of the Blessed Eucharist. " For I have given you an example, that as I have done to you, so you do also."

From the earliest days of the Church the Breaking of Bread implied a communication—a coming together in soul as well as in body. The effect of it on thousands of first converts to Christianity is apparent from the Acts of the Apostles: " The multitude of believers had but one heart and one soul " (Acts iii. 2). All feuds, all animosities, all envy and social distinction disappeared before the heat of the mighty love of the Victim of Sacrifice. One of the most ancient usages in the ritual of the Mass was called the " kiss of peace ". It is still preserved in the ceremony of the High Mass, though now largely confined to the ministers on the altar. Originally, it was given to one another by the entire congregation. Jesus Christ is our peace, Who made peace for us. He sends out His kiss of peace from the altar to-day, as it was long ago sent out into the world from the Cross. In the Sermon on the Mount He emphasized the condition of sharing in sacrifice, which is as true for the new as it was for the old: "If thou offer thy gift at the altar, and there thou remember that thy brother hath anything against thee, leave there thy offering before the altar, and go first to be reconciled with thy brother; and then coming thou shalt offer thy gift" (Matt. v. 23).

8

PEACE ON EARTH

The peace of Christ which is so essential to individuals is still more essential to the world in general. The nations of to-day do not know how to make peace, because they have forgotten, or, what is worse, have refused, the peace which Christ made. He alone is the source and centre of that peace which would, by the very force which it possesses, draw Jew and Gentile, bond and free, to the same table of Divine pacification. A French Bishop aptly expressed the present situation at a Social Week conference: "Armchairs grouped around a table are not sufficient; would it not be more efficacious to draw around a table at which one can adore God?" Mostly the representatives of the disunited nations can think only in terms of things material. They suffer from the sad inheritance of hundreds of years of godless education. Those amongst them who are religious-minded, and they seem to be few, can at best propose what they call "Freedom of Religion". It is good to hear at least the word religion mentioned, but by implication such freedom relegates man's duty towards God to a thing of purely private concern. Let those who wish for religion have it by all means, but it is not a matter for States or groups of States. This so-called basic principle of the Atlantic Charter will not serve to bring peace. What the world needs, and what they should have proclaimed, was "Freedom through Religion"—freedom through obedience to God the Creator, which is the first and most impelling necessity that lies on all created things, and the only basis of that tranquillity of order which is peace. God made man free, but not free in the sense that he could worship if and how he liked. He gave him freedom that his bounden worship of the Creator might assume its most perfect form, coming without restraint from the soul of a free and intelligent being.

The Protestant Reformation destroyed rather than reformed. Its destructive venom was directed against the Mass and the priesthood. They thereby destroyed the very source of all reform. One might as well speak of restoring health to a sick body by removing the heart. The deterioration which set in with the false ideas of liberalism and individualism went on unchecked in a society deprived of the true leaven of the Eucharist. To-day these unsound philosophies have been offset with still more terrible and godless systems of totalitarianism, socialism and communism. The way back from the accumulated disasters of the last three centuries can only lie in restoring the secure foundation which was the basis of a truly Christian civilization in the past. The only complete peace must be a Eucharistic peace. Pope Pius X declared to a world already torn asunder by war greed: "Nothing equals the power of this devotion (Eucharistic) to establish in hearts these bonds of peace and mutual understanding of which Christian society has such great need."

In the midst of darkness there is a bright ray of hope. Jesus watches over the world as the Head of the Church. His *"Misereor super turbam"* still sounds out over the earth. He sends out His inspiration into the hearts of men, recalling them to the source of their spiritual recovery, on which the material recovery so greatly depends. "Seek ye first the kingdom of God and his justice, and all these things shall be added to you" (Matt. vi. 33). From the beginning of the nineteenth century there has been a notable revival of Eucharistic devotion. In the first half of that century no fewer than six new congregations were founded for perpetual adoration. St. Peter Julian Eymard stands out like the prophets of old pointing the way. "This cult," he said, "is necessary to save society. Society is ageing because it has no longer a centre of truth and charity, but it will grow strong as soon as all its members gather around life—around Jesus in the Eucharist." After his death in 1868, a woman apostle, Madame Mary Martha Tamisier, took up the cause. She literally tramped through the towns and villages of France, seeking new adorers of the Blessed Sacrament and public expression of that worship, not only in France, but throughout the world. She wended her weary yet untiring way into Holland and Belgium. After ten years of labour her great desire was realized in the first International Eucharistic Congress held at Lille in 1881. Since that first Congress, year after year, except during the turbulence of great wars, nations have begun to find their true foundation of international peace around the Sacred Host. The dominant note in all these assemblies re-echoes the sentiments of St. Peter: "Lord, to whom shall we go? Thou hast the words of eternal life" (John vi. 69).

The world can be saved only by Christ: "Other foundation no man can lay, but that which is laid; which is Christ Jesus" (1 Cor. iii. 11). But, seeing that the world no longer goes to Him, He must be brought to the world. He gave Himself to His Church, to His Apostles clerical and lay that they might give Him to men. The international Eucharistic Congresses, and others of more local character, are a part—and no mean part, of that giving. De-Christianization was a gradual process. So also the re-Christianizing of society must make its slow progress. Year by year the influence goes out—Christ conquers more and more souls through the Sacrament of the Eucharist. Each international Congress but emphasizes what each nation, each diocese, each parish, each Christian soul must fulfil, namely the enthroning of the Eucharistic King in His Eucharistic reign. Pope Pius XI expressed that hope in prayer at the Roman Congress of 1922: "May it please Jesus, Prince of peace, to extend His kingdom to every social assembly so that the souls of men, being united in a brotherly embrace of faith and love, the beautiful rainbow of peace may shine forth on earth, and from the mystic ark of the Holy Tabernacle may go forth the dove with the olive branch."

9

CATHOLIC ACTION

Catholic Action is yet another sign of the power of the living Christ. Providentially, the Church, inspired of the Holy Ghost, has mustered her full army, calling on the reserves of the Christian laity to face the menace of the evil with the power of the Spirit. This apostolate of the laity flows from their sharing in the priesthood of Christ, especially from the precise participation in that priesthood which comes to them from the character of Confirmation. "Jesus loved the Church, and delivered himself up for it" (Eph. v. 25). So the lay apostle seeks to give himself in the same way in defence of truth and life. Catholic Action is, moreover, a sharing in the mission entrusted by Christ to His Apostles and their successors. Its power comes out from the episcopacy, who share in the fulness of the priesthood of Christ. For that reason it is in every sense a priestly work. What comes from the priesthood must be derived also from its inseparable sacrifice. The Apostolate of the laity must find its ardour and its endurance in the Mass in which the entire priestliness of Christ, of His ministers and of His faithful is energetically engaged.

The organizations of Catholic Action must be like the Church herself, whose life is centred in the Eucharist. They must form well-compacted bodies, resting ultimately on the chief corner-stone, which for us is the altar-stone of His perpetual sacrifice. If the hope of nations lies in refinding Christ, especially through the sacrament of His love and union, those who would teach the world must already possess Him deeply in their souls. He must be in them both light and fire. Where better can this spirit of Catholic Action be engendered than before the Tabernacle? At the first great congress of the Jocist movement in France, one of the leaders during Mass lit his candle from the candle on the altar. The light and fire was passed on to each one present, until nearly one hundred thousand candles, held on high, illumined the world about them. It was a symbolic representation of what the altar means, and how great a light and zeal is possessed by those who understand its holy action. One Mass contains our entire faith and life. One Mass enfolds and gives forth the vast redemptive design of God.

Eighth Chapter

SACRIFICE OF PRAISE ALWAYS TO GOD

(Heb. xiii. 15)

1

SUBLIME THEME OF THE PASSION

A MYSTERIOUS theme opens simultaneously with
the entry of Jesus Christ into His Passion. The
departure of Judas from the Upper Room was the first
signal of the powers of darkness. There were few
sadder moments in Our Lord's life than when the
Traitor, "having received the morsel, went out immediately". The Evangelist describes it in a few
graphic words: "And it was night." Jesus, though
He was fully aware of what that departure was to let
loose upon Him, seems to have waited for it deliberately before entering into His supreme sacrificial work.
The hour was at length come—"The hour so long
desired "—the hour of baptism of blood for which His
soul longed: " How am I straitened until it be accomplished." With the darkness of His sorrow closing in
around Him, He rose to the sublimest heights of religious worship. He put aside all thought of Himself,
and of what He must so shortly endure. All the energy
of His soul was directed to the purpose of His Passion
and death in the sight of the Father. Considering His
perfect knowledge of the events which were to follow,

humanly speaking, one would have expected a gloom to have settled down on the little company. Sad He undoubtedly was, with a great sadness. That was apparent to the Apostles. But He rose above it, and became wholly absorbed in presenting the fruit of suffering which would be gathered in Him by the Father.

The supreme purpose of the Passion was the glory of His Father. In that glory, given and accepted, the Beloved Son would also find His own glory—the glory of " obedience unto death, even unto the death of the Cross ". That is the mysterious theme which dominates all else. He asserted it in the presence of the Apostles the moment Judas had gone out: "When he therefore had gone out, Jesus said: " Now is the Son of man glorified, and God is glorified in him. If God be glorified in him, God also will glorify him in himself, and immediately will he glorify him " (John xiii. 31, 32). When He had completed His final discourse to them, He turned to His Beloved Father and expressed the same preoccupation in fervent prayer: "Father, the hour is come, glorify thy son, that thy son may glorify thee. . . . I have glorified thee on earth. I have finished the word thou hast given me to do. Now glorify me, O Father, with the glory which I had, before the world was, with thee " (John xvii. 1, 4, 5). The Eternal Father and the Word Incarnate were both engaged in this work of the salvation of man. The Love which is the Spirit made them one.

A striking testimony of the perfect accord of Jesus with the will of His Father in the high purpose of establishing perfect worship had already been given on the Sunday preceding. A mysterious tribute of His people was associated with His triumphant entry into

Jerusalem. "Blessed is he that cometh in the name of the Lord, the King of David." Jesus knew whither this triumph was to lead. He knew the exact value of it in the heart of this fickle people. His glory was not dependent on such short-lived enthusiasm of men. Yet He would not silence them at the dictation of the Pharisees. They were expressing what was so clearly involved in His own death, the most urgent necessity that lies on all things of giving glory to God. His reply to the Pharisees revealed how great is that necessity: "I say to you, that if these hold their peace, the stones will cry out" (Luke xix. 40). Jesus entered the Holy City as the Victim of sacrifice. Like the victims of the ancient sacrifices of the Jews, which, bedecked with flowers, were driven into the Temple for the holocausts, so Jesus was hailed by the crowds; His way was strewn with palm-leaves to proclaim His engagement in sacrificial service of God Almighty. His triumphant way would soon become the way of the Cross; the cheers of the crowd would soon be changed to clamours for His death. When the acclamation of that Palm Sunday had ended, Jesus again emphasized the true meaning of His death It will be His glory in the sight of the Father. He addressed all who had assembled for the festivity, including some Gentiles, who were particularly anxious to see Him: "The hour is come that the son of man should be glorified." His solemn declaration again leads to prayer: "What shall I say? Father, save me from this hour. But for this cause I came unto this hour. Father glorify thy name." As was befitting the tremendous solemnity of the occasion, the loving acceptance of the Father was made publicly manifest, so that none might doubt the truth of His mission. "A voice therefore came from heaven:

I have glorified it, and will glorify it again " (John xii. 27, 28). The Incarnate Son did not need any such assurance—He knew that His prayer, always in such perfect conformity with the will of His Father, never went unanswered. "I know that thou hearest me always, but because of the people who stand about have I said it; that they may believe that thou hast sent me" (John xi. 42).

2

GLORY IN THE CROSS

The Cross is glorious to Jesus Christ because it proclaims on earth His love of the Father: "Therefore doth my Father love me because I lay down my life" (John x. 17). The glory of this mutual love in its final testing supersedes all other considerations in the soul of the Saviour. "In the head of the book it is written of me: that I should do thy will, O God" (Heb. x. 7). The Passion and death on the Cross would open out that book before all men in everlasting testimony of His obedience, as High Priest and Victim. "When you shall have lifted up the son of man, then shall you know that I am he, and that I do nothing of myself, but as the Father hath taught me" (John viii. 28). His death by crucifixion, though most cruel and horrible, rises above its outward appearances in the glory which it proclaims from the Cross. "We see Jesus, who was made a little lower than the angels, for the suffering of his death, crowned with glory and honour: that through the grace of God he might taste death for all" (Heb. ii. 9).

Prior to His Passion He favoured the Apostles with a glimpse of the glory of His Humanity. Glory shone out from Him Who is "the image and glory of God" (1 Cor. ii. 7). Had they but known, a still greater glory radiated from the bruised and mangled body through His exaltation on the Cross. The thought of this glory lay deep in the soul of the Saviour as He continued to offer Himself with arms outstretched, raised between heaven and earth. The majesty of God is revealed on the Cross, because "God is love". St. Paul understood the Cross and its glory: "God forbid that I should glory in anything save in the cross of our Lord Jesus Christ" (Gal. v. 11). Like Christ of Whom he became the imitator, his work is concentrated on bringing home the lesson of Calvary: "The word of the Cross, to them indeed that perish is foolishness; but to them that are saved, that is, to us, it is the power of God. . . . We preached Christ crucified, unto the Jews a stumbling-block, and unto the Gentiles foolishness: but unto them that are called, both Jews and Greeks, Christ the power of God and the wisdom of God" (1 Cor. i. 17 seq.).

Through the glory of the Cross was realized the glory of the Resurrection. Jesus left the fruits of His death in the hands of His Father. He said: "If I glorify myself my glory is nothing. It is my Father who glorifieth me" (John viii. 54). The response of the Father to the merit of His life's work of the establishment of the glory of God on the earth was to raise Him from the dead—"Risen from the dead by the glory of the Father" (Rom. vi. 4) "God hath raised him up and given him glory" (1 Pet. i. 21). "He humbled himself, becoming obedient unto death; even unto the death of the cross. For which cause also hath God exalted him, and hath given him a name which is above all names " (Phil. ii. 8, 9). Henceforth His place is on His Father's right hand. "Who being the brightness of his glory, and the figure of his substance, and upholding all things by the word of his power, making purgation for sins, sitteth on the right hand of the majesty on high; being made so much better than the angels, as he hath inherited a more excellent name than they " (Heb. i. 3, 4).

From His throne on high as from the throne of the Cross, the "Lord of glory" (1 Cor. ii. 8) continues to be the mouthpiece of all creation in the praise of God. But by reason of a most perfect association this glory still remains on earth. He established the glory of His Father as "The Liturgist of the good things" (Heb. viii. 2). He in Whom was the fulness of worship willed that it be continued on earth after He had returned to His Father. The word Liturgy comes from two Greek words meaning a public work, or a work which includes a participation by the people under the guidance of a competent head who was called the Liturge. This is the most essential work of the Redeemer. This is His Father's business. He completed that arrangement of worship whilst on earth and handed it all over to His people of whom He ever remains the Head, both human and Divine. "Wherefore it behoved him in all things to be made like unto his brethren, that he might become a merciful high-priest before God, that he might be a propitiation for the sins of the people" (Heb. ii. 17). Christ not only founded the Liturgy on the Cross. Through the Sacrifice of Himself He became that Liturgy, because He is Himself the Image of the Father's glory, as the Divine Person Who made the oblation. He is also the image of that same glory as man in the grace of His hypostatic union by which His human nature participates in His glory as God.   By reason of the Incarnation the body and soul of Jesus became the vehicle of a glory that is essentially Divine.   "In him dwelleth all the fulness of the Godhead corporeally" (Col. ii. 9).   Thus the glory of God came down, lived and walked amongst men.   "The Word was made flesh and dwelt amongst us."   By His death on the Cross He merited for all men to enter into His glory in time and in eternity.   By the grace of adoption which He poured out, He made it possible for all men to lift their lives of every day, of every occupation, as He lifted His, to the glory of the Father.   "Whether you eat or drink, or whatsoever else you do; do all to the glory of God" (1 Cor. x. 31).

3

CHRISTIAN SOCIETY OF PRAISE

In His prayer to the Beloved Father Jesus spoke in two ways of the inheritance which He had left to His Apostles for the whole Church.   "I have given them thy word" (John xvii. 14)—that word was not only His teaching, His power, His prayer; it was also the gift of Himself Who is the Word Incarnate.   It is ever in that Word that the Church acts, speaks and prays. "The glory which thou hast given me, I have given to them" (ibid. 22).   The institution of the Church had for its high aim the founding of a society of everlasting praise, which would continue what He established.   But this work of the perpetuation of worship must continue even as it began. It is always through Him, and with Him, and in Him. The prayerful petition of the Church releases again the power of His redeeming action, unto the continuing of the glory of the Father. "Whatsoever you shall ask the Father in my name, that I will do: that the Father may be glorified in the Son" (John xiv. 13).

This is the wide framework of the Christian religion. It was in such terms that Our Lord described it to the woman at the well of Jacob. All is directed to the Father: "True adorers will adore the Father." It will not be confined like the religion which preceded it to any one place or temple. The new adoration will be in "spirit and in truth". It has its source in the perfect revelation of the Word of God Who is truth itself—"Last of all in these days he hath spoken to us by His Son." The Spirit sent by both Father and Son is the motive power of this perfect worship of God. What is so perfect cannot be confined. "God's name is great among the Gentiles." Finally, Christ places the fullest seal of Divine authority on this holy linking of man with God, by uniting it with the will of His Father; "The Father also seeketh such to adore him" (John iv. 23). By reason of that loving desire of the Father, and our own abiding in spirit and truth, a welcome is assured to our praise and prayer before the throne of God.

By Divine arrangement the chain of glory rising from earth to heaven becomes complete. We glorify the Son, both God and man, because he is the ambassador of the Father. Our glory is in the Spirit Whom He has poured out upon all flesh. He, in turn, uniting our glory with His own, offers His entire society to the Eternal Father as the Head and "the first born of many

brethren ". " The Father hath given all judgment to
the Son, that all men may honour the Son, as they
honour the Father. He who honoureth not the Son,
honoureth not the Father who sent him " (John v.
22, 23). To Christ, "ever living to make intercession
for us," the Church is closely knitted. On Him it is
totally dependent. Of every praise that is offered up,
He is the way, the truth, and the life. His Headship
and High-priesthood remain the source of the
Christian power of prayer. " By him therefore let us
offer the sacrifice of praise always to God, that is to
say, the fruit of lips confessing to his name " (Heb.
xiii. 15).

There are two phases of the life and work of the
Church. The final phase belongs to the Church
Triumphant in heaven where it enters into the glory
of God revealed, and where the glory it offers is nearest
in resemblance to the glory that is God's within Himself. In the clear vision of the Most Holy Trinity,
Christ as God and man leads His brethren into the
everlasting and consummated sacrifice of praise before
the throne of His Father. The intermediate phase
belongs to the Church on earth, pursuing its way,
generation after generation, " unto the measure of the
age of the fulness of Christ" (Eph. iv. 13). But,
whether on earth or in heaven, the glory is the same,
differing only in the mode of its offering. On earth,
indeed, "Our God is a hidden God". But the presence of the Incarnate Son, with Whom is the Father
and the Spirit, is not less real because so hidden. He
has left us the sacramental signs of His presence, the
chief of which makes present even His Humanity on
the altar, and in our souls.

Christ gave His own prayer to the Church: " Lord

teach us how to pray." In that prayer is contained all the accumulated worship of God by way of expectation, which He fulfilled, and presented in its perfect form before the Majesty of God. He is the founder and fashioner of all the praise which is enclosed in what we call the Liturgy. For that reason the Church always prays: "Through Christ Our Lord." "In order that God might be worthily praised by men," says St. Augustine, "God first praised Himself, and because He deigned to praise Himself, man discovered how he might praise Him." The true worship of God springs, indeed, from the purity and holiness of each heart, but all these hearts are joined in the immensity of the Heart of Jesus. "Our fellowship," says St. John, "is with the Father and His Son Jesus Christ" (1 John i. 3). "The Church prays, not in the name of any individual, nor as the sum of individuals, but as a fellowship, as a priestly unity, as the visible priesthood of Christ. And so the fruits of prayer belong to all those who in Christ are consecrated to the Father, to the 'chosen generation, and kingly priesthood'" (Karl Adam). With such thoughts in mind we can appreciate Pope Pius XII's definition of the Liturgy: "The public worship which Our Redeemer renders to the Father, as Head of the Church, and the worship which the society of the faithful renders to the Head, and by means of Him to the Eternal Father. Briefly the Liturgy is the entire work of the Body of Jesus, Head and members. . . . The priesthood fulfils its office down the centuries, and for that reason the Liturgy is nothing else than the exercise of the priestly office."

4

SACRIFICE OF PRAISE

Launched upon its way in the fulness of the Spirit, the Church had within herself every requirement for a perfect work. The Mass which was the centre of her life became also, by the very nature of things, the centre of its prayer. The new life was in prayer and the sacraments, "in the communication of the breaking of bread and in prayers" (Acts ii. 42). From the day of Pentecost the Church entered into legitimate possession of all divinely established praise, both old and new. With a freedom and spontaneity inherited from Christ, yet with an unerring instinct, she built up her liturgical life around the divinely founded nucleus of Christ's own fashioning. Out of reverence for that inner "substance of things" she created her own special ritual to make better known and loved the all-holy mystery within. St. Thomas declares that the Church was guided by the Holy Ghost in the arrangement of her Liturgy. The inspiring centre around which her prayerfulness grew and developed was the Most Blessed Eucharist. Even as all the prayer of Christ led Him to the prayer and action of the Sacrifice of the Cross, and came forth from it, so from the beginning the Church drew up its forms of prayer, as it did for its sacramental ritual, so as to lead to the Most Holy Sacrifice of the Altar by way of preparation, or to come out from it by way of thanksgiving. "The Eucharist," says the Angelic Doctor, "is the sacrament in which is comprehended the whole ecclesiastical unity, and therefore in this, rather than in the other sacraments, mention should be made of all the things that concern the whole Church." As a society of praise the Church found in the Holy Mass the prayer of all prayers, the highest point to which she could reach in fervour on this earth.

The spontaneity with which liturgical prayer began continued to guide its development down the centuries. That development goes on unceasingly, because the Church, as a living, praying body, grows in her appreciation of the wonders of the mystery which she holds and explains. Liturgical prayer, which developed into the Divine Office, was already in evidence in apostolic times, though obviously in rudimentary form. "At the date of the final separation between the Christians and the Synagogue, about the year A.D. 65 (date of the first Epistle to Timothy), the Apostles had adopted, in addition to the Liturgy and the Mass, at least one hour set apart for prayer, and probably even two, i.e. Lauds (originally called Matins, because celebrated in the morning or at dawn), and Vespers. Certain psalms, reading of the Sacred Scriptures, along with certain chants and prayers, not yet reduced to a fixed form, but composed under the inspiration of the Holy Ghost, formed, with the preaching of the word, the basis of these devotional practices" (Baumer O.S.B.).

Prayer coupled with the "ministry of the word", in preaching, celebrating Holy Mass, bestowing the other sacraments, was of such paramount importance to the Apostles, that material preoccupations, such as the care of widows, were entrusted to specially appointed Deacons: "It is not reason that we should leave the word of God and serve tables. . . . We will give ourselves continually to prayer, and to the ministry of the word" (Acts vi. 2, 4). That prayerful liturgical worship took more and more definite shape in the following centuries. It assumed more precise form under the influence of the monks of Thebaid, and may be said to have reached its perfection under the guiding hand of St. Benedict, who is justly named the Father of the Divine Office. But the living centre of the Blessed Eucharist which inaugurated it continued to inspire it. Its purpose to-day in the full flowering of its perfection is identical with that of apostolic times. It continues to gather devout men and women around the altar of sacrifice by way of preparation that they may enter worthily into the sacrificial worship, and by way of thanksgiving for the gift of its most holy Victim.

Festive commemorations, which gave rise to the yearly calendar, developed also around the Altar of Sacrifice. To-day in a perfect sequence we celebrate the entire life of the Saviour within the year. About Him as the Head is grouped the galaxy of saints and blesseds, presided over by the Queen of them all, His Most Blessed Mother. The Mass honours the entire Mystic Body, since it contains the whole ecclesiastical unity. In the prayer and sacrifice of the Head, the Communion of saints in heaven and on earth is deeply concerned. The Passiontide, followed by Easter, with its preparation of fifty days, would seem to have been the first and most distinct celebration in the early Church. Later, as anniversaries came around, the commemoration of other events in Our Lord's life were added, and took their liturgical place. Certain thoughts, certain sacred memories of mysterious events stirred in the hearts of the Apostles and found expression in suitable forms of prayer. Like the Mother of

Jesus, they kept all these things and pondered over them in their minds. Such things formed the subjects of their discourse. Eventually they formed the proper of the Holy Sacrifice in the shape of prayers, instructions, and Gospel readings. In the Catacombs, the sepulchres of the Martyrs formed fitting altars for the celebration of the Mass, since their sacrifice in blood brought them very close to the Victim of Calvary. As the anniversary of each martyr's death was commemorated the place of sacrifice moved from one altar to another, and the ritual became enriched by the memory of his life and death, so the cult of the saints grew side by side with the worship of God in the mysteries of His Beloved Son made man. The Liturgy is Christian dogma prayed, just as faith is that dogma lived.

5

RITUAL SYMBOLISM

The Church as a mother leads her children into the mysteries of faith. She has her own special paedagogy which never loses sight of the realities of our human ways and needs. We require the visible and material to guide us into the knowledge of the invisible and the spiritual. The ritual of Holy Mass enfolds "the mystery of the great action", as it was anciently called. The purpose of all ecclesiastically approved rites, which have been arranged around that inner mystery, is to lead the faithful into the *arcanum*, the secret, which is enclosed. The Mass is a visible sign of the hidden sacrificial action of the living Christ.

Leading to that central sign there are many other signs and symbols, which form the external ceremonial. All these secondary signs have their own precise meaning, and the Mass as we celebrate it to-day cannot be fully appreciated without some knowledge of their significance.

Too frequently this Mass symbolism fails to attain to its purpose because it lacks meaning to the greater part of the congregation. Its purpose is prayerful. The altar, the vestments, the lights, the incense, are all meant to rivet attention on Christ, the principal offerer. "Let this mind be in you, which was also in Christ Jesus" (Phil. ii. 5). The priest at the altar resembles a choirmaster, leading the faithful by voice, hands and bodily worship into a fitting disposition of devotion. All these external gestures are prescribed by the Missal, and give deeper expression to the prayers which they accompany. The wider use of the Missal should lead also to a greater appreciation of the signs of the Great Sign. This appreciation should be regarded as an essential part of our liturgical revival. It will help mightily to foster what Pope Pius X called "active participation in the liturgical service", which he declared to be "the primary and indispensable source of the true Christian spirit". This closer following of the priest on the altar in the might of sacrificial prayer, expressed even in signs, will convince pious Christian souls that, though private prayers are both essential and efficacious, their power of intercession is far greater when, one with the priest, they are associated in the public worship of the Church.

St. Vincent Ferrer declared that the Mass is the highest act of contemplation that is possible. The gateway into that contemplative act is the external rite. St. Thomas teaches that the entire liturgy of the Mass helps in this work of contemplation, since it has for its purpose " to excite devotion and reverence for the sacred mysteries, and to explain their effects ". Again he says: " Since the whole mystery of our salvation is comprised in this sacrament, therefore it is performed with greater solemnity than the other sacraments." The Fathers of the Council of Trent also emphasize the importance of the external setting, of the candles, incense, vestments, music, and other such things, as being "derived from Apostolic discipline and tradition, whereby both the majesty of so great a sacrifice might be recommended, and the minds of the faithful excited, by these visible signs of religion and piety, to the contemplation of the most sublime things which are hidden in this sacrifice ".

Of the many material requisites for the Holy Sacrifice, the altar on which it is celebrated is the most evident of all the symbols. The Roman Pontifical calls it the symbol of Christ Himself. Its orientation is indicative of Christ's coming after the long ages of waiting. It faces eastwards towards the rising sun, as a type of the Messiah, according to the Prophet: "Unto you that fear my name the Sun of Justice shall arise " (Mal. ii. 4). St. Ambrose says that the altar of the Church is a type of Christ's body. On it are five crosses in memory of the five wounds. In the ceremony of its consecration for use in the Most Holy Sacrifice, oil of chrism is poured on it in memory of the anointing of the body of Christ. The tiny sepulchre contains relics of the saints, as a reminder of the altar tombs of the first martyrs, and of the union of the Mystic Body with the Head. The lighted candles which shine out from it in yet another way signify the Saviour Who said: "I am the light of the world." The Crucifix which surmounts it belongs to it by right of identity of sacrifice. Finally, the vestments worn by the priest, each of which has its own mystic symbolism, add solemnity, and emphasize the altogether sacred and unworldly character of the priestly work on the altar of God.

Against the background of permanent symbolism of the altar and its furnishings, the vested priest must add his own contribution of external observances in the actual celebration of the Holy Sacrifice. In the Mass there are many signs and gestures which claim the attention of the faithful, and increase the fervour of their prayer. A variety of prescribed actions by the celebrant join body to soul in the worship of God. St. Thomas, under the heading of adoration, speaks of bodily worship: "As we are composed of a twofold nature, intellectual and sensible, we offer God a two-fold adoration, namely a spiritual adoration consisting in internal devotion of the mind, and a bodily adora-tion, which consists in an exterior humbling of the body. . . . Bodily devotion is done in spirit, in so far as it proceeds from and is directed to spiritual de-votion." The Incarnate Word deigned to use this form of worship during His life. His Passion and death marked the final excellence of His adoration of the Father in body as well as in soul. His outstretched arms on the Cross were an eloquent symbol of the offering of Himself in universal redemption.

All through the Mass, actions correspond with words. They are given in precise detail in the rubrics, and have been hallowed by ancient usage. The priest standing at the steps prepares himself in the consciousness of his unworthiness to go unto the altar of God. Bowing low before the altar, he assumes an attitude of repentance. He strikes his breast at the "*mea culpa*", as he does again later at the prayer, "Also to us sinners". Having ascended the steps, he kisses the altar in token of his love of Christ. He genuflects at the words of the Creed announcing the Incarnation. After the Consecration he frequently repeats the same act of adoration and reverence to God Incarnate on the Altar. Four times, when there is a special urgency in his prayer, for example, at the supplication to the Eternal Father after the Consecration, he bows down profoundly over the altar with hands joined, or with arms crossed on his breast. During the celebration there is constant movement at the altar, so that the Epistle and Gospel sides are well-known parts of the Church itself. The opening prayers, the Epistle and Gradual, are said for the faithful, who are symbolically represented by the south side, which is warmed by the midday sun. On the other hand, the Gospel is read towards the north, because the message of Christ is addressed to all pagan nations. St. Gregory gives us the symbolic meaning: "The dark cold north is a figure of the heathen world: for idolatry has hardened their hearts, just as the cold has frozen the northern lands."

The hands of the priest are consecrated, because, like Jesus did at the Last Supper, he must take bread into them at the Consecration. These hands which are holy have a large part to play in the external and representative action of the Mass. The priest prays not only with lips but with hands, which add their own eloquence to the impetratory power of the sacrifice. "All we who pray," says St. Augustine, "are but beggars in the presence of God, and stand before the presence of the Almighty." Suppliant hands emphasize our mendicancy. Normally, as the priest moves from side to side of the altar they are joined palm to palm on his breast, and are reminiscent of the ancient oath of fealty to the liege-lord. In most of the prayers, and generally throughout the Canon, they are held wide apart. Originally, Christians found in hands and arms outstretched an outward representation of the Crucified Christ. In the Catacombs the Holy Mother, the Church, is represented as a matron with hands extended beyond the shoulders, standing close to a tripod on which rest the symbols of the Eucharist. St. Ambrose says that outstretched arms are a mystical figure of our Saviour praying for the world's redemption with arms outstretched upon the Cross. Tertullian is a still earlier witness to the same usage: "We Christians pray with eyes raised to heaven, and uplifted hands, because they are pure. We are not satisfied with raising our hands, we even extend our arms in memory of the Lord's Passion." In the Dominican and other rites, this extending of the arms accompanies the prayer which follows the Consecration, and is eloquent of the ancient usage.

The opening out of the hands at the "*Dominus vobiscum*" conveys the idea of salutation, of embracing all in the wide distribution of grace of which the priest is minister: by joining them again whilst still facing the people the celebrant would weld them together in closer union with Christ their Head in the mystery performed on the altar. Perhaps the most significant use of the priestly hands lies in the frequent signs of the Cross which are made at different parts of the Mass in accompaniment with prayer. The priest makes it over the people; he makes it over himself in token of blessing and association with the Cross of Christ. He signs the table of the altar with it to remind him that it represents the crucified body of the Lord. He makes it over the offerings that they may be holy in the sight of God. He makes it over the body and blood of Jesus really present on the altar after the Consecration. St. Thomas declares that the signs of the Cross after the Consecration recall the Saviour's sacrifice on the Cross, and its perpetuation in the Mass. That association of the Mass and Calvary is still more mysteriously signified when he makes signs of the Cross with the Sacred Host over the chalice and over the altar.

6

DIVISION AND PRAYERFUL PREPARATION

Prayer of priest and people is the most urgent need during the celebration of the Most Holy Sacrifice. The Missal presents the most perfect way of joining in the sacrificial act of the Great High-Priest and Victim. Our present rite with all its various parts reaches back in its essentials to the Upper Room, and in the general disposition of its prayers to the first centuries of Christianity. The Fathers of the Council of Trent emphasized this radical continuity of rite: "Whereas it beseemeth that holy things be administered in a holy manner, and of all things this sacrifice is the most holy; to that end that it might be worthily and reverently offered, the Catholic Church instituted many years ago the Sacred Canon, so pure from every error, that nothing is contained therein which does not in the highest degree savour of a certain holiness and piety and raise up to God the minds of those who offer. For it is composed out of the words of the Lord, the tradition of the Apostles and the pious instructions of holy Pontiffs." A modern writer speaks in detail of the Roman Rite: "The Roman Canon which early became that of the universal Church . . . has preserved under the austerity and simplicity of its form the most ancient apostolic tradition. The Litanic prayer, the Preface, the reading of the Diptychs, the recital of the Institution, the final Doxology, the Fraction, the Kiss of Peace, the Communion, such indeed were from the beginning the elements of the Eucharistic assembly" (Cabrol). In support of this claim may be quoted the earliest testimony of the Mass ritual after the time of the Apostles, namely that of St. Justin the Martyr; who gives a vivid description of the early assemblies: "On the day called Sunday, all that live either in town or country meet together at the same place, where the writings of the Apostles and prophets are read. . . . When the reader has done, the Bishop preaches a sermon. . . . At the conclusion of this discourse we all rise up together and pray, and, the prayers being over, there is bread and wine and water, and the president sends up prayers and makes thanksgiving. . . . And the people conclude with the joyful acclamation of Amen."

St. Thomas speaks of the prompt will as a necessary disposition for attending at Holy Mass: "In this sacrament a greater devotion is required than in the other sacraments, because in this sacrament the whole of Christ is contained, and also a more widespread devotion, because the devotion of the whole Christian people is needed, for whom the sacrifice is offered, and not only that of those who receive the Sacrament, as in the other sacraments; and therefore, as St. Cyprian has said: 'The priest at the Preface prepares the minds of his brethren saying, Lift up your hearts, and when the people have responded: We have lifted them up unto the Lord, they are reminded that they should think of nothing else but God.'" Our sacrificial Liturgy constantly reiterates this appeal to prayerful devotion. The "Let us pray" is a kind of refrain, ever urging the faithful to still greater efforts in their desire to be united with Christ. One of the most striking characteristics of the Mass prayers is in their conversational form. The responses now made by the altar-servers were originally made by the entire congregation. Nothing emphasizes so strongly the vital part played by the faithful in the offering of the sacrifice as this sacred dialogue of priest and people.

Following the guidance of the Angelic Doctor we may divide the prayerful ritual of the Mass into five parts. The first two parts are by way of preparation and instruction, and lead priest and people into the third part, which consists in the celebration of the Holy Mystery by changing bread into the body and wine into the blood of Christ, as well as in the prayers that immediately follow the Consecration. The fourth and fifth parts come out from the Mystery present on the Altar by way of gift in Holy Communion and by way of thanksgiving in the Post-Communion. It is noticeable that St. Thomas does not refer to the division of the Mass into that of the Catechumens and the faithful. Whilst it is true that very ancient custom brought the Catechumens to the first part of the Mass, and that they departed after the Gospel, there is some likelihood of misunderstanding in so dividing the Mass. Aquinas emphasizes that the whole Mass, especially the instruction, is for the faithful. There never was a part of the Mass arranged solely for Catechumens. It happened that their attendance in the early Church was not allowed to pass beyond the Gospel, because their souls had not received the Character of Christ's priesthood.

The prayers of preparation are intended according to St. Thomas to aid us in performing worthily what follows. "Before prayer prepare thy soul." At the foot of the altar priest and people express at once both their desire and consciousness of unworthiness to enter into the Holy of Holies of God. Yet confidence in the Divine mercy moves the priest to ascend the altar: "Our help is in the name of the Lord." The Introit is by way of Divine praise. It is composed mainly of the Psalms, and St. Thomas quotes Dionysius: "The Psalms comprise of praise whatever is contained in the Sacred Scriptures." The Kyrie thrice repeated is in honour of the Most Holy Trinity, and "against the threefold misery of ignorance, sin and punishment". The words are a relic of the Greek language in which the Mass was celebrated until the middle of the third century. These invocations are part of the Litany, which is now reserved for special occasions. The "Gloria in excelsis" was originally said only at Christmas. About A.D. 500 it was prescribed for all festive occasions. It develops the theme of the Sacrifice of Calvary, and expresses the four ends for which the Mass is offered—of praise, of thanksgiving, of supplication, and of propitiation. It is omitted in sorrowful offices, which St. Thomas reminds us commemorate our unhappy state in this world.

Before the prayers of the Collect the priest turns towards the people, and with significant gesture invites them to join him in prayer. The "*Dominus vobiscum*" is a most perfect form of Christian salutation, probably in common use in early times outside the Mass. It expresses the desire of the Heart of Jesus of union with Him through His minister at the altar. The fruit of this union is expressed in prayer. The power of these official prayers of the Church lies in the certainty of that union with Christ. "Where two or three are gathered togther in my name, there am I in the midst of them" (Mark xviii. 20). These prayers, says Aquinas, are said for the people that they may be worthy of such great mysteries.

After the Collects begins the instruction, which, again declares the Angelic Doctor, is necessary because the Mass is a mystery of faith. It consists, first of all, in lessons from the prophets and the Apostles, from which is derived "the spiritual joy of the Alleluias, or the spiritual sighing expressed in the Tract". The Gospel is the second part of the preparation, "unto perfect instruction in Christ's teaching". It is the word of the Saviour unto all nations. "He said to them, go ye unto the world and preach the gospel to every creature" (Mark xvi. 15). On all Sundays, greater solemnities, and feast of Doctors of the Church there is added the instruction of the Creed of the Council of Nicea, "because we believe that Christ is the Divine truth". From early times, as evidenced by the words of St. Justin, it was customary to preach the word of God after the Gospel. This was naturally considered the best time for the instruction of the people. The Church, which was soon to break the Bread of the Lord's body, desired to prepare the faithful for a more worthy sharing in the sacrifice by first breaking the bread of His doctrine. The living word of His Gospel is explained and developed that they may fully understand the message of the day.

7

IN DEPTH OF THE MYSTERY

The most solemn part of the Mass is opened by the salutation and renewal of invitation to pray. Once the instruction is completed priest and people return to prayer. The Offertory is generally taken from the Psalms. It is in praise of God's infinite power, on which the Mass depends, and normally linked with the general theme of the Proper of the Mass. In the general Roman Rite the Oblation of the bread follows immediately. The words recited whilst the Paten is raised ask for forgiveness and salutary benefit for the priest himself, for those present and for all the faithful living and dead. The chalice is then prepared. Prayer accompanies this preparation, which reminds one forcibly of the mystic meaning of the water mingled with wine: "That through the mystery of this water and wine, we may be made partakers of His Divinity, Who has deigned to become partaker of our humanity." We have the testimony of St. Justin, St. Irenaeus and St. Cyprian that this mixing of water with wine was observed by Our Divine Saviour at the Last Supper. It symbolizes the water which flowed with blood from the side of the Crucified, out of which the Church was born. The little drop of water may also, according to the accompanying prayer, represent the littleness and unworthiness of our humanity which was assumed, and in a manner absorbed into the immensity of the Divinity.   It also signifies according to the same holy Doctor our longing for intimate and inseparable union with Our Lord.   The Oblation of the "Chalice of Salvation " follows.

The Offertory proper concludes with a prayer of deep humility in which the priest begs God to accept us also with pleasure in the sacrifice about to be offered.   Rising from his profound inclination over the altar, he invokes the Holy Spirit that He may sanctify the gifts already offered.   The washing of the fingers is accompanied by the Psalm: " I will wash my hands among the innocent, and I will encompass thy altar O God."   "We should stand at the altar," says St. Cyril, "with spotless hands and purest hearts." Commenting on the symbolism, St. Thomas points out that the cleansing of the fingers rather than the hands denotes separation from even the last sin.   Having returned to the centre of the altar, the celebrant again renews the offering by joining it to the death and glory of Jesus, by directing it to the honour of God's Holy Mother and the Saints, and to the benefit of the faithful on earth.

On the very threshold of the mystery the priest again turns towards the congregation and appeals for earnest prayer.   The " Orate fratres " is a most intimate mode of address.   In plain terms it reminds all present that the sacrifice is theirs.   The dialogue of the Preface emphasizes the same truth.   It seems to place the res- ponsibility on the congregation for the continuance of the sacrifice.   The celebrant seeks their consent at every step, since it is in their name that it is to be offered. The "Let us give thanks to the Lord our God" conveys the essential idea of Eucharistic prayer, which denotes thanksgiving. It is as if the priest said to them: "Let us proceed with the Eucharistic sacrifice." The reply gives the consent of all, and introduces the opening words of the Preface: "It is truly meet and just." The Preface is a prayer of praise and thanksgiving, which closely connects our ceremonial with that of the Saviour Who before breaking bread gave thanks and blessed. It concludes with the great canticle of jubilation in honour of the Most Holy Trinity, in which we join with the angels and saints before the throne of God: "Holy, Holy, Holy, Lord God of Hosts." The sacrificial worship is about to transport us with Christ before the throne of God.

We now enter what is known as the Canon of the Mass, so called because it is solemnly ordered by the Church. This is the most ancient part of the Mass. It has come down unchanged from the earliest centuries. The last and very slight change was made by Pope Gregory in the sixth century. It is the most perfect prayer in the Church of God. As the priest enters into the Holy of Holies of God the great silence descends on the assembly. The prayers in secret betoken that the mystery is itself unutterable. The silence is most reverent and prayerful. "The Lord is in his holy temple, let the earth keep silence before him," cried out the Prophet (Heb. ii. 20). St. Thomas gives the sequence of thought leading up to the Consecration. The first two commemorations recall for whom the sacrifice is offered, for the Church and its Hierarchy and for the faithful in particular and in general. The third commemoration invokes the intercession of the saints on behalf of those thus mentioned, and the fourth concludes the petitions by asking that the "service of our worship" may be salutary.

The Consecration proper is preceded by the prayer *"Quam oblationem"*, in which the priest asks that it may be worthily done, so that, made effective on our behalf by the power of God, "It may become for us the body and blood of Thy dearly beloved Son Jesus Christ". At the Consecration the celebrant repeats the words of the Institution. He speaks in the person of Christ. His identity seems to become absorbed into Christ. Nothing has been changed. The same words fall from his lips as were pronounced by Jesus in the Upper Room. So earnest were the Apostles to do what their Divine Master had done on that night of the Last Supper—so important was it to hand on that act in its most accurate form, that they carried out His command literally without any change of words. In silent adoration the priest adores, and raises Jesus on high that He may be adored by all the people. The Church prompts her faithful to make their act of faith to the uplifted Christ, as Thomas did in the Upper Room after the Resurrection—"My Lord and my God." "Who can doubt," declares St. Gregory, "that at the moment of His immolation at the voice of the priest, the heavens are opened, the choirs of angels come to attend this mystery of Jesus Christ, the things of earth are joined to the things of heaven, the visible and the invisible are united."

After the Consecration the Victim remains living on the altar under the appearances of bread and wine, continuing to recall in the sight of God the separation of His body and blood in His bitter Passion and death. That same Victim has indeed already entered into His glory of the Resurrection and Ascension. But in His hidden glory on the altar He is appropriated by the priest and the "holy people". He is the "Victim all pure, all holy, all perfect". God is asked to look down upon Him and upon us as forming one victim in His sight, and to be pleased with our common sacrifice, as He was with the ancient sacrifices of Abel, Abraham and Melchisedech. The essential act of sacrifice is contained in the Consecration, but the Liturgical sacrifice of union of priest and people with Christ as Victim continues on the altar. "The sacrifice of the interior contrite spirit," says St. Albert the Great, "is not uplifted unless it is incorporated in the sacrifice of the altar. It is therefore thus 'uplifted to the altar on high' when in the sacrifice the faithful are joined to the Godhead of Christ, Who stands in the very presence of the Divine Majesty." The prayer "Supplices" contains the most splendid expression of this liturgical worship. Bending low over the altar the celebrant beseeches the Eternal Father to accept the mystic offerings—not merely the body and blood of His Beloved Son, so infinitely acceptable of their nature, but with that body the entire Mystic Body of the Church, and especially the bodies and souls of all present, who by their holy dispositions have linked themselves with the Victim on the altar. Led by Jesus, Who from the Altar again ascends to the Father, as the Holy Angel of the Great Counsel, the whole of creation is joined to the Creator, the altar of earth is linked with the "altar above", where in beatific vision there is found the perfect phase of everlasting praise. From that altar on high descends the fruits of sacrifice, that those on earth who share in His body and blood, "may be filled with every grace and heavenly blessing".

During these solemn moments the Church, conscious of the Communion of Saints, turns her attention to the departed souls of the faithful who have not yet been allowed to enter into the glory of God, that He might grant them in His goodness "a place of refreshment, light and peace". For the duration of three words the priest breaks the silence. It is again to remind all present that the sacrifice is for them: for we are all in the category of sinners before God—"To us also sinners . . . deign to grant some part and fellowship." The central part of the Mass concludes with the little elevation. It contains the final appeal to the Eternal Father through Christ, with Christ and in Christ for "all good things", "Through Whom is to Thee the Father Almighty in union of the Holy Ghost all honour and glory world without end." To which prayer, St. Justin reminds us, all the people answered, Amen.

8

COMMUNION AND THANKSGIVING

The fourth part of the Mass contains the Communion Liturgy. Once the essentially sacrificial work has been completed, the minds of priest and people are focused on preparation for a worthy reception of the Sacrament. This is first done, St. Thomas declares, by the common prayer of the congregation. The "Our Father" is the Lord's Prayer. He made it the family prayer of the Church. "Directed by His own precepts", we are emboldened to recite it in the Mass. There can be no grander setting for the recital of this prayer, which is the sum total of all Christian prayer, than to recite it officially with God's minister, in the real presence of Jesus Christ, Who recites it for us, as He did long ago for His Apostles. In confidence in the merits of His sacrifice, already renewed on the Altar, we ask the Father to grant us a share in the establishing of His glory, and of the kingdom of His Son, and, above all, to give us on this very day our daily bread—the living Bread that cometh down from heaven, which gives life to the world. Private prayer again follows. Inspired by the final petitions of the "*Pater Noster*", we ask for peace, which can only be established in us by deliverance from evil and freedom from sin and from all disquiet. Peace in the soul is the keynote of the entire liturgical preparation for Holy Communon.

The "*Fractio Panis*", which follows, is now confined to the Sacred Host which is used for the Mass, and entirely consumed by the priest himself. Originally sufficient bread was consecrated at each Mass for all those present, and then broken and distributed. That early ritual was more symbolic of St. Paul's idea that all are one bread, who partake of one bread. But the symbolism is not lost, though now more restricted. The Holy Sacrifice is still the "breaking of Bread", the sign of Divine hospitality. The actual dividing of the Host is accompanied by the concluding formula of all official prayer: "Through the same Jesus Christ Our Lord." The petitions for all needs contained in the "Our Father", and in the secret prayer which followed, are at that moment rendered still more efficacious through the accompanying action of the breaking, which is a Eucharistic sign in the sight of the Father, and which recalls, St. Thomas says, the division of Christ's body which was made at the Passion, and is therefore a solemn pledge of the Divine mercy and love. Peace is the message which goes out to the world from that divided Host. From it is sent the kiss of peace, and the prayer of mercy and peace of the "*Agnus Dei*". Again, the Angelic Doctor states: "The people are prepared for Holy Communion by the '*Pax*' which is given with the words of the '*Agnus Dei*', because this sacrament is the sacrament of unity and of peace."

Three secret prayers are prescribed for the more immediate preparation. All three are directed by name to Jesus Christ really present on the altar. They are redolent of that intimacy which St. John enjoyed in such close proximity to His Divine Master at the Last Supper. All three are also very personal. The celebrant no longer prays in the plural, but in the singular. Seeing that in the Blessed Eucharist Jesus comes wholly and personally to each one, so also the preparation should be in the prayerful striving of each one individually. The silence which again falls on the assembly is indicative of the reverence and recollection needed for the worthy reception of the body and blood of Jesus Christ. In the first prayer peace is again the burden of our petition. In the second we ask for forgiveness of our sins by virtue of the sacrament. In the third that the Holy Communion may be a safeguard for both soul and body. Thus prepared, the celebrant again takes the Sacred Host into his hands, and, on the point of receiving, his sense of unworthiness is admingled with confidence in the healing power of Christ: "Lord, I am not worthy that thou shouldst enter under my roof, but say only the word and my soul shall be healed." The Missal is the most perfect of all prayer books, and no better way of preparation can be found than to recite devoutly these prayers of the priest.

The celebrant receives Holy Communion under both species and the separate formulas of the Roman Rite express his desire in partaking of the body and blood of the Lord that his soul may receive the essential fruit of the Eucharistic Bread, and be preserved unto life everlasting. The same formula is used for the Faithful. "He that eateth my flesh, and drinketh my blood hath everlasting life, and I will raise him up on the last day" (John vi. 55). During the ablutions which follow, and which are themselves a testimony to the holiness of this Bread of Angels, the priest continues his silent prayer to Jesus within his soul: "that what we have taken through our mouths, we may receive with a pure heart." What is taken under the appearance of food should nourish the soul and increase its love. At the second ablution he prays that the body and blood of Jesus may cleave to his innermost soul and dissolve all that is sinful within him.

The fifth part of the Mass consists in a service of thanksgiving. The Communion said by priest and people is, like the Offertory, a hymn of praise. It is taken from the Old or the New Testament, but most frequently from the Psalms. St. Thomas refers it to the hymn said by Christ after the Last Supper. "All the people rejoice in the receiving of the mystery." The prayer or prayers called the Post-Communion are said on behalf of the people, and correspond to the Collects and Secret prayers. This prayer refers again to the Holy Communion, and asks in various ways according to the time or festivity for its salutary effects.

S

At the end the Eucharistic salutation is again given and replied to. Then at all Masses at which the "*Gloria*" has previously been recited, the priest, still turned towards the people, addresses them with the words, "*Ite Missa est.*" This phrase has been called the dismissal, but it is more than a dismissal. It is an echo of the Christmas hymn of the angels. It is the joyful announcement that the sacrifice has been perfected to the very end. St. Thomas explains the words as referring to the "*Hostia*" or the Victim, Who has been sent. Jesus was first sent to men by the Father. Through the Mass the priest on the altar, on behalf of the people, has sent the Incarnate Word in His sacrificial guise back to the Father again with the message of our need of redemption. The "*Ite Missa est*" announces that the Victim has been carried through our liturgical worship of earth even unto the altar on high. So splendid was this formula considered by the Church that it became in time the name for the entire sacrifice. The "*Missa*" is the Mass.

Though he has declared the Holy Sacrifice completed, the priest seems loath to leave the altar. In a final bowing down before the Tabernacle he thinks again of his unworthiness to engage in so holy a mystery, and makes supplication on his own behalf to the Most Holy Trinity, that that unworthiness may not stand in the way of complete acceptance of the sacrifice by God, or of the bestowal of its fruits on those for whom he offered it. At the end he kisses the altar-stone in token of his loving farewell. The priest's farewell to the people is in the form of a blessing. The Last Gospel, which is the prologue of St. John, was originally recited on the way back to the sacristy. It is now part of the Mass. It thus becomes included in the thanksgiving, recalling the glorious economy of God in man's salvation, which is perfectly renewed and applied in the Most Holy Sacrifice. The Mass is the renewal of the mystery of the Incarnation, of the life, Passion and death of the Saviour, and the pledge of everlasting glory. "The Word was made flesh and dwelt amongst us." By becoming bread that dwelling is perpetuated. The fruits of His coming are poured out upon mankind. The action of the Mass draws the people of God into this immensity. All the cares, all the trials, all the sufferings, all the desires of our hearts, are lifted up with Jesus on the altar. There we not only ask in His name, but He, being raised up again for our sakes in all the power and glory of the Cross, asks urgently for us of His Eternal Father. Nowhere better are our petitions made known and heard than when thus made His own by the Immaculate Lamb of God, " Who offers the prayers of all the saints upon the Golden altar, which is before the throne of God" (Apoc. viii. 3).

Ninth Chapter

THE PROMISE OF ETERNAL INHERITANCE

(Heb. ix. 15)

1

SAVED BY HOPE

THE Passion and death of the Divine Saviour leads to the joy and triumph of His Resurrection. He said: "I have power to lay my life down, and I have power to take it again" (John x. 18). He showed forth the first power by deliberately abandoning Himself into the hands of His enemies in obedience to His Father's will. He proved possession of the second by rising in glory from the tomb. The Church meets Him on Easter Sunday with her triumphant Alleluias. "Christ my hope is risen. He will go before you into Galilee. There you shall see Him" (Matt. xxviii. 7). The reason of this rejoicing is not far to seek. "The Lamb that was slain, is worthy to receive power, and divinity, and wisdom, and strength, and honour and glory, and benediction" (Apoc. v. 12). The Christian Easter presents us with an historical and irrefutable record of His Resurrection from the dead, and with it a Divine pledge of our own glorious immortality. In Christ's Passion earth was united to heaven. The things of time were made to touch the things of eternity. In this "admirable commerce" was born the new hope. In Him, first, all that was mortal put on immortality. Jesus is not only the "First born of many brethren", He is also the first risen. "Christ is risen from the dead, the first fruits of them that sleep" (1 Cor. xv. 20).

Christ preceded us into Galilee—into the greater Galilee of His everlasting kingdom. "There you shall see Him." He hid His Divinity beneath the Sacred Humanity, which He assumed at the Incarnation. He now hides both the Divinity and Humanity under the appearances of bread and wine. But the concealed reality has not changed. Our faith reveals Him. Our hope, which gives us a foretaste of His sweetness, makes us desire Him. Our charity, which joins us to Him in friendship, already gives us union with Hm. But He will not remain always hidden. Provided we are faithful to Him in life, He will lift the veil that now hides Him from our mortal eyes, and will show Himself in all the glory of His Divine Majesty revealed. "The veil shall be taken away" (2 Cor. iii. 16). For the follower of the Risen Christ the laying aside of the body in death is the doorway to everlasting life. Not even the body will be laid aside for ever. He will come again and take it also unto Himself, as He will have already taken the soul. "They shall see the Son of man coming in the clouds of heaven with much power and majesty" (Matt. xxiv. 30). This immense hope is the fruit of His own bodily resurrection from the dead.

Yet, though the Church celebrates her Easter and rejoices in the hope of resurrection, she does not forget the road which led her so securely to His triumph. Her Liturgy of paschal time emphasizes the great truth, namely, that Christ's exaltation came from His

Cross: "Wherefore hath God exalted Him." Our Divine Lord explained this mystery of glory through the Cross to the disciples at Emmaus on the Sunday of His Resurrection: "Ought not Christ to have suffered these things, and so enter into his glory?" (Luke xxiv. 26). Our joy in the risen Christ becomes more secure when we have willingly watched and suffered with Him during the long and weary hours of His sufferings and death. "If we suffer with him, that we may be also glorified with him" (Rom. viii. 17). We rejoice in the Resurrection of Jesus as an accomplished fact, and in it we look forward to our own. "If the Spirit of him that raised up Jesus from the dead dwell in you; he that raised up Jesus Christ from the dead, shall quicken also your mortal bodies, because of his Spirit which dwelleth in you" (Rom. viii. 11). Yet we realize only too well that hope is not possession; it is at best only its foretaste. There is yet this life to be lived in this mortal flesh which wars against the soul. We must pursue the road of holiness, such as He marked out for us. "Everyone that hath this hope sanctifyeth himself, as he also is holy" (1 John iii. 3). This road is that on which He himself travelled: "Who having joy set before him, endured the cross" (Heb. xii. 2). St. Paul emphasizes the close relation of cross to crown: "Always bearing about in our body the mortification of Jesus, that the life also of Jesus may be made manifest in our flesh. . . . Knowing that he who raised up Jesus, will raise up us also with Jesus" (2 Cor. iv. 10, 14).

The hope of resurrection is a most magnificent and certain future event. But it depends on our co-operation with grace, and patient working out of our salvation in dependence on God. "We are saved by hope. But hope that is seen, is not hope. But if we hope for that which we see not, we wait for it with patience " (Rom. viii. 24). The motive of this hope can only be found in Christ's own power of rising from the dead, and of his return to His Father and to our Father. His promise is very definite: " I shall go and prepare a place for you. I will come again, and will take you to myself, that where I am, you also may be " (John xiv. 3). It is this hope engendered in each one by Christ that urges us onwards. " I press forward towards the mark, to the prize of the supernal vocation of God in Christ Jesus " (Phil. iii. 14). Now is not the time of rest, since the battle is yet to be won. But Christ is the strength of the soul, in Whom it possesses confidence of final victory.

With St. Thomas the Apostle we may be tempted to ask: " Lord, we know not whither thou goest: and how can we know the way? " (John xiv. 5). Heaven seems far away, and the immensity of its promise baffles our understanding. Yet, though the heaven of God's glory is as yet inaccessible, the way to it is made both visible and approachable. " Jesus saith to Thomas: I am the way, and the truth, and the life. No man cometh to the Father except through me " (ibid. 5). " By him," says St. Paul, " we have access to the Father " (Eph. ii. 18). Jesus continues His work of redemption through His Church, of which He ever remains the Head. He was the first to enter through the door of God's eternal sanctuary, which by the merits of His death is thrown wide open to all. He said to Peter in token of that opened door: " I will give to thee the keys of the kingdom of heaven " (Matt. xvi. 19). The Church possesses the infinite deposit of all the accumulated good wrought by the Saviour, that it may be poured out upon souls until the end of time. All grace has the gift of everlasting life as its final purpose: "The grace of God, life everlasting in Christ Jesus Our Lord" (Rom. vi. 23).

2

THE NEW HEAVEN AND THE NEW EARTH

When the work of Redemption is completed, and the last soul saved, then will come the final consummation. The things that are in part will pass away, and only the perfect and everlasting things will remain. "For we know in part, and we prophesy in part. But when that which is perfect is come, that which is in part shall be done away. When I was a child, I spoke as a child, I understood as a child, I thought as a child. But, when I became a man, I put away the things of a child. We see now through a glass in a dark manner; but then face to face. Now I know in part, but then I shall know even as I am known" (1 Cor. xiii. 9-12). The glory which Christ established upon the earth is but a prelude to the full light of that glory which is to be revealed. When the sign of the Son of Man shall appear in the heavens, there shall be a new heaven and a new earth. "I saw a new heaven and a new earth," says St. John, "for the first heaven and the first earth were gone" (Apoc. xxi. 1). Once the day of the Lord has come, all the sanctifying mechanism of the Church on earth will disappear. Then the supreme Head, Jesus Christ, seen in all the glory of His Divine Majesty, will take the place of sacraments, of dogmas, of discipline, of law, of ecclesiastical government. The Church Militant will entirely cease, once the Church Triumphant in God's appointed time shall have attained to the full measure of its growth—"unto the measure of the age of the fulness of Christ" (Eph. iv. 13). Then there will be but the perfect fruit which has shed its outer covering, which here below holds the fruit concealed. This fruit is the union of all the elect in Christ in the vision and the love of God. "The glory thou hast given me, I have given to them: that they may be one, as we also are one" (John xvii. 22). Thus the charity of the Blessed in heaven is the full realization of the love infused into the soul in Holy Communion. "Charity never falleth away" (1 Cor. xiii. 8). The soul confirmed in charity will find the perfection of its loving Communion of earth. There, inseparably united in the Head, will all be also perfectly united in one another.

The Holy Sacrifice of the Altar, which is the greatest glory of the Church on earth, will cease to be said when the Last Day has come. His command will then have been fulfilled—"Do this until he come." The Mass, like all other things appointed as means of eternal salvation, is only in part. It is, indeed, the most perfect form of sacrifice, as conditioned by our earthly existence. It is the highway through the immolation of the Cross towards the Resurrection. But, once the last soul is saved, it too must cease. The Passion and death of Christ are the means of redemption and of sanctification. But neither Christ nor His members are to suffer eternally. The faithful in Christ precede one another into the glory which He has prepared for them, and which is the fruit of His sufferings. There all await the General Judgment and the resurrection of the dead. That day will mark the triumph of the Cross. Not only Christ, but His followers, will be vindicated. Our churches, our altars, our pulpits, will disappear. There will be but one great temple of Christ and His Elect in the glorious vision of God revealed. St. John describes this new heaven: "I saw no temple therein. For the Lord God Almighty is the temple thereof and the Lamb. And the city hath no need of the sun, nor of the moon to shine in it: for the glory of God hath enlightened it, and the Lamb is the lamp thereof" (Apoc. xxi. 22, 23). Thus the liturgy of earth, the sacrifice of our veiled praise, attains to its fullest and most perfect liturgical expression when the veil is taken away, and the revealed splendour of God is eternally glorified in the Eternal Priesthood of Christ, around Whom are gathered all His saints.

There will be no shadow of imperfection to mar the praise of the Blessed in heaven. Jesus will destroy all evil. What is being wrought now in generation after generation through the power of His grace will then be perfectly accomplished in the power of His glory. "Then the wicked one shall be revealed, whom the Lord Jesus shall kill with the spirit of his mouth, and shall destroy with the brightness of his coming" (2 Thess. ii. 8). Nothing defiled can enter heaven. Purgatory provides the final expiation of guilt and of all debt to God which is not fully paid before death. Once all the elect are gathered together from the four corners of the earth, in body and soul, all expiation will cease. The expiatory character of the Sacrifice of the Mass will no longer be required. It will have no place in the perfect charity of the saints, whose wills are entirely absorbed by the beauty of the Beatific

Vision, and confirmed in good by the Light of Glory which will permeate body as well as soul. "There shall be no curse any more; but the throne of God and the Lamb shall be in it, and his servants shall serve him, and they shall see his face, and his name shall be on their foreheads" (Apoc. xxii. 3. 4).

"In the state of the Blessed," says St. Thomas Aquinas, "nothing in regard to the worship of God will be figurative." All that is figurative will pass away, but not the innermost reality, which it presages and in part contains. Not all that belongs to our Sacrifice of earth will disappear. The essential purpose of the Mass will be everlastingly continued. The Mass is our most sublime way on earth of the worship of God. It is "the sacrifice of praise always to God". But the earthly Sanctus is only the prelude to the heavenly and eternal Sanctus. In heaven Jesus will be the visible Head, the Universal Pontiff of the Church Triumphant. He will lead His brethren in adoration before the throne of His Father. He "Who by the Holy Ghost offered Himself unspotted unto God", never ceases from that offering, which He established on the Cross. Understood in this way, the Holy Mass is an eternal sacrifice of praise, begun on earth, but consummated and perfected in heaven. "It is only the external form which differs. The Church Triumphant celebrates the sacrifice unveiled, while the Church Militant celebrates it in faith. But there is only one Liturgy, which He inaugurated on the Cross" (Bernadot, O.P.). The priesthood of Christ and our sharing in it are eternal. "And I heard," says St. John again of the new heaven, "the voice as it were of a great multitude, and as the voice of many waters, and as the voice of great thunders, saying Alleluia; for the Lord our God the Almighty has reigned. Let us be glad and rejoice and give glory to him " (Apoc. xix. 6, 7).

3

THE PLEDGE OF GLORY

During our time of expectation on earth the Holy Mass continues to be our greatest comfort. It is the sanctuary of God on earth which touches that of heaven. It contains the assurance of the permanence of Christ's priesthood, in which St. Paul declares: " We may have the strongest comfort, who have fled for refuge to hold fast the hope set before us, which we have as an anchor of the soul, sure and firm, and which entereth even within the veil, where the forerunner Jesus is entered, made a high-priest for ever according to the order of Melchisedech " (Heb. vi. 18, 19). The things which are in part contain within them the things which are perfect, and have, though hidden beneath types and figures, the substance of eternal life. They have power to bestow upon us everlastingly what they promise and possess. When by God's grace we shall finally enter through the sanctuary of the Mass into the eternal sanctuary of heaven, we shall see for our-selves how efficacious was our devotion to the Most Holy Sacrifice in the working out of our soul's salva-tion and sanctification. We shall cry out joyfully with St. John: " Blessed are those that wash their robes in the blood of the Lamb: that they may have a right to the tree of life and may enter into the gates of the city " (ibid. xxii. 14).

The Preface of the Mass of the Dead expresses this hope very beautifully: "In Him there hath shone upon us the hope of a happy resurrection, so that we, saddened by the knowledge that we must die, are comforted by the promise of immortal life to come. From Thy faithful, O Lord, life is not taken away, it is but changed; for when their dwelling place in this earthly exile shall have been destroyed, there awaiteth them an everlasting home in heaven." Whilst the Celebrant holds his hands over the offerings immediately before the Consecration, the same hope is expressed. We pray with the priest: "Do thou establish our days in Thy peace, nor suffer that we be condemned, but rather command that we be numbered amongst the flock of Thine Elect."

Whilst awaiting the "Eternal Inheritance", we must lay firm hold on the pledge of the Blessed Eucharist, as we mention frequently in the antiphon composed by St. Thomas. "We have confidence in the entering into the sanctuary by the blood of Christ" (Heb. x. 19). By our assiduous attendance at Holy Mass we are enabled to press forward more speedily towards the mark of our supernal vocation through fellowship in the sufferings of Christ. By being made conformable to His death through union of heart and mind in His Sacrifice, renewed on our altars, we enter most realistically into the power of His Resurrection. "It is the essence of a pledge that it should represent to us the value of the thing promised, and for this purpose nothing is more perfect, nothing is more true and certain than the Holy Eucharist. For in this pledge there is more than a likeness to things eternal, there is an identity of aim and intention. Both in heaven and at the Holy Table, it is God Who gives

Himself, it is God Who dwelleth in us, it is God Who gives us life " (Monsabré).

What is prayed in Sacrifice is realized in Sacrament. Through the action of the Mass we move towards the intimate union of Holy Communion with the Victim. " May the body of Our Lord Jesus Christ preserve thy soul unto life everlasting." The formula expresses vividly the hope contained.   " He that eateth my flesh and drinketh my blood, hath everlasting life: and I will raise him up on the last day " (John vi. 55). What we possess within ourselves in Holy Communion is substantially what we shall possess eternally.   " I am thy reward exceeding great " (Gen. xv. 1). Only the manner of possession differs. The heavenly Communion in Christ is the full flowering of the earthly. In the state of the Blessed we shall know Him, no longer as the Disciples knew Him at Emmaus—" In the Breaking of Bread;" " We know that when he shall appear, we shall be like unto him; because we shall see him as he is " (1 John iii. 2). Jesus desires for us both the Communion of earth and of heaven. He desires the latter through the former. He prayed for this final perfection to His Eternal Father: " I in them, and thou in me; that they may be made perfect in one " (John xvii. 23). Heaven is the consummation of Divine love, and in love of closest union of the one who loves in the beloved. There we will live Jesus in all the completeness of the indwelling of His communicated glory. " I live now not I; but Jesus liveth in me " (Gal. ii. 20). There the Spirit of adoption of sons will give us the inheritance of which Christ made us joint heirs with Himself, and in the fulness of our joyous union with Him we will cry *Abba*, Father. We have not to wait until death to possess eternal life, but we must wait until then to see it "face to face".

Blessed Raymond of Capua, who was for many years St. Catherine's confessor, narrates in his life of the Saint how a certain Donna Semia, a close friend of hers, had a vision at the moment of Catherine's death. A young child led her into the church, where another child opened the Tabernacle with a golden key. Out from it stepped the Virgin of Siena, but rejuvenated and of wondrous beauty. Turning to her friend, the Saint said to her: "Remember what you have now seen and what you have known before." The lesson is obvious. Our entry into the tabernacles of earth ensures our entry into that of heaven. The Eucharist is our way of abiding in Christ here below. What our eyes behold in outward sign, the soul possesses in reality. To receive the Blessed Sacrament, to live it on earth is to lay hold on eternal life.

Jesus is the price of our crossing from earth to heaven. He is our Viaticum, St. Thomas declares, in life and death. Through our devotion to the Eucharist we may say with St. Paul: "Whether we live, we live unto the Lord: or whether we die, we die unto the Lord. Therefore whether we live or whether we die, we are the Lord's" (Rom. xiv. 8). The Church unerringly gave the name Viaticum to the final reception of Holy Communion. He would accompany us even to the last step of the way, which ushers us into eternity, as the Victim offered for our redemption. "Death is swallowed up in victory"—the victory of the redeeming Christ. "You were bought with a great price" (1 Cor. vi. 20). By giving Himself to us in life and death we have the wherewith to pay for what is entirely beyond our means. St. Thomas says that the Eucharist is capable of bringing us to eternal glory, both as a sacrifice and as a sacrament. " The refreshment of the spiritual food, and the unity signified by the species of bread and wine are possessed even here below, though only imperfectly. But they will be perfectly possessed in the state of glory. Thus Augustine, commenting on the words of St. John: " My flesh is meat indeed and my blood is drink indeed," says: " Men seek by food and drink that they may hunger and thirst no more, but that is not obtained except through that food and drink which makes those receive it immortal and incorruptible in the society of the saints, where peace and perfect unity will reign."

In this blessed hope the Liturgy of the Mass instructs and prepares us for the everlasting Liturgy of heaven. The Lenten season, which is a figure of our earthly existence, opens with emphasis on the lowly origin of that flesh which is so much part of our composite nature: " Remember man that thou are but dust, and must return to dust." In token of this truth we are sprinkled with the blessed ashes. But God does not reject this thing of dust. In His love and mercy He deigned to assume it, and in it to accomplish our redemption. On Easter morning in the Risen Christ all such dust is glorified. On that morning the Adorable Sacrament is brought back triumphantly into the Church in token of the Resurrection. In the veiled Ciborium the glorified body of the living Christ is borne along in assurance of the ennobling of all human flesh. He has made it the temple of the Holy Ghost in Baptism. He has made it the tabernacle of His real abiding presence in Holy Communion. But that presence is an active presence which pours out its immortalizing virtue to body as well as soul, and penetrates by its power into flesh and bones and blood, that He may "raise it up on the last day". As we approach the Holy Table all our hope is concentrated in the words which brought Him down again from heaven for our sake—"This is my body." It is His body by virtue of the Incarnation; it becomes my body, my most personal possession by virtue of the mystery of the Eucharist.

4

MAY THEY REST IN PEACE

Not only during life, but even after death has summoned the soul, the Holy Sacrifice pursues its purpose of bringing men to the enjoyment of their "Eternal Inheritance". The value of the Masses which have been offered for the eternal repose of souls since the dawn of Christianity will be known only in the next world. The power of the Church reaches even beyond the grave, and enters efficaciously into that abode of God's mercy, where souls are finally fitted for their entrance into the all-pure vision of God. The Council of Trent declared against the Reformers: "The souls in Purgatory are helped by the prayers and good works of the faithful, but especially by the acceptable sacrifice of the Altar." Christ is never separated from His Elect. His redeeming power over the members of His Mystic Body will never cease until they are all gathered together before the throne of His Eternal Father. The splendid doctrine of the Communion of Saints is a most consoling one for all Christians. The Head of this Divine communication is Christ, in Whom all the

T

members have amongst themselves a strong inter-communication. "If one member suffer anything," says St. Paul, "all the members suffer with it; and if one member glory, all the members rejoice with it" (1 Cor. xii. 26). In and through Christ bitterness is taken out of death not only for those who are called away, but for those who are left behind. The Altar is, for both living and departed, the greatest comfort. The strong mediation of the Redeemer follows the soul even after death. Jesus Christ is all powerful in the continued offering of Himself to the Father. He desires to draw all the departed souls unto Himself irrevocably when, once again, He is lifted up in the Mass, and to apply to them the infinite merits of the shedding of His precious blood. Through our part in Holy Mass we can direct this holy and powerful desire of the Saviour to certain souls for whose eternal rest we pray.

The Most Holy Sacrifice is for the living and the dead unto eternal life. After the Consecration the priest prays that God may command that the sacrifice be lifted to the Altar on high by the hands of His Holy Angel. Then, almost in the same breath, he beseeches God that the merits of it may be applied to the souls of the faithful departed: "For them, O Lord, and for all who rest in Christ, do Thou, we beseech Thee, appoint a place of refreshment, light and peace; through the same Christ Our Lord." The ancient sacrifices of the Jews were, as we read in the Book of Machabeus, of value to the dead. How much more "holy and wholesome" must be the sweet odour of the sacrifice of Christ, "that they may be saved from their sins".

The instinct of a believing people bears testimony

to the dogmatic truth of the value of our Christian Sacrifice for the dead. For hundreds of years, dating back to the Roman Catacombs, Christians sought to bury their dead near the Temple of God, and as close as possible to the altar of His everlasting sacrifice. As they proceeded along the dark passages of the subterranean cemeteries of Rome, torches now and again illumined the name of some friend or relation, whose memory they brought with them to the Altar of Christ's Sacrifice. With the same instinct, in Catholic England, cemeteries were called God's acre. The ancient graveyards of Ireland have the Teampall inevitably in the centre.

In the Christian rite of burial all that is mortal is reverently committed to the good earth, whence it originally came, and there it is left to the care of God, Who will raise again to life to the glory of Jesus Christ. For them we pray in the voice of the Church: "Grant, we beseech Thee, O Almighty and merciful God, that the souls of our brethren, kindred and benefactors, for whom we have offered this Sacrifice of praise to Thy Majesty, being purified of all sins by virtue of this sacrament, may by Thy mercy receive the happiness of perpetual light, through Our Lord Jesus Christ."

St. Thomas says that the beatification of the soul is the final offering of itself to God. Through Jesus Christ in the Mass we practise the offering of ourselves until the final offering comes. The Holy Sacrifice is now the way to the glory that lies beyond. It contains the spirit and truth in which we adore the Father, Who "seeketh for such to adore Him". It is life— eternal life already begun, containing in itself the promise of perfect possession. With the ordained priest on our altars we look forward confidently to His coming. "To him who is able to preserve you without sin, and to present you spotless before the presence of his glory with exceeding joy in the coming of our Lord Jesus Christ: to the only one God our Saviour through Jesus Christ our Lord, be glory and magnificence, empire and power before all ages, and now, and for all ages of ages. Amen" (Jude 25).

Appendix

THE DOMINICAN RITE

"ISN'T the Mass the same everywhere?" A question like this is not infrequently asked by those to whom the celebration of Mass by a Dominican Father, or by a priest of some other Order which possesses a distinct Rite, comes as a surprise. To those who have some knowledge of liturgical development and a keener perception of what is meant by uniformity of Catholic worship such differences present no difficulty. They mark the phases in the progress of ecclesiastical ceremonial with which the Church from the beginning surrounded and adorned the essential worship which was instituted by Jesus Christ. It must be remembered that the Liturgy of the Church, though fundamentally Divine, has been enriched by a splendid ceremonial of ecclesiastical origin, whereby, as St. Thomas remarks, the mind is better prepared to enter into the mystery itself.

To-day, we are accustomed to what is called the Roman Rite as governing the prayers and rubrics of the Most Holy Sacrifice, the administration of the Sacraments, the saying of the Divine Office, etc. As a result there may be a tendency to regard any departure from that precise ritual as non-Roman. There may even exist the feeling that one should be rather apologetic for being in possession of any dissimilarity, as if such were barely tolerated by the Church. We might, for instance, be inclined to think that the Order of Preachers was a kind of "Society of Odd Fellows" which managed to set up something liturgical of its own just for the sake of being odd and therefore conspicuous, and succeeded in getting away with it.

To understand the why and wherefore of the now distinctive Dominican Rite it is essential to bear in mind that there occurred a liturgical evolution within the Church. The Liturgy, as we know to-day, which has now become stabilized and seemingly impervious to further change, was the outcome of that evolution which goes back to the days of the Apostles. It grew out of the piety of both priests and people. The Apostolic origin of the Canon of the Mass is mentioned by the Council of Trent. It was natural that the simple Rite of the days of the Catacombs of Rome should blossom out into more grandiose forms with the new freedom of worship under Constantine. As the Church expanded, so also did her Liturgy. Whilst the main apostolic and traditional source was everywhere upheld during these early centuries, local customs, always with at least Diocesan approval, were gradually added to the ceremonial. These in turn, such as the very early Rite of Gaul or Gallic Rite, influenced that of Rome itself. It is known also that Charlemagne in the eighth century endeavoured to establish the Roman Rite of his time in all the Churches of the Holy Roman Empire. Up to the eighteenth century this very ancient form of the Roman Rite was used in Lyons and is still the Rite of the monks of Chartreuse, who adopted what they found in the Lyons of their day. Unification of the Liturgy which had been in part accomplished by preceding Popes, was finally established by Pius V in the year 1568. The Bull which he issued made the present Roman Rite compulsory on the entire Western Church unless it could be proved without doubt that the Rite in use had the sanction of at least two hundred years of tradition. This preserving of what was ancient has ever been the policy of the Church.

From the date of approval of the Order in 1216 St. Dominic centred his religious organization in Rome, whither he chose to go after the scattering of the first Brethren. To Rome we must also go to find the beginnings of what is now known as the Dominican Rite. In the Rome of St. Dominic's days there had just occurred a most important development which was to affect profoundly the entire course of Liturgical development. Up to the twelfth century there existed a more or less uniform Liturgy in the Eternal City, which was maintained in its full splendour in the important Roman Churches, which were known as Basilicas. In the ancient Choirs of these Churches were the great tomes for the Office and the celebration of Holy Mass. The solemn rites of the Basilicas required the permanent residence of the ancient Orders, such as the Benedictines, who were mainly responsible for their maintenance. Early in the twelfth century there was begun a movement of simplification of the Liturgical Offices and Books which was inaugurated by the Papal Court itself. The Roman Curia had frequently to move from place to place and found it most inconvenient to carry about the large choral books. To suit the new need, a shorter liturgy was arranged and the Breviary or briefer form of the Office emerged, as also the portable Missal. This new form was called the Rite of the Roman Curia as distinct from the

Rite of the Basilicas. Father Batiffol states: "The influence of the Curia on the (liturgical) movement was great and decisive." Both Rites were Roman.

By the beginning of the thirteenth century the distinction between these two Roman Rites was already definitely established. With the rise of the two great Orders—Franciscans and Dominicans—the divergence became even more marked. In 1223, St. Francis of Assisi ordered that all his brethren should follow the Rite of the Roman Curia. St. Dominic chose the Rite of the Roman Basilicas. This latter choice was not a merely arbitrary one. He and his followers from the very beginning were recognized as Canon Regulars as well as Preachers. Canonical life was to play a large part in the shaping of the Order's apostolate. Choral recitation of the Office and the solemn celebration of the Conventual Mass, with other monastic observances which were to be the daily life of the Dominican Fathers and Sisters, found their natural counterpart in the more ancient Roman Rite of the Basilicas. The choice was also otherwise determined. In the year 1219—three years after the approval of the Order—Pope Honorius III made over to St. Dominic and his sons the renowned Basilica of Santa Sabina. This Basilica was noted for the splendour of its liturgical observance down the centuries, especially from the time of St. Gregory the Great. By this papal gift the Order was committed to the Basilica Rite. St. Dominic received this new Church as what we might call "a going concern", and naturally continued the tradition and used the choral books which were at hand.

Both the Franciscan and Dominican Orders were world-wide in their apostolic scope. Each Order brought its chosen Liturgy with it into the various countries of Europe. Local customs of these countries quickly began to exercise an influence in the newly founded convents, with the result that within each Order there was soon seen the danger of lack of uniformity. St. Francis tried to avert that danger by ordering all to follow the Curial Rite. It was inevitable that each Rite would be in some measure adapted to the needs and spirit of each Order. Three Franciscan Generals, in particular St. Bonaventure, were responsible for the Franciscan adaptation of the original Curial Rite. Their efforts were so successful that, in 1277, Pope Nicholas III made this adapted Rite obligatory on all the Churches of Rome, including the Basilicas. Three hundred years later, a Dominican Pope, Pius V, was to make it obligatory for all the Churches in the West. "Thus," says Father Batiffol rather regretfully, "the grand old Roman office of the time of Charlemagne and of Adrian I was suppressed." Yet what was so ancient was not lost, since it came to be preserved in the Dominican Order.

The Dominican Order also left its impress on the Rite, which, as much by force of circumstances as by choice, had come into its possession. The Order was world-wide, and the old Roman Calendar was made more universal. The Fathers had to travel on their missionary work, and study in preparation for preaching became essential activity, so that the need of shortening the Office and adapting the chant to the exigencies of Dominican conventual life was soon felt. Lack of uniformity had also to be met at an early date. It is probable that St. Dominic himself inaugurated the movement towards unification in the Chapter of 1220. Various efforts were made in the same direction at the command of subsequent General Chapters, until the work was definitely completed by the fourth General of the Order, Blessed Humbert, of the Romans. The original Codex of Humbert, which contains all the necessary books of Dominican Liturgy, is preserved in the Archives of the Order in Rome. Another copy, most probably that used by Humbert himself, is to be found in the National Museum of London. In the following quotation from Blessed Humbert's letter to the Order in 1256 we find valuable information both as to the intent and content of this unified Liturgy, which has remained practically unchanged to the present day:

"The variations in our Liturgy, which were the object of no little care on the part of many General Chapters, have now by the grace of God been reduced to conformity in certain exemplars. You are asked to correct the Office according to these exemplars, so that the uniformity so long desired in the Order may be found everywhere. You must realize that the wishes of the brethren concerning the Office were so conflicting that it was impossible in arranging the Liturgy to accede to the desires of each petitioner. Hence, you should bear it patiently, if you perchance find in the Office something that is not in accord with your ideas.

"That you may ascertain whether or not you have the complete Office, know that it comprises in all its parts fourteen books: namely, the Ordinary, the Martyrology, the Antiphonary, the Lectionary, the Psalter, the Collectarium, the Processional, the Gradual, the Conventual Missal, the Pulpitary and the portable Breviary."

A detailed study of the ancient Dominican Missal would show how the rubrics and prayers which are distinctive belong for the most part to the more ancient form of the Roman Rite. The preparation of the Chalice at the beginning of the Mass was probably introduced into the Roman Rite when the difference between the Mass of the Catechumens and that of the Faithful fell into disuse. It was definitely in use in Rome before St. Dominic's time and is found in the eighth century Rite of Chartreuse. The shorter prayers at the foot of the Altar, the reciting of the *Gloria* and *Credo* at the side of the Altar, the brief *Confiteor* are all found in ninth-century Missals. The prayers and manner of making the Offertory is older than in the present Roman Rite, which was further influenced by the Gallican Rite in the twelfth century. The old Lyons Rite of Charlemagne or what is now the Chartreuse Rite preserves also the shorter form. The extending of the arms immediately after the Elevation would seem to have crept in from the early Ambrosian Rite of Milan, which influenced other Rituals in the twelfth century. It represents Christ's Sacrifice upon the Cross. The Communion in the Dominican Rite in which the priest holds the Sacred Host in his left hand is mentioned in the Roman Ordo, a MS. of the twelfth century, as being the proper ceremonial for Cardinal Bishops. It is to be presumed that it was even more widely practised since it found its way into the Dominican Rite.

The peculiarities of the Dominican Rite are not confined to the Most Holy Sacrifice. As is clearly seen from Blessèd Humbert's list of liturgical books, the entire choral observance was the adapted form of the old Rite of the Roman Basilicas. Though many changes have been made in the Office since his time, notably in the adopting of the present Psalter in the reform of the Breviary by Pope Pius X, yet the Dominican Breviary is still very distinctive. The Gregorian Chant which was adopted by the Order in Blessed Humbert's time has also preserved the ancient simplicity of the original Gregorian. In the Order all the ceremonies of Reception, of Profession, of elections, of visitations, of chapters, of festive processions, of blessings for travellers, for the sick and for the dying, of burial for the dead, present an ancient monastic tradition which has been handed down to the sons and daughters of the great Patriarch, Dominic of Gusman, who founded an Order at once canonical and apostolic.

www.ingramcontent.com/pod-product-compliance
Lightning Source LLC
Chambersburg PA
CBHW020436130626
46549CB00001B/171